PREHISTORIC COMMUNITIES
OF THE BRITISH ISLES

PREHISTORIC COMMUNITIES

OF THE

BRITISH ISLES

By

V. GORDON CHILDE
D.Litt., D.Sc., F.B.A., F.S.A.

*Professor of Prehistoric European Archaeology
and Director of the Institute of
Archaeology in the University
of London*

GREENWOOD PRESS, PUBLISHERS
WESTPORT, CONNECTICUT

First published in 1940
Second edition originally published in 1947
by W. & R. Chambers, Ltd., London and Edinburgh

First Greenwood Reprinting 1971

Library of Congress Catalogue Card Number 76-114498

SBN 8371-4732-8

Printed in the United States of America

PREFACE

FOR more than two centuries specialists have been gathering materials illustrating the development of civilization in the British Isles prior to the Roman conquest. During the last two decades the harvest has been augmented by a burst of activity surpassing qualitatively and quantitatively all previous efforts. Systematic excavations, conducted on an unprecedented scale and with matchless precision, have brought unexpected discoveries and filled in many gaps. Monographic studies have reduced to order the products of this activity in restricted regions and for limited periods. Parallel advances in archaeology on the Continent and in the Near East have opened up the possibility of viewing insular prehistory as part of a world process. But no attempt has been made to embrace the result of partial studies in a comprehensive survey of the whole natural unit as such, nor to present in detail its articulation with world history.

Meanwhile material continues to accumulate, whether in museums or in excavation reports, till it threatens to assume unmanageable proportions. The first year of a great struggle, when all the original documents are packed away in cellars, is not altogether a favourable moment for the adventure of synthesis. The present writer, who has contributed to the work of collection and construction only in a minor way and in a small corner, feels himself particularly ill-fitted for the task. Still someone must try it. The war, having largely arrested discovery, offers a breathing space for digestion. Even the deficiencies in the author's mastery of detail may enable him to help the average man to see a general, if incomplete and even distorted, picture. His work embodies no erudite research in museums and periodicals: it is frankly based on the partial syntheses and monographs published by his predecessors and colleagues. To the latter the author is indebted not only for the facts and ideas, acknowledged in the text and footnotes, but also for many explanations and suggestions conveyed in converse and correspondence.

To the Trustees of the British Museum, to the National Museum of Antiquities of Scotland, to the National Museum of Ireland, to the National

Museum of Wales, to the Ashmolean Museum, the Cambridge University Museum of Archaeology and Ethnography and the County Museum of Somerset we are indebted for photographs of, and permission to reproduce, objects in their charge, as also to Mr W. J. Hemp, F.S.A., Mr O. G. S. Crawford, and Mr Alexander Keiller for photographs taken by them.   For permission to reproduce figures from their illustrations we make grateful acknowledgement to the Trustees of the British Museum, the Society of Antiquaries of London, the Society of Antiquaries of Scotland, the Prehistoric Society, the Royal Irish Academy, the Royal Anthropological Institute, the Royal Archaeological Institute, the Wiltshire Archaeological and Natural History Society, Dr A. Bulleid, F.S.A., and Mr H. St George Gray, F.S.A., Dr Grahame Clark, Mr O. G. S. Crawford, Dr Cecil Curwen, Mr G. C. Dunning, Sir Cyril Fox, Mr C. F. C. Hawkes, Mr Alexander Keiller, Mr E. T. Leeds, F.S.A., Mr S. Piggott, and Mr W. J. Varley.   Mr Arthur J. Edwards and Mr R. B. K. Stevenson have kindly assisted by reading proofs.

V. G. CHILDE.

EDINBURGH, 1940.

CONTENTS

LIST OF ILLUSTRATIONS

LIST OF PLATES

CHAPTER I

THE THEME AND ITS BACKGROUND

1. The Materials and their Interpretation

THE drama-cycle of prehistory and history has for its theme Man's conquest of Nature. We are concerned, however, only with that part staged in the British Isles. When the Romans arrived to raise the curtain on history, they found these islands' inhabitants far removed from naked savagery. English agriculture was already so flourishing that Britain was exporting corn in addition to metal, slaves and fat stock. Commerce was facilitated by media of exchange—minted coinage as well as a bar currency—guaranteed and sanctioned by the authority of small but genuine States. Evidently the Roman conquest was not the beginning of the drama of British history, but only of one play in a trilogy. The preceding spectacle, which is our subject here, must be more than a mere curtain-raiser. It must present the primary human achievement—the conversion of a wilderness of trackless forest and marsh into a semi-civilized land with many fields and populous villages in forest clearings connected by tracks over which trade had passed for centuries before the Romans built their roads.

But if the general theme be the same, the several episodes and the actors are different not only in name but also in kind. The prehistorian cannot compete with the historian in presenting individuals, exposing their motives and judging their achievements. For his characters, *ex hypothesi*, did not express their thoughts and aims in written documents as well as in deeds. But their actions had concrete and sometimes enduring consequences which the prehistorian can decipher. His materials are in fact just these realized thoughts and embodied deeds—the tools and weapons, the houses and tombs, the personal finery and decorative designs—in which illiterate and nameless persons expressed concretely their plans for getting a livelihood here, their hopes for a hereafter and their aspirations for beauty and refinement.

Yet the individual will still escape him. Archaeology can deal only with classes of objects; a unique product can find no place in such a science. The disability must not be overestimated. The steam-engine has more

1

enduring significance than James Watt, Buddhism than Gautama Buddha. In any case, prehistory is not bereft of actors. Its content is not a mere linear progress or regression.

In classifying remains of prehistoric man the archaeologist must of course consider first age, function, material and environment. The total assemblage of materials, functionally classified, would disclose at any given time the equipment of the prehistoric islanders for securing a livelihood and attaining the good life. But if use be the primary basis of classification, it never entirely explains the object. Any tool is a social product; its manufacture and use, and therefore its form too, are conditioned by the traditions of social groups which make and use it. American table-knives and forks are quite different from those current in Great Britain. The difference in these everyday utensils, serving the same simple purpose, reflects one divergence in traditions, in habits of eating, between two kindred peoples. Prehistorians interpret in the same way slight differences in the forms of axes, knives or pots, and more marked variations in house-plans or burial rites as reflecting the divergent traditions of distinct social groups.

Thus prehistory can recognize peoples and marshal them on the stage to take the place of the personal actors who form the historian's troupe. Their interactions are no less a part of the drama of prehistory than are their reactions to the external environment. The total assemblage of archaeological material classified from this standpoint can be recognized as the *culture* of a people or social group — communities devoted to a specialized occupation like coal-mining and members of a church may have a distinguishable culture as much as members of distinct nations. Such a culture doubtless represents the adjustment achieved by a human group to a specific environment. But in the British Isles we shall find that traditions evoked by many different environments—the Arctic tundras, the North European plain, the Eurasiatic steppes, the Mediterranean and Biscayan coasts—embodied in distinct cultures, were blended and themselves adapted to our insular environment. So we can exhibit the fusion of traditions instead of the mere accumulation of novel independent adjustments to the British environment.

Did we know the homes, working-places and graves of a prehistoric community, together with a large selection of its tools, weapons, ornaments and cult objects, we should be able to form a fair idea of its economy and numerical strength and make some reasonable guesses as to its social structure, religious and artistic ideals. By plotting on maps the distribution of its distinctive products we could trace the people's territorial expansion.

By comparing these products with those of precursors, neighbours and successors we could evaluate the group's role in local and British history.

These conditions, essential for the complete definition of any society, are never fully satisfied. Not only has an appallingly large proportion of man's handiwork perished—only under exceptional conditions can anything made of wood, basketry or textiles survive—but much of the rest has been destroyed by later successors. The archaeologist has too often to rely on materials gleaned by unsystematic digging or casual collecting, very unevenly conducted or perpetrated in the several counties.

The scientific observation of prehistoric monuments and the systematic collection of relics began effectively only with the eighteenth century [1] and were initiated by romantic antiquaries. These were gentlemen of leisure, trained in the classics and seeking with the spade the panoply of Boudicca and the paraphernalia of the Druids. But they had left the cells of the schoolmen and 'perambulated the countryside, studying at first hand the antiquities of their own forefathers.' The best, like Stukeley, not only collected and preserved many precious relics, but left accurate descriptions of what they observed in the field. Next came the collectors, offspring of Victorian capitalism, not unversed in the new learning called Science. For arranging their collections they borrowed methods of classification from geology and palaeontology. And by classifying they made archaeology a science as well as a diversion. The outline of the chronological framework we still employ was due to the collectors. But their interests were too often in the objects rather than in their makers. They presented an evolution of implements and arms, but left them dead fossils, not the expressions of living human societies.

It was, in fact, not till Abercromby in 1901 used the sepulchral vessel then termed a Drinking Cup to identify a group of prehistoric invaders and to trace these to their Continental home that archaeology really became prehistory. In England the new conceptions did not bear full fruit till after 1920. Three examples must suffice to suggest how very recently prehistory took shape in the British Isles. It was not till 1922, when the Cunningtons excavated All Cannings Cross, that the first Iron Age farmers who really created the rural economy of pre-Roman Britain (Chapter X) were properly defined. The neolithic people, now regarded as the first food-producers in England, were first characterized by Leeds in 1927 (Chapter III). The most distinctive megalithic monuments of Northern Ireland, the

---

[1] After John Aubrey (*obiit* 1683), William Stukeley (1687-1765) heads the list of British prehistorians.

horned cairns of Carlingford type (Chapter IV, 2), were unrecognized before 1932!

As a result of its late inception, our knowledge of prehistory is very uneven. Wessex, Sussex, the Upper Thames, East Anglia, eastern York-shire and South Wales have been thoroughly and scientifically explored. More recently the Orkney Islands and a small district round Kilmartin in Argyll have become well known. Finds are very numerous from Derbyshire, Somerset and parts of Scotland, but their distribution over the several periods is painfully uneven and the number of well-excavated and published sites is defective. Cornwall, Cumberland, Durham and Westmorland, Ayrshire and Ross-shire and most of Ireland are very imperfectly known. In the industrial areas of the Midlands and Clydeside and round London and other large towns monuments and relics have all too often been irrepar-ably lost. Such gross disparities in archaeological documentation are liable to distort prehistory. In particular one must ask at the outset how far the prominence of Sussex and Wessex in prehistory is due to Aubrey, Stukeley, Colt Hoare, Pitt-Rivers, the Cunningtons, the Curwens, Crawford, Hawkes, Stone and Piggott.

2. The Geographical Background

Our drama is staged in the British Isles; its scenery can be read off the map, but not the map we know, for that is an artificial product. Prehistoric man found no moled harbours, no roads, no fields to welcome him. He was indeed the pioneer in making these improvements in a land densely covered with forbidding forest and impassable morass. Mediaeval chronicles, casual phrases in Roman historians, and the tree-stools embalmed in the peat on now treeless moors give us occasional glimpses of primaeval Britain and Ireland. But the vegetation was not everywhere equally inconvenient. The low-lying clay lands supported the so-called *damp oak woods* with a tangle of thorny undergrowth, barriers to settlement and communication that only well-organized and well-equipped societies could tackle in the closing phase of prehistory. Chalk lands and limestone hills when not overlaid with glacial clays supported less intractable vegetation, as did sandy country. Hence the conspicuous importance of the chalk downs of southern England and Yorkshire and the limestone plateaux of the Cotswolds, the Mendips, Derbyshire and Northumberland and the ridges that emerge from the glacial clays in Sligo, Clare and Limerick. And other areas that might seem too bleak for man had in fact been made habitable by their very exposure. The fierce Atlantic gales early cleared of trees the moors of Caithness and the northern isles and the high plateaux of Ulster. These lightly wooded or deforested lands, accordingly, appear as *areas of primary settlement* on which prehistory is focused in contrast to the *areas of difficult settlement*, the clay lands which play the major role in history.

Fox [2] has emphasized the importance for the colonization of Britain of the distinction between Lowland and Highland Zones. The boundary between them, shown in Fig. 30 and roughly coinciding with a line from Teesmouth to Tor Bay, corresponds to the edge of the palaeozoic outcrop in geology.

The *Lowland Zone* is generally of low elevation. It comprises two main areas of primary settlement—the chalk of Salisbury Plain, the Downs, the Chilterns and the East Anglian Ridge together with the limestone plateaux of the Cotswolds and the Mendips on the one hand, and on the other the Lincolnshire and Yorkshire Wolds. Despite interruptions by wooded valleys, ridgeways and navigable streams converging upon Salisbury Plain unify into an island, or rather an archipelago, of easy settlement the chalk uplands and limestone hills of southern England. But this unit is isolated from its smaller counterpart in Yorkshire and Lincolnshire by a wide belt of dense forest and forbidding swamp. Connexion between the two areas was effected, Fox suggests, by the narrow Jurassic Ridge extending north-eastward from the Cotswolds through Northamptonshire.

The *Highland Zone* is built up of old igneous and metamorphic rocks, the soils from which support damp oak woods only on low-lying ground. But they are liable to be boggy and are generally deficient in lime, so that the limestone plateaux mentioned above, as well as the recent moraines in eastern Scotland and the shelly sand of raised beaches in the west, assume an added importance. Mountain ridges impose barriers to intercourse and restrict the habitable area. East of the Spine of Britain, the series of ranges—Pennines, Southern Uplands, Grampians—that divide North Sea from Atlantic drainage, there are still wide continuous areas of moderate elevation in Northumberland, the Tweed valley, the Lothians, Fife and north-east Scotland. But in the West Highlands and to a lesser degree in Galloway, Cumberland and Wales the habitable areas are restricted by sheer physiographical relief to narrow strips of coast and constricted glens separated by rugged mountains and often situated on peninsulas or islands.

[2] *Personality of Britain*, 53-55; his account has been largely used also in the foregoing and subsequent pages.

In the Highlands indeed each such glen, bay or islet becomes a natural unit capable of supporting only a few isolated households.

But facilities for maritime intercourse are contrasted with the difficulties of land communications in the Highland Zone. South-west Scotland in the days before roads and railways was really closer to Ulster than to the Lothians. From Fair Head in Antrim one can see Islay, Jura, Kintyre, Arran and Galloway, and from Cave Hill above Belfast the mountains of Galloway, Man and Cumberland. The sea between, though often terrible, can be as calm as the Aegean for days on end. The Irish Sea with extensions to the Firths of Clyde and Lorne is the natural centre of a province whose several parts it unites rather than divides. So, too, Glamorgan can be reached as well from Somerset across the Bristol Channel as from the Cotswolds. West Highland settlements are even today more accessible by sea than by land. In the past the voyage across the Moray Firth to Caithness as well as to Orkney was much more practicable than the land journey round the three firths and across the intervening mountains.

Now colonists reaching Britain across the Channel or the North Sea naturally arrive in the Lowland Zone. They are welcomed by the Downs, the East Anglian heaths or the Wolds, which offer an environment similar to that which they have just left. For the Downs are just a continuation of the chalk ridges of Artois and Flanders. The plain of eastern England is an extension of the great North European plain only recently interrupted by the North Sea submergence. Settlers from these quarters need not therefore make any drastic change in their equipment or mode of life to adjust it to their island home. 'In Lowland Britain,' Fox writes, 'new cultures of continental origin tend to be *imposed* on the earlier or aboriginal cultures. In the Highland, on the other hand, these tend to be *absorbed* by the older cultures.'

This absorption is due not only to the filtration to which invading cultures are exposed in crossing the Lowland Zone and penetrating the western mountains, nor yet to the conservativism of a region of small and isolated settlements. The Highland Zone of Britain is exposed to other influences too. A natural sea route leads from Portugal and Brittany to Cornwall, the Irish Sea, the Firths of Clyde and Lorne, and so up the Minch to Orkney and eventually Scandinavia. Ireland is an island in the Atlantic while Britain is a peninsula thrust out into the North Sea. The prevalent south-westerly gales might compel voyages in the directions named. Ocean currents and the whales which follow them might entice men to Ireland and even Orkney. The limestone hills of western Ireland would welcome to a familiar environment any mariners who willingly or unwillingly arrived from the Iberian Peninsula. And once landed on our western coasts, gold, copper and tin would lure adventurers to repeat the perilous voyage.

For men need materials for their equipment as well as hunting-grounds, pastures and fields. In this respect the Lowland Zone offered one great attraction. The chalk, so pre-eminently easy of settlement, offers unlimited quantities of excellent flint—the best material for cutting tools and stabbing weapons till metal became not only known but also cheap. The only comparable supply of this precious material in the Highland Zone is the Antrim chalk, capped everywhere by basalt but exposed on the coasts and in eroded valleys. But as soon as the demands of higher civilization began to spread, men sought also metals and precious stones. Of these Ireland and Highland Britain possess a monopoly in quantities which would explain the repetition of otherwise incredible voyages. Tin could be obtained from the granites of Cornwall and was demonstrably exploited by the fifth century B.C., probably much earlier. Copper lodes exist in Anglesey and other parts of Wales, in Weardale, in Galloway, Argyll, Rousay and Shetland, but above all in Ireland—Wicklow, Cork and Kerry. Finally, Ireland ranks as the prehistoric El Dorado of the West, the auriferous sands and gravels of streams flowing from the Wicklow Mountains having supplied material for a wealth of goldwork paralleled only in Hungary or Siberia.

3. THE CHRONOLOGICAL BACKGROUND

As a branch of history, prehistory deals with events in time. But from its very nature it is deprived of the possibility of assigning to its events exact dates in terms of our era such as can be derived from written annals. A sequence of cultures in any locality can indeed be determined by *stratigraphy*; if an inhabited cave, a rubbish pit or a family vault contain, one above the other, several layers of relics, each group distinctive of a different culture, the several cultures at the site must follow one another in the same order, the oldest being that represented in the bottom layer. Such a sequence may be termed a *relative chronology*. It tells nothing about the length of time represented by the several layers. It gives no guarantee that the sequence attested say in Sussex holds good also in Argyll, still less that a given culture in the one area is strictly contemporary with the same culture in the other (unless the unit of time be very large). For early periods a succession of geological and climatic changes affecting the whole of Britain and the rest of Northern Europe provides *an absolute chronology*—an independent framework within which contemporary cultures can be compared in different areas. But the units of geological time thus portioned out, reckoned as they are in millennia, are too long when the drama's tempo has been accelerated as it has in the periods covered by this book. For these we are forced to use a system of *Periods* defined by the cultural sequence deduced from stratigraphy despite its obvious drawbacks.

The well-established sequence of cultures, defined by pottery, on the chalk lands of southern England provides the most convenient standard for the relative chronology of the British Isles, since nearly all the styles are represented elsewhere. *Period I* begins with the settlement on the chalk downs of farmers who built causewayed camps (Chapter III). The earliest silting from the bottom of their ditches comprises pure *Windmill Hill* pottery. At Maiden Castle, Dorchester, a long mound, an anomalous representative of the collective sepulchres termed *long barrows* or *megalithic tombs* (Chapter IV), straddles the abandoned ditches of an older causewayed camp though the barrow-ditches too contained at the bottom only Windmill Hill pottery.[3] So the 'Neolithic Age' may provisionally be subdivided by the addition of a 'megalithic phase' or *Period II*. It is taken as ending with the arrival in several waves of round-headed invaders whose characteristic *Beaker* pottery is found in the upper levels of ditches round causewayed camps and long barrows, and with the latest interments in collective tombs (Chapter VI).

Period III, the first section of the Bronze Age, thus initiated, may itself be subdivided into two phases, by the appearance first of B and then of A Beakers. It ends with the rise on the chalk downs of the *Wessex Culture* (Chapter VIII), distinguished by rich graves furnished with grooved daggers in which Grape Cups and Aldbourne Cups replace Beakers, while contemporary graves contain *Cinerary Urns* of the *Overhanging Rim* family. A rather vague horizon within the Wessex culture may be marked by the importation of *segmented fayence beads*, fashionable in Egypt about 1400 B.C.,[4] which may provisionally be used to divide Period IV from *Period V*. In that case, a new invasion from the Continent, marked in the ceramic record by *Deverel–Rimbury* urns (Chapter IX), about 750 B.C. would define the beginning of *Period VI*. Another invasion of land-hungry farmers, the Hallstatt or *Iron Age A* (All Cannings Cross–West Harling) people (Chapter XI), would initiate the Iron Age and *Period VII*. In the third century B.C. raids by *La Tène* chieftains, some of whom established settle-

---

[3] Wheeler, *Maiden Castle*, 20.   [4] Beck and Stone, *Arch.*, lxxxv, 203-252.

ments in patches and introduced La Tène I brooches (Chapter XII), then
denote the beginning of *Period VIII*, which lasts till the advent of the
Belgae in the first century (*Period IX*).

These periods are defined by cultures, expressing the social traditions
of peoples. Not all the peoples in question spread their cultures from
Lowland Britain to the Highland Zone or Ireland. In so far as they did,
allowance must be made for the time involved in penetrating the Highland
Zone. In such a large area a culture, borne by a slow-moving and conservative society, need not everywhere represent the same period of prehistoric
time. Cultural phases in the several areas can be synchronized only by
commodities that enjoyed a limited currency, actually interchanged between
them. And not all the cultures represented in southern England reached
northern England, Scotland or Ireland. On the other hand, we find there
different cultures, not represented in the south or even spread to the south
from the north and west. The correlation of the several areas will be
discussed in the appropriate chapters, but some of the difficulties should
be mentioned in advance.

Even in Yorkshire we can distinguish no counterparts to Periods I,
VI and IX. The sequence begins with collective tombs, parallel presumably
to those of Period II in the south, but not certainly pre-Beaker. The Beaker
culture of Period III is succeeded not by rich graves of Wessex type but
by poorer interments accompanied by *Food Vessels* (of the Vase form)
(Chapter VII). These were duly replaced by Overhanging Rim Urns
which did arrive in Period V while segmented fayence beads were still
fashionable imports. But the Urn culture must have lasted throughout
Period VI and in parts through Period VII too, since the sole counterpart
of Iron Age A is a single settlement at Scarborough. Period VIII, however,
witnessed the occupation of the Wolds and Limestone Hills by La Tène
tribes who remained in occupation till Roman times.

In Scotland the sequence is further abbreviated, since no distinct culture
whatsoever is yet available to fill Period VII. The Iron Age, in fact, begins
only with the advent of invaders who built *Gallic Forts* and wore La Tène I
brooches. But the Bronze Age tradition characterized by degenerate
descendants of Overhanging Rim Urns (*Cordoned Urns*) lingered on in
remote corners at least. The megalithic tombs with which the sequence
starts certainly contain pottery of Windmill Hill character and were built
before the arrival of round-headed invaders in Caithness and the Western
Highlands, since the latest interments alone are accompanied by Beakers.
Yet the tombs contain so many types that recur in England only in Period IV

(pestle-shaped maces, jet necklaces) as to suggest that conquest by the Beaker folk was delayed till that period.

In Ireland we can recognize only the following parallels with England without other well-defined cultures to fill the gaps: (a) Megalithic tombs, in the North containing pottery in the Windmill Hill tradition; (b) Food Vessels, mostly of the Bowl type; and (c) Cinerary Urns, all save in Ulster the late, Cordoned, descendants of the Overhanging Rim Urns with the contemporary Encrusted Urns. A sprinkling of La Tène chieftains is attested by the fine metal-work from a single site—the crannog of Lisnacrogher in Co. Antrim—and a modest number of stray finds, particularly bits, descended from the Yorkshire type. But Ó Ríordáin's excavations at Cush (Co. Limerick) seem to prove that for funerary vases Cordoned Urns were still current at the beginning of our era when flat rotary querns were already in use. Actual imports to check the ceramic sequence are not available earlier. One Food Vessel was indeed associated with a fine dagger of the Wessex type, characteristic of Period IV in southern England. But even in Wales a Food Vessel of Irish bowl form was accompanied by the segmented fayence beads appropriate to Period V, while in Ireland several Food Vessels have been found in cists together with Encrusted Urns assigned in Britain to Period VI or VII. In several collective tombs of the Boyne group Food Vessels accompanied the latest interments, while the stone pendants, apparently surviving from the primary furniture of such tombs, can be matched in Wessex only in Period IV.

Nevertheless by that period Irish imports in Britain, Denmark and Central Europe show that a metallurgical industry was flourishing in the island. The regular development of metal tools and weapons permits of the establishment of a chronological sequence: Early Bronze Age (or phase 1), Middle Bronze Age 1 and 2 (phases 2-3), Late Bronze Age 1, 2 and 3 (phases 4-6). But only Early Bronze Age, Middle Bronze Age 1 and Late Bronze Age 2 can be correlated respectively with ceramic Periods III, IV and VI. The remaining types are never found associated with pottery in graves or settlements. Moreover, the relevant types are not distributed evenly over the British Isles; those distinctive of the Middle Bronze Age are practically unknown north of the Tay; the carp's-tongue sword and its associates, that best characterize Late Bronze Age 2, are restricted to Lowland England. In other words, many bronze types are distinctive of cultures as much as periods of time, and are to that extent no better guides to chronology than pottery.

Finally, relatively little help towards generalizing our chronological scheme is provided by botanical, geological and climatic studies. In southern England, indeed, the molluscan fauna from Windmill Hill camps and Beaker sites on the chalk discloses a damp 'Atlantic' climate during Periods I-III.[5] Drier 'Sub-Boreal' conditions reigned through Periods IV and V and into VI.[6] But by VII moister 'Sub-Atlantic' conditions had returned. So in East Anglia a marine transgression very conveniently defines a horizon. On the old Lyonesse surface, inundated by the transgression, sherds of Windmill Hill, Skara Brae, Peterborough and B Beaker pottery, but not A Beakers, have been collected.[7] The submergence thus coincides with the middle of Period III. But no conclusive data for correlating cultures in the Highland Zone with those in the Lowlands are yet available, though the climatic sequence, as revealed in peat-mosses, is much the same in both areas. Still, it has been shown that in Ireland both rapiers (of Middle Bronze Age 2) and slashing swords (of the Late Bronze Age) were lost in bogs *after* the Sub-Boreal–Sub-Atlantic transition,[8] whereas in East Anglia a hoard of Late Bronze Age 2 (Period VI) occurs *at* the transitional horizon.[9]

Hence the several columns in the accompanying table can be moved up and down independently.

Period	Southern England	Yorkshire	Scottish Highlands	Ireland
I	Windmill Hill and Causewayed Camps			
II	Windmill Hill and Collective Tombs	Windmill Hill and Collective Tombs	Collective Tombs, Windmill Hill and Beacharra	Collective Tombs, Windmill Hill,
III	B Beakers Lyonesse A Beakers	Beakers	Beakers	Beacharra, etc.
IV 1400 B.C.	Wessex Culture and Segmented Beads	Food Vessels	Food Vessels	Food Vessels
V	Cinerary Urns	Cinerary Urns		
VI	Deverel– Rimbury		Cinerary Urns	Cinerary Urns
VII	Iron Age A 1	Scarborough		
VIII 75 B.C.	Iron Age A 2 Marnians Glastonbury	Charioteers of Arras	Gallic and Vitrified Forts	
IX	Belgae			

[5] *WAM.*, xlvi, 235-238; Curwen, *Arch. Sus.*, 94-96, 232.
[6] *WAM.*, xlvii, 78-79; *PPS.*, iv, 256.
[7] *PPS.*, ii, 209-210.
[8] *PPS.*, iii, 277-278.
[9] *Ant. J.*, xx, 62, 70.

4. THE HUMAN BACKGROUND

In the wings of our theatre lurk ghostly figures who had occupied the stage before the scenery described in Section 2 was set—in other words, when Britain was still joined to the Continent and when, instead of temperate forests, ice sheets and tundras alternated with tropical jungles. Actors such as we have envisaged can first be recognized on the stage of Britain some seven or eight thousand years ago.   Men or man-like creatures have lived on the Earth and in Britain itself for some half a million years. The story of Man's emergence occupies some nine-tenths of his history. Though England has made important contributions to this story, they do not compose a drama such as we wish to present here, and shall be omitted altogether.   It is not till about 50,000 years ago that Men in the full sense, members of the species *Homo sapiens*, can certainly be discerned here. Even then, the remains they have left in Britain do not suffice to allow us to define societies, as do contemporary remains from France or South Russia.   The life of mammoth-hunters in the Dordogne and on the Pontic steppes is adequately described in general text-books of European prehistory. Their kinsmen and contemporaries in Britain are vaguer figures.

Few abandoned the well-stocked hunting-grounds of France and Central Europe to settle in what Professor Garrod [10] happily describes as 'the Ultima Thule of Upper Palaeolithic Europe, a north-west cape, remote and inhospitable, bounded by the great ice sheet under which Scotland and Ireland still lay buried.'   Still, tiny bands of food-gatherers did follow the reindeer, the mammoth and the woolly rhinoceros across the land-bridge and encamp at least temporarily in caves, at first in southern England only, later as far north as Derbyshire and Yorkshire.

The first visitants were Aurignacians,[11] the westernmost outposts of a great migration that can be traced from Palestine and Asia Minor across the Crimea and Bulgaria and through Central Europe to France.   They had developed an effective organization and equipment for communal hunts after gregarious animals, and in favourable environments like the Dordogne they had even leisure and surplus food for the elaboration of a magic art and speculations about the future life.   Their remains in southern England and Wales consist for the most part of flint tools for leather-dressing and carving bone.   Nothing survives to show that they

[10] *Upper Palaeolithic Age*, 191.
[11] I follow the new terminology introduced by Professor Garrod, *PPS.*, iv, 1-26—using Aurignacian as the equivalent of the former Middle Aurignacian and Gravettian for Upper Aurignacian.

were prosperous enough to practise art here. But they did perhaps find time to bury ceremonially those who died here. The famous skeleton unearthed by Dean Buckland in Paviland Cave (Gower) [12] may be Aurignacian. It belónged to a tall man, some twenty-five years old, of the Crô-Magnon race, well known in France. The body lay extended, covered with red ochre and accompanied by ornaments—an ivory bracelet, cylindrical ivory rods and perhaps perforated shells—and by the skull of an elephant. [13]

The Aurignacians may have retreated at the onset of another period of intensified cold, so severe and prolonged over so many centuries or millennia as to cause a considerable extension of the glaciers and ice sheets. Thus the entrance to Cae Gwynn, a cave in the Vale of Clwyd, was sealed up by the moraine of a glacier after it had served as a temporary habitat for man. [14] Eventually other transient visitors arrived—Gravettians whose kinsmen and ancestors had specialized in hunting big game on open steppes and tundras in South Russia, Central Europe, France and Spain. They arrived in a late stage of their cultural evolution, termed in France the Font Robert stage, and may already have been accompanied by stragglers of a different people—the Solutreans, who in parts of France and northern Spain succeed the Gravettians in the archaeological record. For at many sites [15] flint implements pressure-flaked in the so-called Proto-Solutrean style [16] occur as well as Gravettian tools.

On their arrival they still found a few mammoth, woolly rhinoceros, [17] bison and reindeer as well as plenty of horses and wild oxen in Britain. But the climate soon—i.e. in the next two or three thousand years—began to grow milder. First the rhinoceros and then the mammoth died out, and at last the reindeer vanished even from Derbyshire. In the meantime the archaeological record in Britain diverges from the classic scheme familiar from the Dordogne and the Pyrenees. It looks as if some Gravettians had established permanent homes in England, adjusted their mode of life to the changing local conditions and developed their industrial traditions in an already insular way.

[12] Buckland, *Reliquiae Diluvianae* (1823), 87.

[13] Garrod, *op. cit.*, 60-63; the skeleton may be Aurignacian or Gravettian.

[14] Garrod, *op. cit.*, 115-117; the relics are too sparse for accurate classification.

[15] e.g. Kent's Cavern, Torquay; Paviland; Wookey Hole (Mendips); Soldiers' Hole (Cheddar, *Ant. J.*, viii, 207); Pin Hole Cave and Mother Grundy's Parlour, Creswell Crags.

[16] True Solutrean forms have been reported from East Anglia, but are not universally accepted; 'two magnificent Solutré leaf-shaped implements' have been recovered from Soldiers' Hole, Cheddar, according to Kendrick and Hawkes, p. 41.

[17] Mother Grundy's Parlour and Aveline's Hole (Mendips).

The resultant has been termed the Creswellian culture, characterized by an essentially Gravettian inventory of flint tools, generally of small size and with emphasis on shouldered points. It takes the place in general of the Magdalenian culture in which the gathering economy of the Old Stone Age reached a brilliant culmination in the exceptionally favoured environment of the Franco-Cantabrian region. But a few products of the late Magdalenian style—harpoons from Kent's Cavern and Aveline's Hole; a baton from Gough's Cave (Cheddar); needles from Creswell Crags and Kent's Cavern; bevelled javelin-heads from Pin Hole Cave (Creswell Crags) and Victoria Cave (Settle, Yorks.)—did reach England.[18] They have been variously interpreted as simple imports from France or as evidences for actual visits by Magdalenian hunters. The baton from Gough's Cave seems to have belonged to a short young man who had been buried contracted in the cave.

One's general impression is that during the closing phases of the last Ice Age southern Britain was occupied by a very sparse and far from prosperous population of hunters and collectors, living for the most part in caves, but also camping on the open plains in East Anglia and Lincolnshire.[19] None of the caves, save Paviland, seems to have been occupied at all intensively nor for long continuous periods. The population must have been very small; Clark's [20] estimate for the winter months of a total of 250 is not extravagantly low!

It is true the skeletal remains of a not inconsiderable number of individuals have been recovered. In addition to the burials already mentioned, parts of a dozen or so persons have turned up—after all, not such a large number from a period of 10,000 years or more! They include a couple of brachycranial skulls,[21] interesting because till quite recently it was believed that round-heads first appeared in Europe in post-pleistocene times. A general tendency to brachycephaly is now, however, recognized in the Crô-Magnon race [22] to which most British palaeolithic men belonged.

The contributions of these few food-gatherers to Britain's cultural heritage were negligible. What contributions, if any, they made to our

---

[18] Garrod, op. cit., 121; the engravings on bone, none entirely convincing, should belong here if anywhere.

[19] e.g. PSEA., vi (1931), 335-339.

[20] Archaeology and Society, 178.

[21] Aveline's Hole; Kent's Cavern: described by Keith, New Discoveries relating to the Antiquity of Man, 406-421. His attribution of the skulls to the mesolithic period is possible only in the first instance and even there unlikely; cf. Clark, Mesolithic Britain, 107.

[22] Coon, Races, 35, 49.

biological heritage is less certain. In Britain their descendants should have been almost swamped out by the relatively numerous later immigrants to be described in subsequent chapters. In Ireland, on the contrary, their cultural traditions can be dimly discerned at a later period, and they may have played a proportionately large part in the population. But in the pleistocene period Ireland was still uninhabited.

CHAPTER II

THE ECONOMY OF THE FOREST PERIOD

1. CHANGES OF CLIMATE AND SEA-LEVEL

THE melting of the glaciers transformed the environment of man positively as well as negatively in the British Isles and the rest of Europe: a landscape dominated by tundra and steppe gave place to one of forests. Throughout North-Western Europe trees spread onto the grassy plains or bare hills and moraines in much the same order.[1] First came groves of birch, aspen and willow, then pine forests soon combined with hazel scrub, next mixed oak woods, to be joined later by alders and last of all by beeches. Of course the above is an ideal sequence, realized only on suitable soils and at appropriate altitudes. It would be absurd to picture a solid phalanx of oak woods breasting the Pennines and crossing the Irish Sea undismayed! The actual composition of any given forest is governed by latitude, altitude, geological nature of the soil, climate, distance from the sea, fauna and other local factors. Historically it is also conditioned by the rates at which the several species of vegetation can be propagated, and by the distance from the refuges where each survived during the Ice Age.[2]

Something like the above sequence is, however, revealed by actual tree-stools and tree-pollen preserved in the successive layers of peat in bogs and mosses, not only in Denmark but also in East Anglia, the Pennines, Wales, Scotland and even Ireland. The peats disclose not only the bare fact of an arboreal migration, but also climatic fluctuations which furthered or retarded it. Five phases have been distinguished in Denmark and Sweden and given names appropriate there—Pre-Boreal, Boreal, Atlantic, Sub-Boreal and Sub-Atlantic. Of course, in an archipelago facing the Atlantic, climate can never be quite the same as in peninsulas washed by the North Sea. So the Scandinavian terms, too well established to be discarded altogether, can only be applied in rather forced conventional senses to the British conditions.

In the *Boreal* phase pine woods did in fact cover the British Isles, to

---

[1] Conveniently summarized by Clark, *Northern Europe* (1936), 1-53.

[2] On the possibility that southern England and Eire provided refuges see Wilmot, *PRS.*, cxviii (1938), 215-225.

round the coast of Britain from Lancashire to Caithness and from Sutherland to County Durham, and in Ireland from Down to Donegal.

The virtual attachment of south-eastern England to the Continent during Boreal times was obviously a factor of vital importance in the colonization of the island. The former existence of coastal tracts is less obviously significant. But many mesolithic societies lived as strand-loopers in Atlantic times and even later. The post-Atlantic transgression has simply erased all traces of their settlements in the areas affected. Forest has always profoundly affected the distribution of settlement. Yet for man the Boreal pine woods were not impenetrable; after all, they are never very close and are interrupted by glades where hazel could flourish. Their decay in the Atlantic phase to make room for oak woods or swamps brought no benefit. And subsequent changes in vegetation due to climatic causes had little effect on man compared with those wrought'by the farmers themselves and by their stock.

The replacement of tundra and steppe by forest involved the disappearance of the large gregarious mammals the pursuit of which had been the foundation of palaeolithic economy in North-Western Europe. The *mesolithic* huntsmen—those who maintained the old gathering economy in the geologists' holocene—had to learn new techniques for catching small game in forests and scrub, to be combined with fishing and fowling and the collection of hitherto unknown nuts, berries and shellfish.

2. EPIPALAEOLITHIC SURVIVORS

In the middle zone of Mother Grundy's Parlour, Creswell Crags (Derbyshire), and in King Arthur's Cave, Wye Valley, a poor flint industry in the Creswellian tradition but associated with a recent temperate fauna [8] seems to denote a survival of the old palaeolithic stock. The latter made shift as best they might, hunting wild pig, oxen, horse, red deer, bears and beavers. They show no sign of devising any sort of axe to help them in dealing with the forest now dominating their environment. Nor, as far as is known, did they have dogs to help them in the chase, though such help would now be valuable.

The extent of this survival in England cannot be gauged accurately, since characteristic equipment is far less easy to recognize than that introduced by Tardenoisian immigrants. But though ill-adapted to the new

[8] Clark, *Mesolithic Britain*, 20, 38.

conditions, some societies did survive, untouched by the new-comers, and even colonized Ireland.

In Northern Ireland various pure blade industries, for the most part in the Atlantic 25-ft. beach, seem to carry on upper palaeolithic traditions, unaffected by the innovations which distinguish intrusive mesolithic industries. No bones survive in most cases, and we have to rely entirely on the flint-work in estimating the origins and status of the societies concerned. The flint, bounteously exposed along the Antrim coast, provided ample material for the development of local styles among parties of fishers and hunters adapting themselves to novel conditions. The earliest groups known, from Island Magee and Cushendun, arrived in late Boreal or more probably early Atlantic times.[9] Their characteristic tools, broad blades and heavy scrapers, that might have been useful in wood-working, are found at the base of the raised-beach deposits. Some members of the same groups crossed over to Kintyre, where similar implements, made of Antrim flint, have been collected in the 25-ft. beach at Campbeltown.[10]

The traditions thus introduced persisted in Ireland throughout the Atlantic period; they are still dominating the flint-work incorporated in the beach at Glenarm when the sea was receding after the maximal transgression.[11] Some fragmentary bones of red deer and a bovid may disclose the game pursued.

3. TARDENOISIAN IMMIGRANTS

In Boreal times the food-gathering population of Britain was augmented by infiltrations of immigrants still practising the old economy, who may have absorbed or expelled the Creswellians. The introduction of true microliths is attributed to two waves of Tardenoisian invaders,[12] both coming from Gaul, where their tools are abundant: they get their name from the type patent station, Fère-en-Tardenois in Dept. Aisne. Microliths are small flint blades trimmed (generally blunted) along one edge or more by secondary chipping, but devoid of secondary flaking on the faces. Untrimmed chips are not technically microliths just because they are small. Nor are all microliths so minute as to deserve the name of pygmies, nor necessarily of geometrical form.

In any true Tardenoisian assemblage a rather small oblique graver—

---

[9] *PSEA.*, vii, 366; *PRIA.*, xliv, C, 120; *JRSAI.*, lxvii, 209.
[10] *PSAS.*, lvi, 261.   [11] *JRSAI.*, lxvii, 181-209.
[12] Clark, *Mesolithic Britain*, 38-52; *Northern Europe*, 190-218.

the micro-burin, Fig. 2—is associated with the microlithic blades. All microliths must have been mounted in wooden or bone shafts to form points, barbs or blades for composite tools or weapons; the care devoted to blunting the backs remains, however, quite inexplicable.

Tardenoisian tools are always found on sandy soils both on the Continent and in Great Britain; even on the Pennines they are lacking on the grits and restricted to sandstone formations. There the implements are often found 1200 to 1500 ft. above sea-level in patches, some 4 sq. yds. in area, with traces of hearths. Such doubtless mark the sites of what must have been temporary summer camps [13]; in the winter the hunters must retire to lower elevations and find more efficient shelters—where possible, caves. Their implements, together with Pendleside chert from the Pennines, have in fact been found in the upper middle zone at Creswell Crags. In default of caves, Tardenoisians dug themselves shelters in the sandy soil on the

Continent, and probably in England too. Nina Layard found remains of such in the Colne Valley (Essex) — irregular pits about 4 ft. deep and 8 ft. wide; and Clark subsequently explored four comparable pit-dwellings near Farnham (Surrey).[14] In these English pit-dwellings, however, Tardenoisian equipment is mixed with relics more appropriate to the Maglemosean tradition. So the dwellings cannot be attributed to Tardenoisians without qualification.

For the rest, Tardenoisians have left little beyond their puzzling microliths. In these a sympathetic study reveals a remarkable divergence of traditions between local groups. Two main series stand out. In the one,

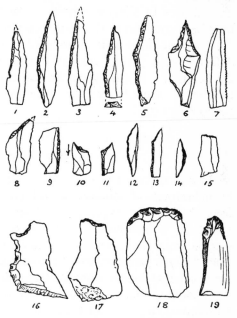

FIG. 1. Non-geometric Microliths, Warcock Hill. ¾. After Buckley.

while geometric forms are absent apart from the micro-burin, the blades, blunted in true microlithic style, tend to be relatively broad (Fig. 1). This

[13] Clark, PPS., v, 102.   [14] PPS., v, 61-100.

'broad blade industry,' as Buckley calls it, is represented all along the Pennines and on the coasts of Northumberland and Durham.[15] In southern England it occurs only as a component of the Maglemosean complex described in Section 5.   Clark has shown that it corresponds closely to the Early Tardenoisian of Belgium, and Raistrick infers that it was introduced into northern England by colonists come direct thence.   The Belgian Tardenoisians still hunted reindeer, and must therefore have flourished in early post-glacial (? Pre-Boreal) times.   Even in Yorkshire their sandy camp sites are often covered with peat the formation of which is generally supposed to begin in early Atlantic times.[16] In that case they must have reached Britain in Boreal times, naturally in boats but not necessarily after any serious voyage on the open sea (p. 18).

The second group laboriously trimmed small narrow blades to neat geometric figures—triangles, rhomboids, crescents and, later, trapezes (Fig. 2).   Some of these could conveniently be made by chipping two notches in a little blade and snapping it obliquely at the notches.   The stumps left are indistinguishable from micro-burins.   Makers of geometric microliths camped on sandy ridges bordering the fens in Cambridgeshire,[17] and on sandy heaths in Suffolk [18] and Lincolnshire,[19] and spread as far north as the Cleveden Hills and Pennines in Yorkshire without apparently reaching County Durham.[20]   They did, however, spread westward into North Wales [21] and reached even the Isle of Man, naturally by boat.   In the south geometric microliths have been collected from many sites on the greensand of Surrey, Kent and Sussex, but generally as elements in a composite culture dominated by Forest traditions.[22]

Our geometric microliths agree very closely with those characteristic of the Middle Tardenoisian of Belgium.   It is generally assumed that the fashion was introduced by immigrants from that quarter.   These, too, should have arrived during the Boreal phase.   In Cambridgeshire characteristic products have been found in a zone of fen peat just below 'the transition from Boreal to Atlantic.' [23]   In North Wales, on the contrary, the context of the microliths seems to be rather Atlantic.   This might be due to the slowness of the hunters' penetration to the west or to an earlier onset of moist conditions there.

[15] Raistrick, *YAJ.*, xxxi, 151.

[16] So Clark and Raistrick, but Godwin, *PRS.*, 118 (1935), 213, suggests these Pennine peats may be later.   [17] Shippea Hill: Clark, *Ant. J.*, xv, 303-305.

[18] e.g. Wangford and Lakenheath.   [19] e.g. Scunthorpe.

[20] *YAJ.*, xxxi, 151.   [21] Prestatyn, Flints., *PPS.*, iv, 330-334.

[22] Clark, *PPS.*, v, 62-104.   [23] Godwin, *Ant. J.*, xv, 310.

The fashions in flint-work favoured by Tardenoisians seem to have developed in Africa and were doubtless popularized by immigrants from that Continent.[24] These may, however, have joined forces with disintegrating

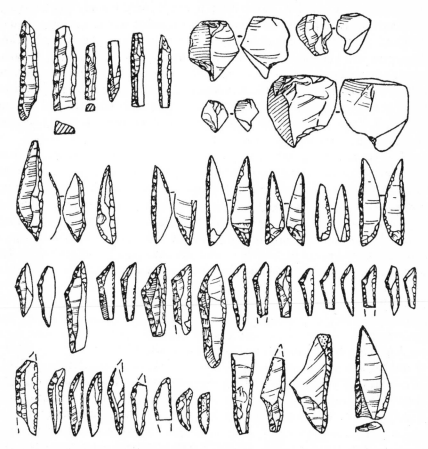

Fig. 2. Geometric Microliths from Farnham; top right, micro-burins. ¼.
After Clark and Rankine in *PPS*.

European Upper Palaeolithic societies and have been virtually absorbed therein before reaching Britain. There is a little evidence that dogs had already attached themselves to the ancestral African communities. So the first dogs in Britain may have followed the Tardenoisians. But no direct evidence to this effect is available.

[24] Childe, *Dawn*, 7.

Archaeology represents—perhaps misrepresents—Tardenoisians as minute groups eking out a precarious existence with an unpractical equipment and largely isolated from one another by marshes and forests. But they certainly were able to survive, if not to multiply, and succeeded in maintaining their industrial traditions even after immigrant farmers had introduced a new economy and the Neolithic Age. In the Mendips groups of hunters, making microliths, lived on into the Early Bronze Age, perhaps to become subjects of the new Beaker invaders. There are hints of a similar survival in Staffordshire. In the north of England many assemblages of microliths lack the micro-burin, as do the late Mendip groups; such doubtless belong to descendants of the Boreal immigrants living in Atlantic or Sub-Boreal times. Such belated groups spread into Scotland. On sandy stretches in Tweedside and Ayrshire, and even along the Dee in Kincardineshire,[25] assemblages of microliths, many of them geometric, attest the immigration of Tardenoisian families. But the micro-burin is excessively rare, while small blades, pressure-flaked on the faces in neolithic technique, often accompany the microliths. At Shewalton Moor (Ayrshire), an arrow-head of Bronze Age form had been imitated in microlithic style. The Tardenoisian settlement of Scotland is thus late; it may be post-mesolithic in time though the mesolithic economy was presumably kept intact.

4. AZILIAN STRAND-LOOPERS

A series of settlements on the west coast of Scotland is generally attributed to Azilians from France (named after the Mas d'Azil in Ariège). Near Oban they once inhabited two shallow rock-shelters, now destroyed; on the little island of Oransay they camped, perhaps only in summer, on the sandy shore with a mere windscreen to protect them from the gales. In each case the settlements are close to the 25-ft. raised beach, but they seem to have been occupied first when the sea was receding again after the maximum of the transgression.[26]

The Scottish Azilians lived by hunting red and roe deer, boar, badger, wild-cat and seal, fowling, collecting nuts and shellfish, and catching fish, including deep-sea species. They were assisted in the chase by dogs, and must have had boats to reach Oransay and for fishing. The fisherman relied on a harpoon or fish-spear with a head of bone or antler, generally double-barbed (Fig. 3). Flint being very rare in Scotland, every scrap was

[25] *PSAS.*, lxx, 419-434.   [26] Childe, *P.S.*, 13-17; *Dawn*, 4-5.

utilized till worn out, so that the flint-work seems poor. But Breuil [27] has recognized a few gravers, including a micro-burin. The commonest surviving artefacts are stout chisel-shaped slices of bone or antler rounded and blunted at both ends, and elongated beach-pebbles of the same shape, also battered at both ends. They are popularly mis-named 'limpet-scoops,' but Breuil plausibly argues that they served as *fabricators* in working flint. Clark

FIG. 3.   Azilian 'Harpoon,' Oban.   ½.

suggests less probably that they could be used in carpentry, but a chisel-shaped implement made from a stag's cannon bone [28] might have been so used as a wedge, since its edge is sharp. Apart from the latter—which has counterparts in Azilian sites in France—the Azilians throughout Atlantic Europe seem no better equipped for dealing with forest than the Tardenoisians.

In Britain, therefore, they appear as a predominantly littoral population. In addition to the coastal settlements preserved by the subsequent marine regression, distinctive 'harpoons' from a river near Shewalton (Ayrs.),[29] from the Dee near Kirkcudbright, from Victoria Cave in the West Riding and from Whitburn on the Durham coast attest occasional visitants with the same traditions.[30]   Farther south, traces of such a littoral population have less chance of survival since the coast-line has continued to sink since Atlantic times (p. 18).   Nevertheless, elongated pebbles, treated just like the Scottish fabricators, have been found with atypical microliths near Aberystwyth, on the Pembrokeshire coasts [31] and at Penwith, Land's End.[32]

The Azilian culture developed from the local Magdalenian in Cantabria and South France, where its authors may have acquired dogs and the trick of making micro-burins from Tardenoisian immigrants.   Presumably they spread thence northwards along the coasts, though no reliable memorials of their journey survive between the Dordogne and Yorkshire.   Ample time is available for a migration by short stages.   In Cantabria and Ariège the Azilian occupations follow immediately upon the Magdalenian, presumably in Boreal times; the settlements in Scotland are relatively late Atlantic.   And some Azilians may have preserved their identity as long as Tardenoisians; on Colonsay at a sandhill site pebble fabricators were found

[27] *PSAS.*, lvi, 265.
[29] *PSAS.*, lxxiii, 48-49.
[31] *Arch. Camb.* (1915), 179; Grimes, *Guide*, 45.
[28] Childe, *P.S.*, Figs. I, 7.
[30] Clark, *Mesolithic Britain*, 14-16.
[32] Clark, *op. cit.*, 45.

together with arrow-heads of Bronze Age type,[33] and similar associations are reported from Pembrokeshire.

5. FOREST FOLK

The population of the great plain of Northern Europe [34] in Boreal times specialized in hunting, fowling and fishing on the banks of the numerous lakes, meres and streams that interrupt the forest. To this end they developed a highly specialized equipment of bone fish-hooks, fish-spears or harpoons, and at the same time evolved a 'heavy industry' in bone, stone and flint for dealing with the timber that constituted such a conspicuous element in their environment. Those termed Maglemoseans (after the 'Big Moss' near Mullerup, Zealand), living west of the Baltic, in Boreal times took over the micro-burin and other articles from Tardenoisian neighbours.

As south-eastern England was then still effectively a continuation of the plain, it is to be expected that Maglemoseans should reach Britain too. Conditions here have indeed been generally unfavourable to the preservation of the bone-work that is so distinctive of the Continental societies. Yet typically Maglemosean harpoons have been collected from the Leman–Ower Banks off the East Anglian coast (Fig. 4), from two sites in Holderness

FIG. 4. 'Maglemose' Harpoon of Bone, Leman–Ower Banks. ⅓. After Mrs Burkitt.

(Yorks.), from Royston (Herts.), and from the Thames near Battersea and Wandsworth, while heavy tools decorated in Maglemosean style were recovered from the Thames and from the Test (Hants).[35]

Moreover, several settlement sites can be recognized by characteristic stone tools though all organic remains have perished. All are located on low-lying land adapted to the Maglemosean economy. That best explored, at Broxbourne (Herts.),[36] was situated on a ridge of sand and gravel in the flood plain of the River Lea. The occupied area covered only some 15 ft. and could hardly have accommodated more than a family group. Of the

---

[33] *Geological Magazine* (1911), 171.   [34] Childe, *Dawn*, 8-13.

[35] *BMQ.*, viii (1934), 144; Maglemosean types of antler adzes and chisels were made and used right into the Iron Age, so that undecorated specimens, common in the Thames and elsewhere, cannot be used to prove Maglemosean settlement.

[36] *JRAI.*, lxiv, 101-128.

hunters' equipment survive microliths, mostly conforming to the 'broad blade' Tardenoisian type; a few true gravers in addition to micro-burins allow one to infer a kit of bone points and hooks as complete as was current on the Baltic. Club-heads of stone, perforated by percussion from both sides, were used on the Baltic. Such have been found in southern England too, but on sites where the Maglemosean tradition persisted into Atlantic times.

The carpenter's equipment is represented by the *core-axe*, the first effective wood-working tool found in the British Isles (Fig. 5). The

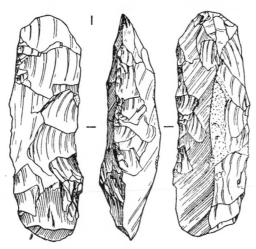

FIG. 5. Core-axe, Farnham. $\frac{1}{2}$.
After Clark.

working edge is formed 'by a special blow struck transversely at one corner of the extremity'—the so-called *tranchet blow*; flakes thus detached often turn up. And the implement could be resharpened by simply repeating the tranchet blow.

The Maglemoseans reached Britain in Boreal times; the Broxbourne site is covered by a Boreal peat, and the North Sea harpoon was embedded in a peat of like age. In that period, too, they had spread up the Thames valley as far as Newbury on the Kennet. On the coast they can be traced northwards to West Hartlepool, County Durham, where Trechmann [37] has found a core-axe, a micro-burin and other tools in a submerged forest.

They were subsequently cut off from their Continental relatives by the

[37] *PPS.*, ii, 161-168.

marine transgression of Atlantic times, but none the less preserved and developed the old traditions.   At Lower Halstow, Burchell [38] found a settlement on the shore of the Medway estuary beneath Atlantic peat. Presumably the old economy was retained, but only the carpenter's equipment is available for study.   The core-axe now assumed a special form peculiar to Britain, termed the *Thames pick*; it is longer and narrower than the Boreal variety.   With it appears the flake-axe or *grand tranchet* (Fig. 6);

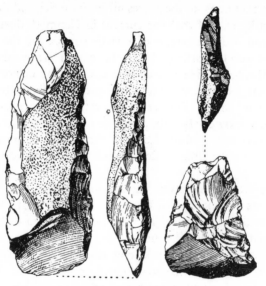

FIG. 6.   Flake-axe, Lower Halstow.   -½.
After Burchell.

one face is the bulbar surface of the flake; the intersection of this with the bed of a flake previously detached from the core by a transverse, tranchet blow forms the working edge.   Such axes were occasionally used by Maglemoseans on the Baltic in Boreal times and were very popular among their descendants in Atlantic times.

Judging by the number of Thames picks, the late Maglemosean population must have flourished in the Thames valley during the Atlantic phase.   And they can be traced elsewhere.   The *Horsham culture* of the greensands in Essex, Kent, Surrey and Sussex is essentially a 'geometric Tardenoisian' enriched by a carpenter's kit of core- and flake-axes and by percussion-perforated club-heads.[39]   It is thus a blend of Maglemosean and Middle

[38] *PSEA.*, v, 73-78; 217-223; 288-296.   [39] Clark, *PPS.*, v, 61-118.

Tardenoisian traditions. The settlements, including the pit-dwellings described on p. 21, are restricted to the sands and located by preference beside springs; they thus reflect a Tardenoisian rather than a Forest economy. Yet the idea of tackling and exploiting the forest environment has been adopted. It was not restricted to south-eastern England.

At the Nab Head and elsewhere in Pembrokeshire,[40] and even in Cornwall, core-axes have turned up to attest the penetration of Maglemoseans, or at least of their traditions, to the shores of the Irish Sea and the Atlantic. In Scotland an antler axe, of the type current in Denmark during the Atlantic phase, was found with the carcase of a whale stranded in the enlarged Forth estuary, 5 miles west of Stirling. It may have been left by mesolithic whalers from beyond the North Sea or from the coastal sites of northern England. And Lacaille has recently reported a few core-axes from the Tweed valley and Loch Lomond side.[41] On the Solway estuary, too, core- and flake-axes in the Forest tradition disclose the presence of Forest folk at the time of the marine transgression.[42] Most probably these crossed over from eastern England, since we have already encountered them on the coasts of Durham and Yorkshire.

Presumably from the Solway mouth some sailed or paddled over to Ireland. The axes, long known from the beach at Larne,[43] might be the result; for here the old Creswellian tradition is blended with that of Forest folk. At Glenarm Movius[44] found core- and flake-axes being left about *above* the old Atlantic raised beach long after the epi-Creswellian industry (described on p. 20) had been incorporated *in* the beach. But at Glenarm the flints include fish-tailed scrapers and other types that can be matched better in North France than in Britain. And with them go the bones of sheep and cows as if their makers had been food-producers. So at Ballynagard on Rathlin Island axes were accompanied by Western pottery with the curious club-rims so common in the later Windmill Hill ware of Britain.

Hence Whelan[45] holds that the North Irish culture is a branch of the so-called Campignyan, introduced by immigrants from France together with the neolithic arts and a food-producing economy. The French Campignyan itself is, of course, just the classical Western Neolithic infused with local Forest traditions. Did not a similar infusion occur in Northern Ireland,

---

[40] Grimes, *Guide*, 13-15.

[41] *PSAS.*, lxxiv, 6-10.

[42] *Mem. Geol. Survey G.B.: Geology of Carlisle and District* (1926), 79. The implements were not certainly found in the Raised Beach gravels.

[43] Whelan, *PRIA.*, C, xliv, 120, Pl. II.

[44] *JRSAI.*, lxvii, 196, 208-210.

[45] *PRIA.*, C, xlii, 130-142.

though here both the Forest folk and the neolithic farmers would have come via Britain? In any case we have now left the Mesolithic, even as a division of the local British time-scale, behind us, and reached the full Neolithic when causewayed camps were inhabited in southern England.

What proportion did survivors from mesolithic food-gatherers form in the later population of the British Isles? What contributions did they make to the cultural capital of the islanders? Admittedly an unusually large proportion of mesolithic equipment was made from perishable materials; the more durable products are not particularly attractive to amateur collectors; large areas of settlement have been made inaccessible by the sea's encroachment. Yet mesolithic industries cover on the geochronologists' estimates a period of at least 3000 years—as long as is allowed to all subsequent prehistoric periods put together. The surviving material is exiguous when compared with that assigned to the New Stone, Bronze and Early Iron Ages. It suggests an extremely small population. Yet, if they adopted a new economy from neolithic immigrants, tiny scattered groups might multiply quite fast.

Survivals of mesolithic traditions into later periods have already been mentioned. The cases cited, however, suggest conservative groups in cultural backwaters obstinately clinging to an obsolescent economy. The earliest food-producing communities we can recognize in Britain owe nothing in the way of equipment to the mesolithic societies who lived or had lived in close proximity. The same is true of the next intrusive group, the Beaker folk. But in their sanctuaries and barrows microliths occur as if residual Tardenoisians were included among their subjects. Even earlier in the Peterborough culture of eastern England, as in the North British Food Vessel culture later, we shall recognize components derived from the Forest tradition. In Ireland the aboriginal mesolithic element may prove to be more prominent, but even here it is not easy to assess its strength. In any case, the notorious insularity of British and Irish neolithic and later cultures must be partly due to absorption by older established cultures. The latter did represent adjustments, albeit only for the purposes of gathering, to the islands' peculiar environments. It would be odd indeed if the later arrivals failed to profit by the experience of their humbler precursors.

CHAPTER III

THE NEOLITHIC REVOLUTION

1. THE FOOD-PRODUCING ECONOMY

DURING ninety-nine per cent. of his existence on the earth, Man had subsisted by hunting and collecting what nature provided. Though he exceeded other animals in cunning and dexterity, his attitude to his environment was effectively as passive and negative as that of the beaver or the fox. Perhaps only 7000 years ago one or two societies adopted a more aggressive attitude to their surroundings. They began actively and successfully to increase their food-supply by cultivating edible plants and breeding animals to yield meat or milk. About the same time, and in obedience to the same urge, they began creating materials that do not occur in nature—pottery and threads. Agriculture and stock-breeding initiated an economic revolution; for they allowed population to expand beyond the narrow limits imposed by the naturally available supplies of game and wild fruits. In theory, by merely extending the area under cultivation and sparing the natural increase of the herds, provision could be made for an indefinite number of new mouths.

All the available data indicate that the neolithic revolution [1] started somewhere in that East Mediterranean zone which extends from Egypt to Iran. Wild grasses, ancestral to wheat and barley, would grow on the arid uplands of Palestine and Iran. Sheep, ancestors of the stocks from which our oldest domestic sheep are derived, still roam wild on the Anatolian-Iranian mountains. Only on the edge of the Nile, in Syria and in Iran, does archaeology reveal communities of farmers unquestionably before 4500 B.C. Their economy was still transitional: farming was on a par with, if not subordinate to, hunting and fishing, whereas among the oldest farmers in Central and Western Europe such gathering activities had been relegated to a position of minimal importance.

The neolithic revolution had to spread. Under the simple rural economy that at first prevailed, farming involved migration. The same plot will not yield good crops for many years in succession. The simplest solution of

[1] Cf. Childe, *New Light on the Most Ancient East* (1934) and *Man makes Himself* (1939).

31

the contradiction, one still adopted by many African tribes, is to start cultivating fresh lands as soon as the old plots show signs of exhaustion. When all the land in a district has been used up, the community migrates with goods and chattels to fresh fields. In any case, new land was needed for new families as long as population was growing; and growing flocks and herds will also be requiring fresh pastures. But suitable land, neither too dry nor marshy, not excessively stony and free from heavy forest, in fact is available only in patches. Expanding under the pressures just sketched, even by the shortest stages, primitive farmers must soon spread from the Nile to the Atlantic, from the Straits of Gibraltar to the Straits of Dover. Naturally they would not expand *in vacuo*. They would meet other communities, still mesolithic in economy. Some of these might adopt the new economy, swell the army of landseekers and accelerate its progress. Even so, it might take 2500 years for the first farmers to reach the English Channel.

In the interval another revolution had occurred in the Orient. Communities cultivating the alluvial plains of the Nile, the Tigris–Euphrates and the Indus valleys had no need to shift periodically to new fields; the silt brought down by the annual inundations restored to the land what the crops had taken out. Such farmers could produce more food-stuffs than were needed for domestic consumption, and with the surplus support labourers to dig bigger canals, artisans to manufacture more efficient tools, merchants to import raw materials and priests to conciliate imaginary supernatural powers. The attack upon external nature could be continued with augmented resources. It led to the harnessing of the winds and the strength of oxen, to the invention of the sail, the wheel and the plough, to the discovery of metallurgy. A second economic revolution was accomplished. By 3000 B.C. populous and wealthy cities had grown up in Egypt, Mesopotamia and India. The demands of these metropoles for metals, luxuries and magic substances involved the propagation of the new economy and the rise of new urban centres of demand in ever-widening circles around the original foci. By 2000 B.C. repercussions of the new commercial activity were probably reaching Britain. Though a true urban economy was not established here before the Roman conquest, the general use of metal that characterizes what is termed the Bronze Age finally destroyed the self-sufficiency that neolithic communities might enjoy. This economic change was doubtless due, however indirectly, to the commerce of the Oriental cities.

There is a time-lag of 3000 years between the first literate cities of the Orient and the rise of like institutions in Roman Britain. A comparable time-lag may have intervened between the first trading ventures of Oriental metal-merchants and the impact of their activities upon islands which even to classical Greece appeared the uttermost outpost of the known world.

2. THE BRITISH ISLES AS FIELDS FOR COLONIZATION

The neolithic economy was first established in dry hot climes. The plants and animals on which it is based are derived from wild species at home on continental steppes. Drought was the principal handicap to Oriental–Mediterranean husbandry and stock-breeding. It must have been a long and difficult task to adjust a rural economy evolved to meet such conditions and plants adapted to the steppe to the temperate regime of Atlantic Europe. Deep ploughing, unprofitable or even dangerous on shallow Mediterranean soils, is essential for the best results on the clay lands of England and Northern Europe. Exhaustion is slow where the surface layers are not leached by abundant rain. The steppes are treeless, the Mediterranean forest light compared with the dense oak woods that covered the plains of Atlantic Europe. Though some sort of axe or adze is rightly regarded as a hall-mark of neolithic culture, it was too fragile a tool to make much mark in clearing these temperate forests. Even the metal axes of the Bronze Age, though more durable, were too expensive for such rough work. Only cheap iron tools gave men effective mastery over this aspect of Atlantic environment. Before considering the colonization of Britain by food-producers we should consider the environment as they would find it.

The moist Atlantic climate with its cool wet summers would be unfamiliar; only the stoutest calves could survive the long cold winters unstalled. Everywhere forest alternated with bog. The clay lands supported 'damp' oak woods with thorny scrub that constituted insuperable obstacles to settlement and imposed formidable barriers even to communications. Though the clay lands include the most productive soils of the British Isles, their exploitation requires equipment, social solidarity and capital expenditure beyond the range of the colonists here envisaged. They constitute what Fox [2] terms 'areas of difficult settlement.' On the other hand, chalk downs, limestone plateaux, some recent moraines support less intractable vegetation, and the gales of the Atlantic period had already cleared of trees some sandy tracts along the coasts, exposed uplands and the north of Scotland (p. 5). They offered 'areas of easy settlement' where small communities, poorly

[2] *The Personality of Britain*, 76.

equipped, could find patches of arable land and pasture with a minimum expenditure of social effort.   In particular, the chalk downs of southern England, that just continue the same formation from France, would offer a familiar environment to farmers crossing the Channel.   At the same time, the limestone ridges rising above the drift in western Ireland would welcome to a veritably Mediterranean landscape any adventurous groups who arrived by sea-ways from the south (Pl. III, 2).   It was, however, from the chalk lands of Gaul to the chalk downs of Sussex and Wessex that the first farmers to till and graze the soils of Britain came.

3. The Windmill Hill Culture

Immigrants from across the Channel brought, fully formed, the oldest neolithic culture recognizable in the archaeological record.   Apart from encampments of the same folk on the Fen margins and the Essex coasts, the oldest settlements of food-producers yet recognized in the British Isles are causewayed camps, strung out along the Downs and uplands from Sussex to eastern Devon.[3]   The first to be recognized as neolithic (by Keiller), Windmill Hill (Wilts.) (Fig. 10, No. 5), may appropriately give a name to the whole culture they represent.

The camps' occupants relied for a livelihood chiefly on breeding cattle, but kept also sheep or goats and pigs, and cultivated barley and wheat.[4] Their cattle are larger and have longer horns than the later Celtic short-horn (*Bos longifrons*), but are smaller than the native wild ox or *urus* (*Bos primigenius*). They cannot, therefore, be the results of taming wild oxen, but the herds may have been recruited by crossing imported short-horns with wild cattle.[5] The corn plots may have been cultivated with a hoe or a digging stick or an antler pick similar to that used in mining and ditching (p. 38).   The grains were ground with bun-shaped rubbers pushed round and round a flat-topped stone slab till an oval depression was worn in it.[6]   (Such will be termed *saucer querns* in contradistinction to the later *saddle quern*.)

In comparison with these 'productive' pursuits, food-gathering activities were surprisingly inconspicuous.   Among the food-refuse of the camps the

[3] Coombe Hill (Jevington), Whitehawk (Brighton) (Fig. 10, 7), The Trundle (Goodwood) (*ib.* 6) in Sussex; Abingdon, Berks., Windmill Hill (*ib.* 5), Knap Hill and Robin Hood's Ball, in Wilts.; Maiden Castle, Dorchester (*ib.* 4); and Hembury, near Honiton in Devon (*ib.* 3).

[4] Jessen and Helbaek, 17, 63.

[5] *CISPP*. (London, 1932), 155.

[6] *Antiquity*, xi, 135.

bones of domestic beasts greatly exceed those of game. They give no hint of a transition from the mesolithic to the neolithic economy.

The fortified settlements suggest permanent occupation of the same site, or at least a return thereto at regular intervals. The 'camps' are

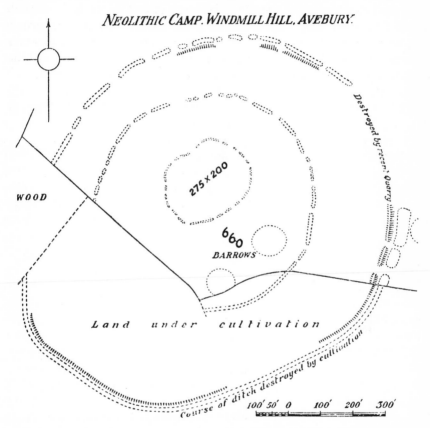

FIG. 7. Plan of Causewayed Camp of Windmill Hill, Wilts. After Keiller.

normally surrounded by one or more irregular flat-bottomed ditches interrupted at frequent intervals by causeways left unquarried in the chalk or subsoil (Fig. 7). The material from the ditches was piled up on the inner side in a bank which served as the basis for a stockade.[7] At Whitehawk there were four concentric ditches which enclosed a total area of $11\frac{1}{2}$ acres though the innermost enclosure measured only 2 acres. The outer ditch

[7] Curwen, *Arch. Sus.*, 83.

at the Trundle (Goodwood) enclosed 14 acres, the inner 3 acres. Part of a small curvilinear hut was uncovered at the inner margin of the rampart at Hembury.[8] A series of elongated pits, arranged in a sort of spiral, between the inner and outer ditch of the Trundle are interpreted by Curwen [9] as hut-foundations. One was an irregular oval, 25 ft. long by 10 ft. wide and about 4 ft. deep, with five stake-holes along the edge for the supports for a roof of, possibly, skins. The same author found on the open downs an isolated dwelling of rather similar form—an oval pit 8 ft. long by 6 ft. wide by 2 ft. deep, connected with a round depression 4 ft. in diameter but only 9 ins. deep.[10] On the other hand, at Halden, in Devon, Willard [11] traced the foundations of a rectangular house, built above ground like the Hembury hut. So Windmill Hill folk did not live exclusively in causewayed camps nor in one single type of dwelling, even in southern England.

For carpentry they used axes and adzes of local flint on the Downs, but in Devon and Dorset also axes of fine-grained stones imported from Cornwall.[12] None were perforated for hafting, nor were any mounted in antler sleeves as was customary among mesolithic Forest folk and neolithic Westerners in France and Switzerland. Arrow-heads of leaf-shaped form (Fig. 24, 1-3), characteristic of Windmill Hill culture, may rank as hunters' weapons. The mesolithic transverse arrow-head occurs exceptionally in Sussex camps and at Windmill Hill, and derivatives of it at Maiden Castle, but only in late layers. For leather dressing innumerable scrapers were made of flint and very curious bunched combs [13] of stags' antler. So presumably skins were used for clothing, as nothing attests a textile industry.

The pots, too, are clearly inspired in the first instance by leather models. What Piggott [14] regards as the oldest forms, represented at the bottom of the Windmill Hill ditches, at the Trundle in Sussex and at Hembury in Devon— Group A 1—are plain round-bottomed baggy dishes and bowls with simple rims and small lug handles (Fig. 8, 1-2). Carinated forms (Fig. 8, 3) are said to appear rather later at the type site and are classed as A 2. They are common at Whitehawk and farther east, but are missing in Dorset and Devon. Piggott,[15] followed by Hawkes, attributes them to a different group of colonists more closely allied than the first to the Michelsberg branch of the Western population. The A 2 pottery of Wessex and Sussex shows a distinctive insular development in the squashing down or rolling over of

[8] *PDAES.*, ii, 161.   [9] *SAC.*, lxxii, 105; *Arch. Sus.*, 92.
[10] *SAC.*, lxxv, 154.   [11] *PDAES.*, ii, 249-251.   [12] *Ant. J.*, xvi, 266.
[13] Found at the Sussex camps, Windmill Hill, Maiden Castle, Abingdon and Maiden Bower (Fig. 10, 9).   [11] *Arch. J.*, lxxxviii, 82-85   [16] *PSEA.*, vii (1934), 373-381.

the rim to form *club rims* (Fig. 8, 4). Moreover, it is often decorated. By drawing her fingers lightly over the wet clay the potter produced shallow *finger-tip fluting*, compared to the wrinkles of leather, the hammer-marks on beaten copper, or the chisel-marks on wood; a blunt bone point produced rather wide shallow *channelled* lines, generally grouped in parallel bundles

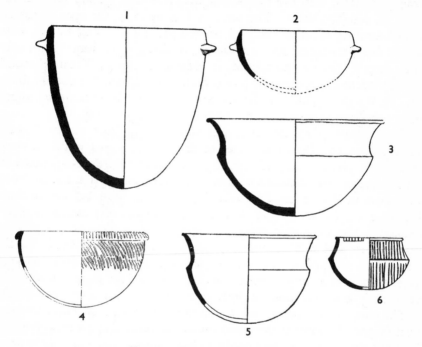

FIG. 8. WINDMILL HILL VASES.

1, Form B; 2, Form A; 3, Form G; 6, Form J.

1. The Trundle = Form B; 2. Hembury = Form A; 3. Hanging Grimston (Yorks.) = Form G; 4. Sandy Hill Smithy (Eday); 5. Hanging Thorn Cairn (Ulster); 6. Hanging Thorn Cairn = Form J.   All ⅓.

and arranged in panels; finally, pricks with a point, or even a comb, produced *punctured* patterns. Instead of the A 2 ware at Hembury and Maiden Castle, we may find associated with A 1 vessels bowls with *trumpet lugs*, i.e. horizontal tubes expanding at both ends.[16] They were fashionable in Brittany, as also in Mediterranean lands, and have hence been hailed as heralds of a third, Armorican immigration.[17]

[16] *PDAES.*, ii, Pl. XXXVII.   [17] Hawkes, *Foundations*, 146.

It would seem an over-refinement to subdivide the Windmill Hill culture and reconstruct three distinct migrations on the strength of the relatively minor ceramic peculiarities, each of which may be found equally in camps or long barrows associated with arrow-heads, distinctive of all three groups in common.   These local ceramic styles may indeed suggest the variety of traditions impinging on England in Period I.   They equally disclose the divergence of traditions between regional groups who by virtue of their neolithic economy itself were to a large extent mutually isolated.

For all the equipment described could be made in the consumers' households from local materials so that each community could be self-sufficing.   In fact, this neolithic self-sufficiency was only potential.   There is evidence for communal specialization and trade.   Some Windmill Hill communities specialized in the extraction of flint by mining.   Now flint-mining was practised by peoples of similar traditions in Egypt and Sicily, and nearer home by the kindred Westerners of France, Belgium and Holland.   So that it is likely that the mining technique formed part of the ancestral Western tradition brought to England by the Windmill Hill people themselves.

The flint nodules that lie about the surface of the chalk are seldom large enough for making into axes and are flawed by frost.   Satisfactory nodules of good flint occur in seams in the chalk, which are sometimes exposed by sections cut by streams or by marine erosion.   To reach these layers more conveniently the miners sank shafts from the ground surface, often through several feet of overburden.   The simplest shaft is a mere pit expanding at the bottom where the desired nodules lay.   Then shallow lateral excavations were cut into the pit walls along the seam.   Finally, complicated subterranean galleries have often been driven along the seam from the pit bottom.   Most mines in Sussex and Wessex belong to the galleried type.   But at Grimes Graves in Norfolk (Fig. 10, 10) all three types are found within a small area.   Armstrong [18] believes that they form a chronological sequence beginning with the simple 'primitive' pits.   Clark and Piggott,[19] however, contend that the form of a mine is conditioned not by age but by the conditions of the site—depth of the seam, solidity of the chalk for a roof, and so on.

The shafts and galleries were dug, like the ditches of neolithic camps, with the aid of an *antler pick*, i.e. a red-deer's antler deprived of all but the brow tine.[20]   It was not really used as a pick but as a lever.   The projecting tine was hammered into the chalk by blows on the back of the antler, which was then used as a lever-handle in splitting off the lump of chalk.

[18] *PSEA.*, v, 93-123.   [19] *Antiquity*, vii, 181.   [20] Curwen, *Arch. Sus.*, 113.

However, in the 'primitive pits' at Grimes Graves, Armstrong found only wedges made from the marrow-bones of deer and oxen instead of antlers.[21] Rakes made of antlers with two lateral tines and shovels made from the shoulder-blades of oxen were appropriately used. The dark galleries were feebly illuminated by lamps quarried out of lumps of chalk, such as are found also in the camps at the Trundle, Whitehawk and Windmill Hill.[22]

When all the nodules that could safely be quarried had been extracted, the dump was shovelled back into the shaft. The hollow remaining was used as a sheltered working-place. For flint was not only mined but partially worked up on the spot. Often there are in one shaft several working-floors marked by flakes and wasters, animal bones and hearths. The 'celts' found in the mines are seldom polished; they were exported in the rough unfinished state. Axes of the type common in the Cissbury mines turn up all over the Sussex Downs. The numbers turned out were far in excess of the miners' needs. They must have been produced for export. In fact, the flint-miners of Norfolk, Sussex and Wessex formed specialized industrial communities, bartering their products over a wide area. Indeed, these pioneers of British mining must have waxed rich from their industrial enterprise.

Rare sherds of Windmill Hill ware from the shafts suffice to show that the miners belonged to that society. But sherds of a different kind from Grimes Graves suggest that another group, the Peterborough people to be described below, shared at least in the trade with their products.

The flint-mines are not the only proof that Windmill Hill folk were the founders of British industrialism. On the slopes of Penmaen Mawr in North Wales, Hazzledine Warren [23] found the debris of a regular factory where axes were manufactured on a large scale from the local augite-granophyre (Graig Lwyd rock). The products have been unearthed on Windmill Hill sites in the vicinity, and even in Glamorgan and Wessex.[24] They reached the latter regions mainly in Period III, and it is again likely that Peterborough folk were engaged in their distribution.

The superstitions of Windmill Hill folk are illustrated by phalli and female figurines, carved in chalk [25] (Fig. 9). Both are fertility charms used in magic rites to ensure the germination of the grain and the multiplication of the herds and flocks. The miners who laboured in the dark and eerie galleries observed like cults. Armstrong found in pit 15 at Grimes Graves

---

[21] *PSEA.*, iv (1923), 120; (1924), 187. [22] *Antiquity*, vii, 172.
[23] *JRAI.*, xlix (1919), 342; li 165. [24] *Arch. Camb.*, xc (1935), 208.
[25] Figurines, Maiden Castle and Windmill Hill; phalli, Whitehawk Camp, the Trundle, Blackpatch flint-mines, Thickthorne long barrow: *PPS.*, ii, 87.

a sort of altar on which may have stood a female figurine and a phallus of chalk [26] for rites designed to restore earth's fertility in good flint too.

Skeletons of Windmill Hill folk have been exposed, buried quite unceremoniously, in the ditch of Whitehawk camp and in the shaft of a flint-mine.

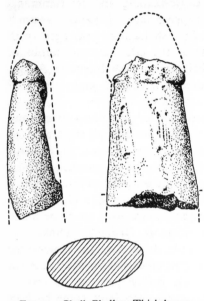

FIG. 9.   Chalk Phallus, Thickthorne Down. ⅓. After Piggott in *PPS.*, ii.

But their chiefs at least were sometimes buried in communal ossuaries—long barrows. On each block of Sussex downland there is a causewayed camp, a group of flint-mines and a cluster of long barrows.[27] And Windmill Hill pottery has been found in the ditches of many long barrows and in the megalithic chambers that some cover. Piggott [28] indeed holds that the rite of long-barrow burial was the traditional practice of the Windmill Hill folk from the first, while Hawkes [29] suggests that it was introduced from Brittany together with trumpet-lugged pottery. Others hold that it is a secondary trait in the Windmill Hill culture, symbolizing its authors' conversion to a new megalithic religion reaching southern England from the West. This religious movement will occupy us in the next chapter   Till then burial rites cannot be used to define the origins or distribution of the Windmill Hill colonists.

The culture just described is not the result of the autochthonous development of any local mesolithic culture. The new economy appears abruptly fully perfected; the animals and plants on which it is based are exotic. Save for a handful of *tranchet* arrow-heads, not a single item from any mesolithic equipment occurs in causewayed camps. The distribution of mesolithic and neolithic settlement in southern England is sharply contrasted when plotted on a large-scale map.[30] On the contrary, the Windmill Hill culture is just an outpost of the great cycle of Western neolithic societies

[26] Described to British Association at Dundee, 1939; owing to faulting this pit missed the usual seam of good nodules.

[27] Curwen, *Arch. Sus.*, 96-99.   [28] *PPS.*, i, 121.

[29] *Foundations*, 147.   [30] Clark, *Mesolithic Britain*, 90.

represented beyond the Channel in the oldest Swiss lake-dwellings, the Michelsberg settlements of Belgium and the Rhine valley, Fort Harrouard and le Campigny in the Lower Seine basin, and the pre-megalithic graves of Brittany.[31] The whole economy is strikingly similar, with its preference for upland sites, its reliance on cattle-keeping and its communal specialization for flint-mining and manufacturing axes. Jaquetta Hawkes [32] has shown in detail how accurately the English leathery pots agree with those from Switzerland and France. Even the odd bunched combs of antler can be matched at Spiennes in Belgium and Ombrieve in Ariège. The earliest Swiss lake-dwellers had used bun-shaped grain-rubbers.[33] Leaf-shaped arrow-heads are common in eastern Gaul.

The Western culture itself can be traced not only to South France and Spain, but even to Egypt. Merimde on the western edge of the Delta and sites round the Fayum reveal already in the Vth millennium B.C. the essential Western features, perhaps even the cradle whence semi-nomadic farmers set out on the long trek that eventually brought them to the Channel. It is not irrelevant to recall that the nearest modern analogies to illustrate the economy of the British Isles in the Stone and Bronze Ages are to be found among the 'Hamitic' Nilotes of the Sudan—Shilluk, Hadendoa, Dinka.

Peake [34] maintains that our migrants could drive their stock along the Kent–Artois ridge onto the Downs. But most geologists consider that the Straits of Dover were cut through too long before 3000 B.C. to leave a ridgeway for neolithic cattle-men. These must then have come by boat and did not necessarily all land at the same port nor all start from the same parts of Gaul. We have already seen how keeled bowls with everted rim, found only at Windmill Hill and farther east, resemble Belgian Michelsberg forms, while the trumpet lugs from Dorset and Devon have special affinities with Normandy and Brittany.[35] Be that as it may, Windmill Hill culture exhibits a marked insularity when compared with its continental counterparts. Local specializations and divergences in fashion and tradition are indeed a natural counterpart of the neolithic economy which divided society up into small self-contained communities marooned on islands of pasture in a waste of trackless forest and marsh. Nevertheless the potter's early penchant for club rims, and her restricted repertory of shapes, the huntsman's exclusive preference for leaf-shaped arrow-heads and the failure to use

---

[31] Childe, *Dawn*, 271-278, 285-289.   [32] *Antiquity*, viii, 26-40.
[33] Vouga, *Le Néolithique lacustre ancien*, 19.
[34] *Mem. & Proc. Manchester Lit. & Phil. Soc.*, lxxxi (1937), 63-65 ; cf. *PPS.*, iv, 230-231.
[35] *PSEA.*, vii (1934), 379.

antler for axes and axe-mounts, constitute obvious differentiae to distinguish the Windmill Hill culture positively, and still more negatively, from other groups of the Western complex. Some ancestral Western traits had been lost. Now such loss of traits is a regular accompaniment of dissolution of culture normally associated with transmarine settlement while water transport is still rudimentary.

The relative age of the arrival of Windmill Hill colonists in southern England is reasonably well defined. Pot sherds recovered from the peats show that they had settled on the edge of the Cambridgeshire fens soon after the transition from the Boreal to the Atlantic phase of climate and before the marine transgression that deposited fen clay on the older peat bed.[36] In Essex, too, they still found available for settlement the so-called Lyonesse surface, which was submerged, probably by the same transgression.[37] In the silt of the ditches of Windmill Hill and Whitehawk camps Windmill Hill sherds occur much deeper and earlier than any Beaker ware, so that the culture they denote began before Period III. At Maiden Castle, Dorset, an anomalous long barrow straddles the ditch of the Windmill Hill camp, so that the latter existed before Period II—if such a period be admitted at all. On the other hand, Windmill Hill pottery stratified below Beaker ware in the primary silting of the ditches bordering this and other Wessex long barrows demonstrates that the culture flourished also in Period II. Part of a flint dagger from Abingdon [38] and a 'sickle' from Hembury [39] would indeed seem to mean that the Windmill Hill culture persisted till the A Beaker culture had penetrated to Berkshire and Devon, i.e. into Period III.

The neolithic farmers would seem then to have rapidly colonized tracts all over the area of easy settlement in southern England. How far did they cross the forests and marshes that confined this favoured area? Causewayed camps seem confined thereto. Yet relics conforming to those just described have been recovered in the comparable areas of Lincolnshire and eastern Yorkshire, in Cornwall, the Mendips and Cotswolds and South Wales, in North Wales and Cumberland, on Man, on the western and northern coasts of Scotland including the Hebrides and Orkney, in Northern Ireland and even in Co. Limerick. But most finds come from collective tombs. While the relation of megalith-builders to the inhabitants of causewayed camps remain in suspense, relics from such tombs cannot be accepted without qualification as proof of Windmill Hill settlement. Moreover, Western equipment exhibits so much uniformity over the whole of Belgium, Switzer-

[36] *Ant. J.*, xv, 317.
[38] *Ant. J.*, vii, 448.
[37] *PPS.*, ii, 210.
[39] *PDAES.*, i (1932), 177.

land and France that relics very similar to those found in causewayed camps might have been left by bodies of Western immigrants who had no direct connexion with the societies inhabiting Sussex and Wessex. This latter difficulty may be discounted if the positive and negative traits cited as differentiae of the Windmill Hill culture be taken as criteria of its presence. In a stratified society divergences in funerary architecture or ritual might denote differences in the ruling classes alone, while common traditions in domestic arts would reflect the underlying unity of the masses. It will, then, be convenient to refer briefly here to settlements that have yielded relics illustrative of an underlying unity and to regional variations in pottery that disclose divergent traditions within it. The peculiarities of funerary architecture will then be considered separately in Chapter IV.

Westward some doubtful sherds, now lost, from hut-circles on Legis Tor near Plymouth [40] may possibly prove an occupation of Dartmoor. A few more sherds, together with leaf-shaped arrow-heads, have been collected apparently from sixty circular huts built against and between large natural boulders on the fortified hill-top of Carn Brea [41] in Cornwall. A cave, at Cheddar, in the Mendips, occupied in pre-Beaker times,[42] supplements the evidence from many long barrows for an extension of settlement onto the limestone plateaux of Somerset and Gloucestershire and beyond the Severn into South Wales (the Glamorgan coast and the Black Mountains). North of the 'South English archipelago' there are a fortified settlement at Gwaenysgor above Prestatyn (Flints.) and two burial caves [43] east of the Vale of Clwyd. Occupation of the Wolds in Lincolnshire and Yorkshire is disclosed solely by pottery, arrow-heads and one comb from collective tombs, one erected certainly after the advent of B Beaker folk and none demonstrably anterior to Period III (p. 64). Then there comes one such tomb in Northumberland,[44] a shore settlement at Hedderwick near Dunbar [45] in East Lothian where Beaker sherds have been collected too, a 'domestic site' near Falkirk, and, apart from megalithic tombs mentioned in Chapter IV, a settlement on Wideford Hill, Orkney.[46] On the Cumberland coast six hearths beside the now extinct Ehenside Tarn [47] recall the lacustrine settlements of Westerners in the Alps and have, like them, yielded a saucer quern and a wooden paddle as well as stone axes and pottery. Megalithic tombs are of course plentiful on the west coast of Scotland, but a settlement at

---

[40] *TDA.*, xxviii, 174-189. [41] *JRIC.*, xiii (1895), 92-98.
[42] *P.Som.A.S.*, lxxii (1926), 108. [43] Grimes, *Guide*, 28.
[44] *Arch. Ael.* (1935), 149. [45] *PSAS.*, lxiii, 67. [46] *POAS.*, xii, 32.
[47] *T.C. & W.A. & A.S.*, xxxii (1932), 57-62: No. 11 in Fig. 10 here.

Rothesay, Bute,[48] has yielded typical pottery but also true saddle querns. In Northern Ireland, apart from the numerous gallery graves, Windmill Hill pottery has been collected from shore sites [49] under sand-dunes (as also at Glenluce, Wigtownshire), while there was a fortified settlement, 13 acres in area, on Lyle's Hill [50] above Belfast.   Finally, Ó Riordáin [51] has found neolithic pottery on the floor of a house at Lough Gur, Co. Limerick. This house, the oldest known in the British Isles, measured 26 ft. by 18 ft. The walls, with stone foundations, and roof were supported by four rows of seven posts inside with two parallel rows outside, while the hearth occupied the centre of the aisle up the hall.

Within this area of scattered settlement the pottery, which alone has been published in quantities sufficient for classification, reveals the divergence of two easily recognizable regional traditions.   The bulk of the fragments from Lincolnshire, eastern Yorkshire and Northumberland belong to bowls with an S profile but otherwise simple rims with or without a keel,[52] plain or decorated only with finger-tip fluting.   Despite the carination they have an obvious kinship with the A 1 ware of East Anglia and south-eastern England generally.   To the same group belong on the one hand the vases from Falkirk and from a tomb near Burghead (Elgins.), on the other those of Ehenside Tarn in Cumberland and then some from the collective tombs of Man and North Ireland as well as from the North Irish sand-hills (Dundrum) and Glenluce in Scotland.   Only once in Yorkshire, occasionally at Glenluce, often in Cumberland, Man [53] and Ireland (even at Lough Gur) the carination is exaggerated by an applied ridge.   On the other hand, club rims, such as characterize the southern A 2, recur sometimes in the Cotswold–Severn province and South Wales, again in North Wales and at Glenluce, regularly in south-western Scotland and at Hedderwick.   They are encountered in only one site in Yorkshire but are quite common in Ulster.

The first style might reflect colonization of the habitable patches in a relatively continuous province.   But that province itself cuts across the area where club-rimmed types were fashionable.   In Ireland both varieties occur together in the same tomb or settlement.   Yet the Scottish–Irish series of club-rimmed vases are separated by the Yorkshire–Irish group from their relatives in Wales and Wessex.   Moreover, in south-west Scotland pure Windmill Hill elements are blended with so many traits of clearly foreign

[48] *TBNHS.* (1930), 50-54.   [49] *JRSAI.*, xxi (1891), 440.
[50] *Belfast Museum Quarterly Notes*, lxiv (1940), 4-10.
[51] Information from the excavator ; cf. *PRIA.*, xlviii, C, 268.
[52] Newbigin, *PPS.*, iii, 191.   [53] Piggott, *Ant. J.*, xii, 150-154.

origin—not only distinctive megalithic tombs, but also true saddle querns and new ceramic forms and decorative styles—that they can only be regarded as elements in a new culture, named after a site in Kintyre, Beacharra (Fig. 10, 12). It was indeed the Beacharra culture that was transferred to northern Ireland, there to absorb the Yorkshire tradition too. In sand-hill settlements, like Dundrum (Co. Down),[54] we see the squashed-down rims, now richly decorated with cord impressions in Beacharra style, assuming truly monstrous proportions. It was this hybrid tradition with both keeled bowls and club-rimmed pots, now still more exaggerated and decorated with comb instead of cord imprints, that spread south to reappear in the neolithic houses at Lough Gur in Co. Limerick.

Similarly in the north of Scotland we can, on the ceramic evidence, no longer speak of a Windmill Hill culture, but of an Unstan or Pentland culture infected with the ceramic and funerary traditions associated with megalithic passage graves (p. 71). So the mariners who, whether as missionaries or chiefs, spread the megalithic religion had a share in instigating or leading the expansion of Windmill Hill culture over Scotland and Ireland.

[54] Hewson, *JRSAI.*, lxviii (1938), 73-87; influence from the Boyne style and even approximations to Peterborough techniques are observable on some of the pottery, while in the flint-work, despite leaf-shaped arrow-heads, an abundance of hollow-scrapers may denote absorption of mesolithic elements (cf. p. 89); cf. also *UJA.*, viii (1945), 25—Ushet, Rathlin Island.

CHAPTER IV

THE MEGALITHIC RELIGION

1. ARCHITECTURE AND RITUAL

THE course of prehistory in the British Isles was profoundly modified by a religious movement which affected all the coasts of the Mediterranean, the Atlantic and even the Baltic. The content of this religion is naturally almost unknown. But it inspired the construction of elaborate tombs, conventionally miscalled megalithic,[1] to be used as family vaults for interment of the dead in accordance with a single ritual. Strict agreements in arbitrary details of funerary architecture over large tracts of Mediterranean and Atlantic Europe are as good evidences for a megalithic religion as are mosques for Mohammedanism. The distribution of tombs, predominantly along the coasts and radiating from coastal ports, indicates the channels of the religion's propagation and the area of its domain.

Changes of religion are not confined in their effects to spiritual things. The Mohammedan conquests spread not only the mosque and the Koran but also elements of Arabic art, science and economy to barbarized Europe and darkest Africa. Christian missionaries introduced into Scotland not only the Mass but mortared building and an improved rural economy. Throughout Atlantic Europe the first objects of metal and indications of long-distance trade come from megalithic tombs, as if conversion to the new faith often went hand-in-hand with the adoption of a new economy.

Most religions have been racked by schisms which affect not only creeds but also ecclesiastical architecture. You need not wait for the service to distinguish an Orthodox basilica from a Roman Catholic church. Among communities linked, if at all, by precarious and irregular communications minor divagations from orthodoxy are particularly likely. So in the British Isles, as elsewhere in the megalithic province, we can observe local divergences from the traditionally sanctified tomb plans. Indeed, even before the cult reached Britain such divergences had assumed the form of veritable schisms;

---

[1] From Greek μέγας, great, and λίθος, a stone; but the use of big stones is not the decisive criterion of the religion, since tombs of the same plan may be built of big stones on edge, or of smaller stones laid in courses or finally cut in the rock.

46

several distinct traditions of sepulchral architecture were introduced, already differentiated, from various quarters.

The first great schism had perhaps taken place already in the western Mediterranean. The orthodox church maintained that the burial vault must be a distinct, preferably circular, chamber entered by a low, narrow passage—what archaeologists term a *passage grave*. Passage graves may be excavated in the ground, or built with dry masonry and roofed by corbelling, or finally built of upright blocks or slabs (orthostats) directly supporting slab lintels. Another sect may have held that passage and chamber introduced unessential complications; a chamber with a proper portal was enough. The chamber might be a big square box of slabs—a *dolmenic cist*—or a *long cist* or *gallery grave* with parallel sides like the passage of the orthodox tomb.[2] This schismatic sect flourished particularly round the Gulf of the Lion and in Catalonia where passage graves are rare; orthodoxy, expressed in passage graves, dominated southern Spain and Portugal.

Architectural differences do not always reflect differences of faith. The galvanized iron mission chapel in a new suburb may be called a degeneration of the cruciform parish church built of stone; it is not necessarily either later in date or less orthodox than the mother church. A similar degeneration may convert a passage grave into a gallery grave or even a dolmenic cist just because its builders were poorer and less skilled than contemporaries who built passage graves. The family vaults in the British Isles present a very large variety of forms. It is often doubtful how far this diversity is due to different traditions implanted from abroad, to the growth of divergent traditions locally, or simply to poverty, the nature of available materials and sheer clumsiness. We recognize provisionally the following groups:—*A.* Long Cists (or Gallery Graves): 1. the Clyde–Carlingford Group; 2. The Cotswold–Severn Group (possibly Passage Graves); 3. Paris Cists or Wedge-shaped Cairns; 4. Heel-shaped Cairns; 5. Medway Group. *B.* 'Unchambered' long barrows and collective tombs. *C.* Passage Graves: 1. The Boyne Group; 2. The Pentland Group—Caithness type; Unstan type; and Rousay type (Stalled Cairns); 3. The Beauly Group; 4. Entrance Graves. The distribution of the best-defined groups is shown by appropriate hatching in Fig. 10.

Despite all varieties in plan and construction, tombs of all kinds in the

[2] The long cists in South France, like many in other megalithic regions, can also be regarded as degenerate passage graves—in the sense explained above—and could not in that case be taken as evidences of sectarianism. Hawkes (*Foundations*, p. 172) regards long cists as 'galleries of cists placed end to end,' the cists themselves resulting from the native Pyrenaeans' adoption of the orthodox megalithic cult and modifications of it.

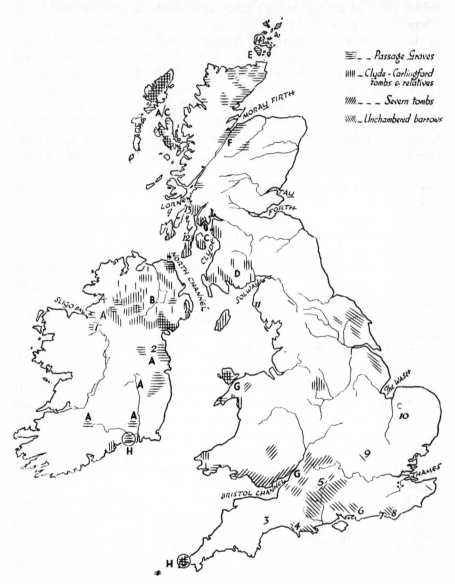

FIG. 10.   Map showing the principal neolithic sites and groups of collective tombs. For explanation of letters and numbers see text, Chapters III-V.

British Isles, as abroad, exhibit many agreements in structure and ritual. These may be mentioned here. No tombs in England have been excavated in the ground in Mediterranean fashion, though excavation would have been easy enough on the chalk downs.[3] But in Ireland Hemp[4] has recognized some rock-hewn chambers which formally recall the Mediterranean collective tombs though no skeletons or grave-goods were found in them. On Hoy, Orkney, a small chamber cut out in a huge boulder—the Dwarfie Stane— agrees precisely in plan with local built passage graves.[5] And tombs on Rousay and Eday, though walled with dry masonry and roofed with lintels, have been erected entirely in artificial excavations.[6] Finally, the dolmenic cist (perhaps once a passage grave with stepped entry) at Pant y Saer, Anglesey, was built in a shallow rock-cut pit above the edges of which its orthostats rise.[7]

The remainder of our collective tombs have been built above ground and artificially buried by a cairn or barrow. As on the Continent, the covering mound was never a formless heap of stones and earth; careful excavation shows that it has been constructed with great care in conformity with ritual prescriptions. The mounds covering passage graves are usually round on the Continent and—with notable exceptions—in Britain too. A long mound would seem an appropriate covering for a long cist, and most tombs of this type in the British Isles are in fact thus covered. But in Catalonia and southern France some gallery graves and most dolmenic cists (including the segmented cist of La Halliade) are buried in round tumuli; Daniel has, however, traced some covered by pear-shaped mounds in Aveyron and Lozère.[8] The dimensions of many British long cairns and barrows are out of all proportion to the size of the chambers they cover. At Yarrows in Caithness chamber and passage together are only 18 ft. long, while the cairn measures no less than 240 ft.! Many long barrows in southern England exceed 300 ft. in length, while an anomalous variant at Maiden Castle, Dorset, extends for one-third of a mile!

All our long mounds are pear-shaped in plan and higher at one end than the other. They are thus differentiated from the long rectangular or oval mounds that cover some long cists and dolmens in Denmark, Holland and Brittany. Piggott[9] and Hawkes[10] contend that the idea of the long mound was introduced from Brittany, where pear-shaped mounds

---

[3] A chamber exposed at Waddon near Croydon in 1902 and since destroyed looks in plan very like a rock-cut tomb : *Reliquary*, xi, 32.

[4] *Antiquity*, xi, 348-350.   [5] *PSAS.*, lxx, 217-230.

[6] *PSAS.*, lxxii, 193-204; lxxiii, 155-162.   [7] *Arch. Camb.*, lxxxviii (1933), 219.

[8] *Ant. J.*, xix, 157-165.   [9] *Antiquity*, xi, 441-452.   [10] *Foundations*, 175.

had covered cemeteries of non-megalithic cists containing pottery very like the Hembury variant of Windmill Hill ware, and that megalithic tombs were intruded into such long mounds locally. It seems to me more likely that the long mound and the long cist were brought from South France together.

Whether round or long, the mound or cairn was always delimited by some sort of kerb; it might be composed merely of big blocks or take the form of a built wall of dry-stone masonry. The revetment walls of long and round cairns in the Cotswolds, Derbyshire and northern Scotland are often beautifully built (Pl. I, 1). On Rousay [11] (Pl. I, 2) the component slabs are in some instances arranged to form herring-bone patterns giving a distinctly decorative effect. There may be two or even three parallel or concentric walls round the whole or part of the mound, the inner now standing higher than the outer as if the whole structure were staged like an early Pyramid.

Yet it is doubtful whether these handsome walls were intended to be permanently exposed. In recently excavated barrows of the Severn type Elsie Clifford [12] and Grimes [13] have laid bare an 'extra-revetment' of stones piled slantwise against the built walls as if the whole exterior had been masked with a blanket of stones and earth. In the same way it seems that the forecourts, described in the next paragraph, were blocked up soon after the erection of the tomb. If so, all this fine masonry must be regarded as purely ceremonial.

Passage tombs in Sicily and long cists in Sardinia may open onto a *forecourt*, semicircular in plan and cut in the rock; and a similar forecourt, framed on either side by upright slabs, is a regular adjunct to the Sardinian gallery graves, termed Giants' Tombs, and precedes some Almerian and Portuguese passage graves. This ritual feature is faithfully preserved in the *horned cairns* of the Clyde–Carlingford group, where the forecourt is defined by a semicircle of unhewn monoliths at the wider end of the cairn. Some passage graves in Sligo and Caithness are also contained in horned cairns, generally with horns at both ends and, in Caithness, bounded by built walls instead of uprights. Vestiges of a similar forecourt may be recognized in the concave timber revetments to the higher ends of the earthen long barrows at Maiden Castle and Skendleby (Fig. 13).[14] A forecourt was also attached to the broad end of barrows of the Severn group, but here the built revetment walls which define it are convex so that the plan

---

[11] *PSAS.*, lxix, 325-350; lxxi, 297-308.   [12] *Arch.*, lxxxvi, 136; *PPS.*, iv, 201.

[13] *PPS.*, v, 125.   [14] *Arch.*, lxxxv, 46.

of the court is not semicircular but cuspidal. A reminiscence of this type of forecourt, defined by a timber revetment, may perhaps be traced in a Yorkshire long barrow of earth.[15]

The entrances to passage graves in southern Spain and to gallery graves in Portugal, Brittany, Central France, Central Germany, Sweden and the Caucasus are often closed by so-called *porthole stones*—i.e. slabs with round or sub-rectangular windows carved in them, or pairs of slabs so trimmed as to form such windows when joined.[16] Two porthole stones, now isolated from any chamber, survive in Cornwall, where Hencken recognizes also a vestigial porthole cut in one corner of a slab closing a ʻdolmen.ʼ[17] There are further portholes in four barrows with cist-like chambers of the Severn type,[18] in cists of the Clyde family at Gretch Veg, Isle of Man,[19] and the Bridestones, Staffs.; a porthole stone stands without any surviving chamber on the edge of the passage grave cemetery of Carrowmore, Sligo,[20] another divides the chamber of a dolmenic cist at Burren, Cavan, while vestigial specimens fulfil this function at Deerpark, Co. Clare[21] and Labbacallee, Co. Cork.[22] So this item of sepulchral furniture is not regularly associated with any specific group of tombs in the British Isles; it may have come to Sligo with the passage grave cult from Portugal, but reached Cornwall from the Paris basin via Jersey.

The erection of tombs of all groups in the British Isles was preceded by an elaborate ceremonial to consecrate the site. Thorough excavation reveals under the barrow or cairn traces of fires and often burnt bones— burnt offerings. Often pits had been dug in the subsoil, in which animal bones or a few sherds may be found.[23] Similar traces of burning and pits have been noted in the forecourts of horned cairns. No similar observations have been recorded in France or Spain, probably only because examination has been restricted to the chambers.

Once built, the vault seems to have been used for several generations just as on the Continent. Most tombs not hopelessly despoiled have been found to contain the remains of from five to fifty individuals. The normal burial ritual is uniform throughout the megalithic province from Cyprus

[15] Hanging Grimston: Mortimer, *Forty Years*, 103.
[16] Childe, *Dawn*, 206.   [17] Hencken, *Arch. Corn.*, 46.
[18] Rodmarton and Avening (Glos.), Lanhill (Wilts.) and Tinkinswood (Glam.). *PPS.*, vi (1940), 150 ff.   [19] *Arch. Camb.*, lxxxiv (1929), 171.   [20] *JRSAI.* (1887-88), 74. [21] Borlase, *Dolmens*, 205 and 70.   [22] *PRIA.*, xliii, C, 78-81.
[23] With passage graves, Baltinglass, Wicklow and Bryn Celli Dhu, Anglesey (*Arch.*, lxxx, 179); in Clyde–Carlingford group, Cashtal yn Ard, Man (*Ant. J.*, xvi, 373-388), and often in Ulster; in English long barrows, Wessex, Lincs., Yorks., Westmorland (*Arch.*, lxxxv, 88).

to Denmark. The latest interments are found lying in the contracted position or squatting against the walls; to make room for them the bones of earlier interments, already skeletalized, have been pushed aside or rearranged in a corner. In at least one Wiltshire tomb,[21] as in comparable tombs in Greece and Denmark, anatomical peculiarities betray a real 'family likeness' between most of the chamber's occupants. The dead were accompanied by offerings of food, vases and ornaments; these do not all belong to the same archaeological period and thus confirm the deduction that each vault was used as a burial-place for several generations. Yet after each interment the tomb's entrance was carefully sealed so that only initiated members of the family could find it.

As elsewhere in the megalithic province, fires were often kindled in the tombs, either for ritual purposes or to provide illumination. Bones, scorched by such fires, have been mistaken for evidences of cremation. But cases of cremation before burial have been reported from Almeria and very commonly from Brittany. In the British Isles cremation was the normal rite in Irish passage graves, occurs commonly in the segmented cists of Northern Ireland and sporadically in their Scottish counterparts, and has been reported from many long barrows in northern England and from a few in the south. In Britain the rite may have been adopted from the Boyne group of Ireland.

The skeletons from our collective tombs belong to a tall variety of the long-headed Mediterranean race. Coon [25] finds 'the type cannot be duplicated anywhere on the European Continent save as an element in a mixed population.' Hence he infers that the megalithic cult was diffused by a race that avoided mixture by coming by sea. The archaeological evidence is not altogether in harmony with this anthropological deduction. There is no megalithic culture, defined by equipment and ornaments, common to all megalithic tombs, and therefore no megalithic people whose mass migrations could have diffused tombs and equipment too. In each area of Europe the grave-goods belong to local types, equally represented in non-megalithic or pre-megalithic contexts. So in Great Britain and Northern Ireland the only elements common to all groups of tombs are native Windmill Hill pottery and leaf-shaped arrow-heads. There must, of course, have been actual migrants who diffused the megalithic religion by settling down long enough and with sufficient prestige to make converts. But the converts retained their own secular traditions; there was no replacement of population.

Megalith-builders must be conceived as families coming by sea from different quarters and settling down among native populations to whom they

[21] *PPS.*, iv, 147; cf. Childe, *Dawn*, 76, 209.   [25] *Races*, 110.

taught their own peculiar version of the faith. Perhaps they formed a spiritual aristocracy of 'divine' chiefs whose magic powers ensured the fertility of crops and herds, of game and fish. If such families practised exogamy but yet married normally within the aristocracy, 'hybrid' tombs— a passage grave in a long cairn for instance—could be explained as a compromise between partners belonging to different sects if no *ne temere* decree prohibited the marriage of a passage grave to a long stone cist.

The shortest way from the Mediterranean to the Atlantic north-west is across the Pyrenaean isthmus, the eastern end of which was controlled by adherents of the long cist sect. Hence their convention was implanted in Britain before the more orthodox passage grave whose partisans took the long sea route round Spain and Portugal.

2. The Clyde–Carlingford or Beacharra Culture

The tradition of the megalithic cist in its purest form was brought by families who settled on both sides of the North Channel to develop the Clyde–Carlingford culture in south-west Scotland, Northern Ireland and Man. They brought with them not only the convention of the megalithic cist—probably in the form of a segmented cist in a horned cairn [26]—but also a new ceramic style, Beacharra ware, which is found in some tombs side by side with Windmill Hill ware. A *segmented cist* is a gallery, framed with megalithic slabs on edge which generally support the dry-stone masonry of a corbelled roof, subdivided into segments by transverse slabs on edge (termed *septal stones*) that never reach to the roof and entered directly through a portal so narrow as to be perhaps merely symbolic. The tall uprights that form the jambs are in classical examples the tallest and central members in a semicircle of orthostats that border the forecourt in the broader end of a long cairn. *Beacharra ware* is characterized by squat carinated pots with a short neck (Pl. II, 1). These and other vases are decorated with panelled designs in which semicircles are prominent, executed by *channelling* (i.e. with a blunt-pointed instrument leaving a U-shaped groove) or incision or with the imprint of a cord or of whipped cords.

Segmented cists occur in Touraine and Haute Poitou, the Hautes Pyrénées, the Basque provinces and Catalonia. But some of the Sardinian

---

[26] Hawkes, on the contrary, maintains that all that was introduced into the British Isles was the dolmenic cist; the multiplication of such cists set end to end to form a segmented cist and the latter's combination with a forecourt and a long cairn would be secondary developments in Scotland (*Foundations*, 179).

Giants' Tombs [27] agree so closely in chamber plan, portal and forecourt with our horned cairns that they may represent the origin of the convention. From Scotland it would have been handed on across the North Sea to be embodied in the first megalithic tombs erected in Denmark, the dysser or dolmens. Pottery,[28] decorated with channelled semicircles like Beacharra ware, is known from Early Minoan Crete,[29] Morocco, Spain, South France and Brittany, always in a pre-Beaker context. The semicircles are derived from magic patterns, current in Sardinia and elsewhere in the megalithic province. But the cord technique must be a backwash of missionary enterprise across the North Sea; for cord-ornamented pots were fashionable in Denmark when the first dysser were built there; in return the semicircle motive was later adopted in Denmark and translated into cord technique.[30]

The Clyde group (Fig. 10, C) [31] comprises 34 well-attested monuments in Arran, Bute, Kintyre, Islay and along Loch Fyne, together with an uncertain number of hybrid types on Loch Etive, Skye and the Hebrides. Eight or nine galleries, 18 to 24 ft. in length and opening onto fine forecourts (Fig. 11, 1), presumably mark primary settlements as all are near the coast. 'Degenerate' variants, occurring over a wider area and even extending into the Tay basin, would then illustrate secondary colonization from these centres. Degeneration is shown in the suppression of the forecourt (i.e. the horns), and/or a reduction of the gallery's length, in compensation for which extra chambers may be built at the side or in the narrow end of the cairn. The dead had been originally deposited squatting against the chamber walls, but the bones are often in disorder, and cases of cremation have been reported both from Arran and Argyll. The grave-goods include seemingly typical A 2 Windmill Hill ware with squashed rims and finger-tip fluting, form B being popular, Beacharra ware, one stone axe, leaf-shaped arrowheads and bones of calves, sheep or goats and pigs. But even in quite early tombs we may find sherds of Beaker pottery [32] or even of Food Vessel,[33] narrow knives with polished edges,[34] plano-convex knives,[35] a jet necklace [36] and a jet slider,[37] types elsewhere associated with Food Vessels and pro-

---

[27] Childe, *Dawn*, 209; Davies, *UJA.*, ii, 160-170.

[28] Jaquetta Hawkes, *Arch. J.*, xcv (1939), 126-173.

[29] Evans, *Palace of Minos*, Figs. 21-22.

[30] Brønsted, *Danmarks Oldtid*, i, 130; Bagge and Kjellmark, *Stenålders Boplatserna vid Siretorp*, 166-174; *PSEA.*, vii (1932), 62-66.

[31] Childe, *P.S.*, 25-32, 64-69.

[32] Giants' Graves, Dunan Beag (Arran), Glecknabae (Bute), Kilchoan and Largie (Argyll).   [33] Dunan Mor (Arran).

[34] Torlin.   [35] Giants' Graves, Dunan Mor, Sliddery Water, Torlin.

[36] Dunan Beag.   [37] Beacharra.

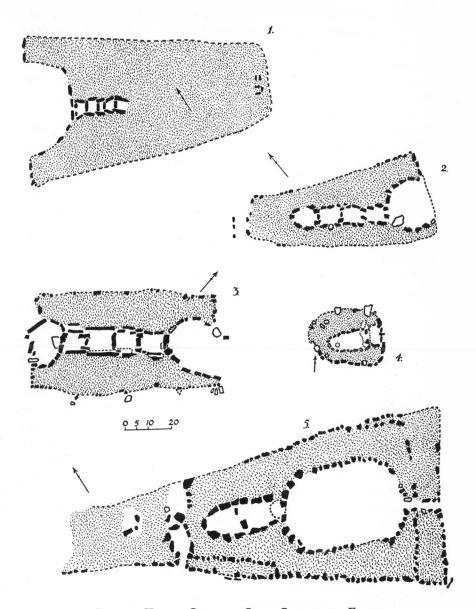

FIG. II. HORNED CAIRNS OF CLYDE–CARLINGFORD FAMILY.
I. East Bennan, Arran; 2. Browndod, Antrim; 3. Aghanaglack, Fermanagh;
4. Loughash, Tyrone; 5. Crevykeel, Sligo.

visionally assigned to Period IV.   Scott has indeed established that interments accompanied by very late Beakers in North Uist were subsequent to those associated with Beacharra vases.   So the 'Bronze Age' relics from Arran and Bute may also be regarded as the furniture of secondary burials. Nevertheless, they probably imply that the family vaults were still in use when the Beaker invaders arrived and when the Food Vessel culture emerged in south-western Scotland.   Bryce indeed has suggested that it was the advent of the Beaker folk with their tradition of individual burial that caused the degeneration of megalithic funerary architecture.   The invaders' short cists eventually came to take the place of the older collective tombs.

In Ayrshire and Galloway tombs of the 'Solway type' (Fig. 10, D) may be regarded as degenerate versions of the foregoing in which the chamber has been reduced to a single segment, sometimes preceded by a passage, several chambers being covered by a single cairn.   Some such cairns near the Solway coast preserve fine forecourts, but quite a number are round. No relics have been obtained from any cairns of this group.

The Carlingford type is represented by over 70 monuments spread right across Ulster and into Sligo (Fig. 10, B).   From the first they differ from their Scottish analogues in that the chamber is normally set skew to the axis bisecting the forecourt and is subdivided by upright jambs as well as by septal stones (Fig. 11, 2).   Cairns covering several chambers, each reduced to a single compartment,[38] and 'dolmens' (cists) with high portals may illustrate a degeneration parallel to that just described in Scotland. But the late and feeble impact of the 'separate grave' culture generally allowed time for elaborations on the traditional theme along three main lines, all best represented in regions away from the shores of the Irish Sea. In Antrim, Derry, Fermanagh and Tyrone some cairns contain chambers at both ends—or a single chamber with portals at both ends—each with a proper forecourt, so that the whole monument appears a 'double-horned cairn' [39] (Fig. 11, 3).   In Donegal and Sligo the horns are extended to curve inwards round the forecourt till they eventually almost meet, enclosing now in the body of the cairn an open oval court—Mahr's 'lobster claw type' [40] (Fig. 11, 5).   Finally, in Tyrone and Derry the façade is flattened out but the chamber shortened but widened and given a double portal [41] (Fig. 11, 4).

[38] Aghnaskeag B.: *Co. Louth Arch. J.*, ix (1939), 1-18; cf. *UJA.*, ii, 39; *Survey*, pp. xiii, xv; such degenerations occur outside Ulster as far south as Co. Dublin.

[39] *PRIA.*, xlv, 1-13 ; *JRSAI.*, lxix, 23-33.   *UJA.*, viii, 21.

[40] *JRSAI.*, lxix, 91-95; *PPS.*, iii, 347.

[41] Largantea, *UJA.*, i, 164-175; Loughash, *ibid.*, ii, 254-268; *Survey*, p. xiii.

Estyn Evans,[42] however, classifies these latter tombs with the wedge-shaped gallery graves described on p. 61 below.

Tombs of all varieties contain cremations more often than inhumations; at Dunloy the bodies seem to have been burned in a trench behind the one-compartment chamber; in the floor of the trench the ashes were buried in pits.[43] All may be accompanied by leaf-shaped arrow-heads, flint axes and pottery of Western type, resembling more often the Yorkshire variety (Fig. 8, 5) with the shoulder accentuated by an applied strip, than the A 2 ware of the Clyde. Beacharra vases (Fig. 8, 6) are found in a few tombs, notably with the cremations at Dunloy, and often ornamented with cord impressions forming pendant triangles in addition to the standard motives,[44] or developing towards the Food Vessel.[45] Disc beads from several tombs have been compared to British Bronze Age types,[46] and two late tombs yielded tanged-and-barbed arrow-heads.[47] Finally, typical Beakers of distinctive North British character were found in both the double-portalled cairns so far explored.[11] So the Ulster vaults must have remained in use as long as their relatives in Scotland. Nay, even longer; for the Beakers are plainly very late. And Davies [48] insists that the Beakers at Loughash were contemporary with an Encrusted Urn (another was found at Largantea) and other objects which in Britain would be assigned to Period V or VI.

On Man at least five cairns are of the Clyde horned type.[49] But the Mull Hill Circle consists of six pairs of single-segment cists arranged on the circumference of a circle, 50 ft. in diameter.[50] In each pair the portal-ends are juxtaposed, and a passage, about 7 ft. long, leads out radially from the gap between them. They yielded pottery of the later Ulster type with Yorkshire affinities.

Outside these three focal areas vaults probably of the same family occur on the limestone plateau of Derbyshire and Staffordshire, along the coasts of Wales and southern Eire, and probably in Cornwall. In the former area the Bridestones,[51] near Congleton (Staffs.), was certainly a long horned cairn of Solway type, and the chambers in the round cairns (bounded with built

[42] Survey, p. xv; cf. Herring and May, INJ., vii (1940), 253-259.
[43] UJA., i, 62-65.
[11] PSEA., vii, 62-64. UJA., vi, 23.   [45] P.B.N.H.&P.S. (1933-34), Pl. 4, 2.
[46] By Hencken, JRSAI., lxix, 79, 93 n., 62-64.
[47] UJA., ii, 39; JRSAI., lxix, 32-33 (double-horned cairn).
[48] UJA., ii, 267; cf. INJ., vii, 257.
[49] Clark, PPS., i, 75-79; cremation seems to have been the normal rite.
[50] Ant. J., xii, 146-157.
[51] C. W. Phillips, Map of the Trent Basin: Long Barrows-Megaliths, Ordnance Survey, 1933.

walls) of Five Wells (Taddington) [52] and Minninglow [53] (Ballidon), Derbyshire, could also be classified in the Solway group. The monuments in Anglesey,[54] Pembrokeshire [55] and Cornwall [56] are too ruinous to be classified. But across the sea once more in Waterford Powell has proved the monument at Ballynamona Lower [57] to be a tripartite segmented cist in an unusually short horned cairn. It contained a keeled vase decorated very elaborately in the Beacharra technique, and a stone disc. While the Derbyshire tombs must belong to families who had spread from the main North Channel foci, the vaults in southern Ireland and England might have been erected by members who separated from the original colonizing party on their way north.

3. THE SEVERN CULTURE

A distinct architectural tradition is illustrated by some 65 pear-shaped long cairns in South Wales from the Gower Peninsula to the Black Mountains and in the Mendips and Cotswolds, extending thence as earthen barrows into the Downs of north Wiltshire and Berkshire with two abnormal outliers in the Conway valley of North Wales [58] (Fig. 10, G). The cairns, bounded by built walls, have cuspidal forecourts in the wide ends, but at Wayland's Smithy (Berks.) the façade is flattened out. The chamber at West Kennet (Wilts.) is an orthostatic passage grave, but round the Severn the classical type is what Daniel calls a *transeptal gallery grave*, i.e. a gallery with three, two or one transept, often roofed by corbelling, on either side (Fig. 12, 1). Crawford, Daniel and Grimes [59] have traced the degeneration of this type: (1) The transepts are suppressed and the gallery contracted to a terminal chamber [60] (Fig. 12, 2); (2) the transepts become independent chambers connected directly with the exterior, the axial gallery being suppressed [61] (Fig. 12, 4); or finally, (3) access is given to the central gallery from the side (Fig. 12, 3).[62] In three Cotswold barrows of class 2 and one of class 1

[52] *Reliquary*, vii (1901), 232; it contained Peterborough ware, leaf-shaped and tanged-and-barbed arrow-heads, two chambers.

[53] Bateman, *Ten Years Digging*, 54, 82 (several chambers, skeletons).

[54] *PPS.*, ii, 119.

[55] *PPS.*, ii, 119; but Pentre Yfan was a single-segment cist covered by a long cairn with a reduced forecourt: *BBCS.*, viii, 271; x, 82-84.

[56] *Antiquity*, xi, 198.

[57] *JRSAI.*, lxviii, 260-271; there are at least two other such tombs in the county.

[58] Maps in *PPS.*, iii, 89; ii, 128.

[59] Crawford, *Ordnance Survey Professional Paper*, No. 6, p. 4; *PPS.*, iii, 85; v, 139.

[60] Tinkinswood (Glam.), *Arch. Camb.* (1916), 295.

[61] Ty Isaf, Lanhill, Rodmarton, Avening, etc.

[62] Capel Garmon (Denb.), *Arch. Camb.*, lxxxii (1927), 1-40.

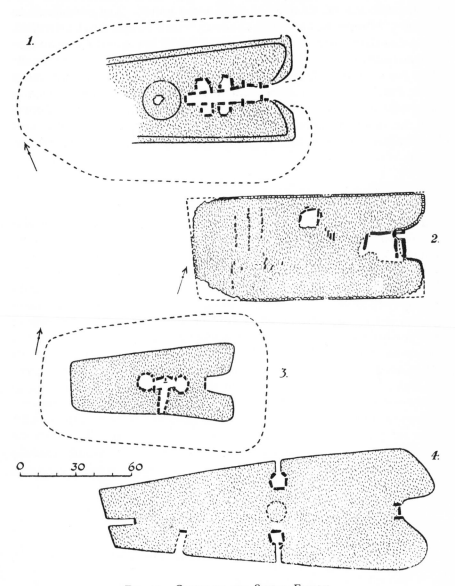

FIG. 12. CAIRNS OF THE SEVERN FAMILY.

1. Notgrove, Glos. ; 2. Tinkinswood, Glam. ; 3. Capel Garmon, Denbigh. ;
4. Belas Knap, Glos.

the lateral chambers are closed by composite porthole stones, approached at Rodmarton not from the margin but by a stepped pit from the surface of the mound [63] reproducing the effect of the 'pit-cave' tombs cut in the rock in Greece and Sicily.   In all cases the forecourt is preserved, though it leads in variants 2 and 3 to a functionless *dummy portal* (Pl. I, 1).   In some cairns covering transeptal galleries or lateral chambers there has been found behind the burial vaults a closed circular chamber or *rotunda* which at Notgrove (Glos.) covered a single burial in a cist but at Ty Isaf (Breck.) enclosed an asymmetrically placed chamber of our variant 3.[61]

The vaults of this family contain inhumation burials of up to fifty persons whose skulls are said by Thurnam to have been 'cleft with a blow in six or seven cases.'   The furniture includes bones of oxen, sheep or goats and horse, Windmill Hill pottery,[65] leaf-shaped arrow-heads, a few globular beads of shale [66] and a couple of stone discs.[67]   But Beaker sherds show that many tombs remained open till the round-headed invaders reached even the Cotswolds and Wales.[68]

The Severn tombs are classed as gallery graves primarily because they are regularly covered with long mounds.   Daniel [69] indeed proposed to derive the type from tombs with lateral chambers round the mouth of the Loire and in Morbihan, but Forde [70] has proved that these tombs are genuine passage graves.   Indeed, passage graves of the Boyne group with three or five cells might have served as the models for the British chambers.   In any case, the architectural tradition here discussed was most probably brought in by way of the Bristol Channel, whether from Brittany, Ireland or farther afield.

4. Miscellaneous Gallery Graves

(a) *Paris Cists.* A specialized form of gallery grave, divided—generally by a porthole stone—into a short ante-chamber and a long chamber, developed in the Paris basin where such tombs are generally built underground, and spread thence to Brittany and Jersey where they are built above ground

[63] Mrs Clifford's excavations, 1939.

[61] Notgrove, *Arch.*, lxxxvi, 125-127; Belas Knap, *T.B. & G.A.S.*, li, 278; Ty Isaf, *PPS.*, v, 128-129.

[65] Treated by Grimes as mostly A 1 in *Guide*, 45, but some sherds are accepted as A 2 in *PPS.*, v, 135.

[66] *Arch.*, lxxxvi, 146.   [67] *PPS.*, v, 132.

[68] *PPS.*, iii, 160-162; Grimes, *Guide*, 33, 35.

[69] *PPS.*, v, 162-165; in addition to the chamber plans the stone discs can be paralleled in these French tombs.   [70] *PPS.*, vi, 170-176.

and covered with long rectangular cairns.[71] Hencken [72] has recognized ruinous derivatives of the Paris type in Cornwall, and some Irish tombs may be inspired from this quarter too. At Labbacallee in Co. Cork Leask and Price [73] examined a gallery, expanding in width and height from one end to the other, without any door, but divided into two unequal lengths by a slab with a vestigial porthole carved in one corner. The tomb contained a scrap of pottery, possibly Windmill Hill, and a skeleton and 'Iron Age' pottery with cremated bones, but none of the relics regularly associated with Paris galleries on the Continent and even in Jersey. A similar tomb at Lough Gur (Limerick) is reported to have contained Beaker sherds. In Northern Ireland tombs, classified in this group by Estyn Evans,[71] though they do have entrances, have been found to contain cremated remains, tanged-and-barbed arrow-heads, and even Food Vessel sherds.[75] Nothing in the furniture and not much in their structure connects these Irish tombs with the Paris group. But architecturally they do strikingly resemble a group of wedge-shaped double cists in Central Germany—a region with which Ireland was in close commercial contact during the Early Bronze Age.[76]

(b) Far away in Shetland, Bryce [77] has recently described what he terms *heel-shaped* cairns. Their characteristics are (1) a long or slightly concave façade, formed of walling or faced with slabs, longer than either diameter of the cairn it faces and marked at its extremities by upright pillar stones; (2) a relatively small chamber approached by a passage and typically trefoil in shape, i.e. with two lateral recesses and a terminal one. The façade connects these monuments with the Clyde–Carlingford group, the chamber perhaps with the Boyne passage graves through variants such as occur in the Hebrides. It is presumably from the latter quarter that some bold adventurers carried the composite tradition to Thule, but no excavation has yet produced any relics to confirm or refute this hypothesis; a little pottery recently discovered by unscientific digging approximates to the Unstan ware of Orkney.

(c) On the Medway a group of small closed chambers in mounds demarcated by rectangular settings of big blocks is not connected directly with any Atlantic series. They conform strictly to the traditions current in Holland and north-western Germany,[78] and no doubt represent a settlement from that quarter. The 'Nordics,' buried in these tombs, seem to

[71] Childe, *Dawn*, 294-297.
[72] *Arch. Corn.*, 46.
[73] *PRIA.*, xliii, 77-100.
[71] *Survey*, p. xv.
[75] *P.B.N.H.&P.S.* (1937-38), 34-48; *UJA.*, iii, 41-55; *INJ.*, vii, 254.
[76] Cf. e.g. Childe, *Danube*, 136.
[77] *PSAS.*, lxxiv, 23-36.
[78] Piggott, *PPS.*, i, 122.

have been of shorter stature than other British megalith-builders,[79] but were
not accompanied by any relics to show when they arrived here.[80]

5. 'UNCHAMBERED' LONG BARROWS

In many tombs in Lowland England, while the funerary ritual of the
megalithic religion was observed, a chamber of big stones is missing.   The
best known of such collective tombs are the earthen long barrows, but
both in Yorkshire and in the Chiltern Hills round barrows cover remains
buried by the same rites and accompanied by the same Windmill Hill
pottery.   Long barrows have been defined by Thurnam [81] as 'immense

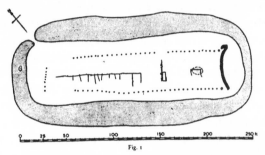

Fig. 1

FIG. 13.   Plan of Long Barrow at Skendleby,
Lincs. (ditch stippled).   After Phillips.

oval mounds, varying from 100 to nearly 400 ft. in length and 30 to 50 ft.
in width.   Along each side of the whole length of the tumulus is a deep wide
trench.   The mound is (generally) placed east and west, the east end being
somewhat higher and broader than the other.'   Modern excavation shows
that the earthen mound is, sometimes at least, delimited by a kerb of upright
posts [82] or of piled sods,[83] comparable to the stone revetments of cairns, and
that the end may contain a timber façade (p. 50) (Fig. 13).   A kidney-shaped
barrow on Whiteleaf Hill (Bucks.) [84] covered a wooden chamber contained
on three sides by tree-trunks laid horizontally and open on the east to a
crescentic forecourt.

[79] Coon, *Races*, 111; there are no grounds for supposing that the people buried in the
Medway tombs were especially connected with causewayed camps.

[80] A Northern flint axe of the early thin-butted type found in Julieberrie's Grave, a
normal unchambered long barrow in Kent, may have been brought over by the Medway
people: *Ant. J.*, xix, 267-269.   [81] *Arch.*, xlii, 172.

[82] Pitt-Rivers, *Cranbourne Chase*, iv, 65; *Arch.*, lxxxv, 49.

[83] *PPS.*, iii, 5.   [84] *PPS.*, ii, 213; iii, 441.

A number of skeletons, usually 'disarticulated,' are commonly reported to have been found under the higher end of the mound. At Skendleby (Lincs.) Phillips [85] found, on a platform of chalk rubble, five bodies laid to rest in the contracted position, while remains of three other skeletons were in confusion like those of the earlier interments in megalithic chambers. But in Norfolk and in some Wessex long barrows cremations are said to have taken place on such platforms.[86] Collective cremations in a 'crematorium trench' have been reported from a famous series of long and round barrows (the latter containing Windmill Hill pottery) in the north of England. The bones lay in complete disorder in a mesial trench 20 to 30 ft. long and some 4 ft. wide. They had mostly been burned but never reduced to the state of fine comminution obtained by Bronze Age cremations.[87] From the trenches Mortimer reported pieces of oak 'charcoal' several feet long and placed horizontally.[88] So the crematorium trenches sound suspiciously like wooden chambers that had caught fire, perhaps accidentally, though a resemblance to the undoubted cremations observed by Estyn Evans at Dunloy (p. 57) must be admitted. Finally, pit-dwellings found by Mortimer under a long and a round barrow in eastern Yorkshire [89] might be interpreted as partial 'rock-hewn tombs.'

The foregoing details, taken in conjunction with the wood and turf revetments and forecourts mentioned on p. 62, suggest that the name 'unchambered' is unfortunate. The earthen barrows may really have covered chambers of perishable materials like turf or timber and were almost certainly used for successive interments, only the earlier skeletons being disarticulated, and that for the same reason as those in stone chambers. However, some long cairns in Northumberland and Westmorland seem equally unchambered,[90] and one in west Yorkshire covered a completely closed megalithic cist (6½ ft. × 3 ft. × 4 ft.) containing a burnt and an unburnt skeleton.[91]

The pottery associated with the primary interments or the construction of the barrow is always Windmill Hill ware,[92] the remaining relics being leaf-shaped arrow-heads and bones of geese, deer and cattle. Beaker and

[85] *Arch.*, lxxxv, 88.   [86] *PPS.*, iv, 335-336.

[87] Thurnam (*Arch.*, xlii, 191), Greenwell (*B.B.*, 501) and Mortimer (*Forty Years*, 300) all insist on this distinction.

[88] Mortimer, *Forty Years*, 239.

[89] *Ibid.*, 336, 333; cf. *PPS.*, i, 124.

[90] *Arch. Ael.*, 4, xiii (1936), 293-309; RC. *Westmorland*, p. xxix.

[91] *YAJ.*, xxx, 252; xxxiv, 226.

[92] Generally A I, form G being prominent in Yorks. and Lincs., but note form J (Beacharra!) from Holdenhurst, Hants: *PPS.*, iii, 9.

Peterborough sherds occur in the secondary fillings of the ditches beside Wessex long barrows. On the other hand, the Skendleby long barrow was erected only after B Beaker folk had reached Lincolnshire, though, as usual, before the advent of A Beakers. And Nancy Newbigin [93] finds no proof that the collective tombs in Yorkshire and Northumberland antedate the Beaker invasion. So too the abnormal long barrow at Maiden Castle ran across the abandoned ditch of a Windmill Hill causewayed camp (p. 8), though pure Windmill Hill ware was still found at the bottom of the barrow-ditches.

On Piggott's theory of the Breton origin of the long mound unchambered long barrows might be older than any megalithic chambers, and indeed coeval with the causewayed camps. The chambered barrows and cairns would result from the grafting of the Atlantic tradition of megalithic architecture onto a pre-existing type of sepulchre (p. 40). The data here adduced afford no proof that any unchambered barrow is older than the earlier megalithic chambers. Indeed they give hints that in eastern England earthen barrows are later than some Clyde and Severn galleries. Perhaps, then, we should prefer Crawford's [94] statement that 'a long barrow is merely the reproduction in earth of a characteristic form of megalithic burial.' When the apostles of the megalithic faith reached regions where suitable stone was lacking, they translated into wood or turfs their architectural traditions. Doubtless the new cult was adopted by the builders of causewayed camps. But it presumably reached Wessex and Sussex from the Severn societies. In Yorkshire and Lincolnshire, however, the inspiration would have come from the Carlingford province and, with round barrows, from the Boyne. Yorkshire is connected with Ireland in the megalithic period by communities of ceramic form and was the eastern terminus of a trade route whereby Irish metal-work was diffused across northern England.

6. THE BOYNE CULTURE

Megalithic orthodoxy, expressed in passage graves, was brought from the Iberian Peninsula to Ireland, where it seems no Windmill Hill farmers were yet established to embrace the faith. But it found expression in imposing tombs, termed, after the most famous cemetery, the Boyne group or, since their mutual agreements are not solely architectural, the Boyne culture. If the votaries of the cult came by sea from Portugal to Sligo Bay they would have been welcomed to familiar limestone country. In any case,

---

[93] *Arch. Ael.*, xii (1935), 149.   [94] *Wessex from the Air*, 11.

their tombs are very numerous round that bay and extend thence across Ireland to Fair Head on the north, to the Mourne and Wicklow Mountains on the Irish Sea, with outliers as far south as Kilkenny and Co. Limerick [95] (Fig. 10, A).

The larger tombs of the Boyne culture are located by preference on mountain-tops and, like the passage graves of Greece, Spain and Portugal, are frequently grouped in small cemeteries. Thus there are at least 14 cairns dispersed upon the four limestone ridges of the Bricklieve Mountains (Carrowkeel, Fig. 10, 1),[96] about 30 on the ridges of Slieve na Caillighe (Lough Crew), and as many as 60 rude chambers at Carrowmore near Sligo.[97] In these cemeteries a degeneration could be traced in the plan of the chambers.

A simple round corbelled chamber, like that on Tibradden Mt., south of Dublin,[98] being the most widespread form outside Ireland, might be taken as the earliest. But at Baltinglass (Wicklow) one such tomb had been built onto an earlier cairn covering a chamber of more complex form. The classical Boyne type, in any case, is cruciform, i.e. there are three small cells grouped symmetrically round the main chamber (Fig. 14). In some cairns on Slieve na Caillighe and Carrowkeel, at Seefin [99] and Baltinglass the plans are complicated by the presence of two pairs of lateral cells like transepts. More usually we can trace a devolution involving suppression of the passage to leave a closed chamber (Slieve na Caillighe), replacement of corbelling by orthostats and lintels (Carrowkeel H), and eventually reduction of the whole to a cist (ibid. O). In the Carrowmore cemetery the degeneration to the so-called dolmen now standing bare at the centre of a ring of boulders graphically refutes older theories that made simple forms the starting-point; a by-product appears in plan a perfect gallery grave in a round cairn.

In the finest monuments, like New Grange (Fig. 10, 2),[100] the chambers are of superb masonry, the roofs being corbelled and the walls faced with huge flat slabs on edge. At Carrowkeel and Slieve na Caillighe transverse slabs set on edge across the passage and the cell-entries recall the septal stones of the Clyde galleries. At Slieve na Caillighe, New Grange, Seefin, Carnanmore (Antrim), [100a] Knockmany (Tyrone) and elsewhere many slabs in chamber, passage and even peristalith are adorned with carved or engraved patterns, including spirals (Pl. III, 1). Though seemingly geo-

[95] Powell, *PPS.*, iv, 239-248.   [96] *PRIA.*, xxix (1912), 311-347.
[97] *JRSAI.* (1885-86), 485 ff.; (1887-88), 20 ff.   [98] *JRSAI.*, lxiii, 252.
[99] *JRSAI.*, lxii, 153-157; lxvii, 313.   [100] Coffey, *New Grange*, Dublin, 1-60.
[101] *PSEA.*, vii (1934), 293-305.   [100a] *UJA.*, viii, 19

metric, Breuil [101] and Mahr [102] have detected in these designs stylized representations of the human form, of a boat and other objects.   The history of

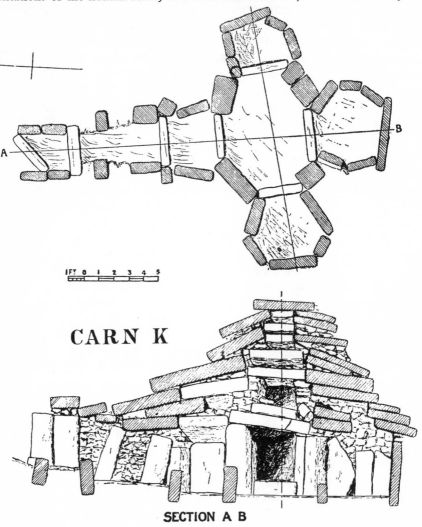

CARN K

SECTION A B

FIG. 14.   Plan and elevation of corbelled Passage Grave on Carrowkeel Mt.,
Co. Sligo.   After Macalister in *PRIA*.

such designs can be traced in carvings or paintings on the walls of Breton and Iberian passage graves and of contemporary cave shelters in Spain, and

[102] *PPS.*, iii, 354-360.

some stones from New Grange (e.g., Fig. 15) 'show exactly the same pattern as the anthropomorphic schist idols' [103] found in Portuguese passage graves. They disclose the chthonic deity to whose bosom the faithful dead returned.

The handsome vaults are covered by round cairns often out of all proportion to the size of the chamber and reaching such imposing dimensions as a diameter of 280 ft. on the Boyne. Some may have been mantled in white quartz pebbles, recalling the whitewashed *mastabas* of Old Kingdom Egypt. All were bounded by a kerb or peristalith which may curve in to form a small forecourt at the mouth of the entrance passage. New Grange is further encircled by a fosse with a ring of free-standing uprights outside

FIG. 15.   Carved Stone from tomb at New Grange.   After *PRIA*.

it. But in monument E at Carrowkeel a cruciform chamber with truncated passage occupies one end of a true double-horned cairn, and at Crevykeel (Sligo) a small oval passage grave (Fig. 11, 5) seems to have been built into the side of a lobster-claw derivative of the Carlingford series behind the appropriate gallery.[104] Even in the Boyne cemetery there seems to be a long barrow.

Some cairns on Slieve na Caillighe had been violated in pre-Roman times, and the plundering of the Boyne tombs by Norse raiders is recorded in the Irish annals. Owing to such disturbance these conspicuous and princely monuments have yielded astonishingly little funerary furniture. The burial rite, with at least one exception,[105] was cremation. The finely comminuted bones were laid upon stone trays or collected in skin bags. The long bone pins or pegs that fastened such wrappings are among the most distinctive of the surviving grave-goods. Multiple interments were the rule; in the Carrowkeel cemetery the average would have been about

---

[103] Coffey, Figs. 14 and 24; cf. *Dawn*, Fig. 127.   [104] Hencken, *JRSAI.*, lxix, 95.
[105] Belmore Mountain; unburnt bones are mentioned also at Carrowkeel.

twelve in each tomb.[106]   Besides the pins, large stone basins, baetyl-shaped pebbles, smooth stone balls, and beads and pendants of jasper, serpentine, steatite and limestone [107] (Fig. 16), seem to be survivals of the original furniture.   No 'neolithic' pottery of the Windmill Hill family has been

found in any Irish passage grave.   On the contrary, small sherds resembling in texture and firing English Peterborough ware, but decorated with horizontal rows of finger-nail imprints, stabs or stab-and-drag lines,[108] may represent a contemporary Irish fabric, quite independent of British ceramic schools.

FIG. 16. Stone Beads from Carrowkeel. ⅓.

So many tombs [109] contained Food Bowls (of types B and C) that it must be admitted that they remained in use till the 'Bronze Age' culture characterized thereby had emerged.   But at Belmore Mountain [110] a second Food Bowl was contained in a cist high up in the cairn above the main cruciform chamber.   And Encrusted Urns came from a degenerate tomb at Carrowmore [111] and from a curious double passage grave at Cairne Grannia (Antrim).[112]   The numerous Bronze Age vases and parallels to the passage grave art on the covers of Scottish Bronze Age cists have led most authòrities to attribute the Boyne tombs to that period, i.e. our Period III or IV.   Moreover, amber pendants, just like the stone ones from the passage graves, recur in the Wessex graves of the latter period.   Mahr and others, however, rely on the exclusive distribution of passage graves over against horned cairns for proving the 'neolithic' roots of the Boyne culture in Period II.   But though the Carlingford cairns hardly spread into the Boyne province, tombs of Boyne type do extend well into the area occupied by gallery graves.

Not only do close architectural parallels to the Boyne tombs occur in Portugal (notably at Alcalá in Algarve), but their ritual art, baetyls, stone basins and stone pendants [113] can all be matched there or in southern Spain, the pendants also in an Early Minoan 'tholos' ossuary in Crete.   Even the stab-and-drag technique of the ceramic decoration can be compared to the Boquique style of the Peninsula.   Moreover, though the only arrow-head

---

[106] Among the bones, principally from five cairns, Macalister could distinguish 31 individuals, which, however, represented not more than half the total.

[107] Belmore Mountain, Carrowkeel, Carrowmore, Slieve na Caillighe: Gogan, *J. Cork H.&A.S.*, xxxv (1930), 90-95.

[108] *JRSAI.*, lxv, 320; so from Baltinglass, unpublished.

[109] Belmore Mt., Carrowmore, Carrowkeel, Tibradden (in cist on chamber floor).

[110] *PRIA.* (1898), 659.   [111] *JRSAI.* (1885-86), 567.   [112] *PRIA.*, xxxii, C, 240.

[113] Alcalá: Estáçio da Veiga, *Antiguidades Monumentaes do Algarve*, iii, Pl. VII, 4; Koumasa, Candia Museum, No. 548.

reported from a Boyne tomb (on Slieve na Caillighe) is leaf-shaped, hollow-based arrow-heads and halberds or javelin heads, polished on the face, of Portuguese style, are common in the province, and Ireland has yielded two curious hanging bowls of Portuguese form.[114] One was found in a short cist with cremated bones at Cabinteely (Co. Dublin),[115] the other in a curious tumulus at Drimnagh in the same county.[116]

Here the hanging bowl, richly decorated in stab-and-drag technique with West Mediterranean ladder patterns, lay with an extended skeleton and bones of oxen, swine and sheep in an irregular cist under a small cairn. This had been covered with a mound of turf and stacked logs, 72 ft. in diameter, that had been deliberately set on fire. A sherd of a keeled Ulster bowl of Windmill Hill ware was found above the turf mound. The mound had been used for a secondary interment with a Food Vessel and subsequently enlarged to cover a burial in a Cordoned Urn.

Moreover, the concentration of rich tombs on the metalliferous Wicklow Mountains, and inferential evidence adduced in Chapter VI, imply that metallurgy was practised in the Boyne societies as among the communities buried in Spanish and Portuguese passage graves. Finally, the distribution of tombs in the Boyne tradition in Britain will suggest that the associated economy was no more neolithic than, but just as commercial as, that of the Peninsula. So not only the megalithic religion and the Iberian architectural tradition, but a recognizable amount of equipment and economic organization too, were brought to Ireland from Portugal.

The rite of cremation, on the contrary, was surely a heresy in the megalithic religion. Cases of cremation have indeed been reported from passage graves in south-eastern Spain, but are common and well authenticated first in Brittany and Ireland. The heresy may well have originated there. If the megalithic religion's spread were partly motivated by a quest for Isles of the Blest beneath the setting sun, votaries who had reached the westernmost limit of the Old World might well transfer their hopes to a new world accessible by the purifying fire already used in funerary ritual.

Outside Ireland passage graves were built in only a few areas significantly located with regard to natural trade routes and in a form or with a furniture that makes them appear like the mission churches of trading posts established by Boyne communities. In Anglesey, Bryn Celli Ddu [117] is an orthostatic passage grave in a large round cairn and surrounded by a buried fosse in which stood the cairn's peristalith. Behind the chamber at the exact centre

---

[114] Estaçio da Veiga, i, 200-202.
[116] JRSAI., lxix, 190-225.

[115] Arch., xliii, 373.
[117] Arch., lxxx, 179 ff.

of an inner ring of uprights lay a stone carved with spirals in the Boyne style. In the same island the ruined chamber, standing in a rock-cut pit at Pant y Saer,[118] may also rank as a passage grave. Sherds of Windmill Hill A 2 ware, a lozenge-shaped flint arrow-head and a stone disc and, probably derived from a secondary cist in the chamber, an A Beaker, were recovered from the ruin by Scott.

Along the sea-way northward round Scotland skirting the Clyde province there is a well-blazed trail of passage graves. Barpa Langas (North Uist) [119] and Rudh'an Dunain (Skye) [120] are orthostatic passage graves. At Callernish, Lewis, a tiny cruciform chamber in a round cairn stands within a stone circle, tangential to the cairn's peristalith, from which radiate four stone alignments.[121] Finally, Clettraval (North Uist),[122] though the primary burials were inhumations accompanied by Beacharra ware, is architecturally intermediate between a passage grave and a segmented cist. For the six 'compartments' grow progressively wider and higher as one proceeds from the outermost (3 ft. wide by 4 ft. 3 ins. high) to the innermost (7 ft. by 6 ft. 3 ins.), and the covering cairn was long, with a virtually flat façade. So both sects of the megalithic religion found supporters in the Western Isles and some accommodation between the two faiths may have been reached.

7. THE PENTLAND CULTURE

Beyond the region where two traditions seem to mingle is a megalithic province on both sides of the Pentland Firth dominated by the passage grave tradition (Fig. 10, E). Maes Howe at Stennis in Orkney, a huge mound, encircled with a fosse and covering a rectangular chamber, entered by a long passage, built and roofed in superb dry-stone masonry and connected with three cells arranged in cruciform fashion as at New Grange, must surely have been the tomb of a chieftain from the Boyne. But it was robbed and used as a shelter by a party of Vikings. A few inferior tombs on Mainland, Sanday and Westray might be derivatives of this plan.[123] All consist of a central corbelled chamber out of which open from three to fourteen small cells. Beyond many skeletons and animal bones, they have yielded no distinctive relics. In the remaining tombs the passage grave tradition seems to have been modified by that expressed in the segmented

[118] *Arch. Camb.*, lxxxviii (1933), 185-228.   [119] RC. *Skye and the Hebrides*, No. 224.

[120] *PSAS.*, lxvi, 182-213; Childe, *P.S.*, 43.   [121] RC. *Hebrides*, No. 54.

[122] Scott, *PSAS.*, lxix, 480-556.   [123] Childe, *P.S.*, 47-49.

cists. For the chamber is regularly divided into compartments by slabs
projecting from the side walls.

The *Caithness type* [124] is represented by about 100 cairns, mostly on the
Scottish mainland, three or four scattered on the Orkney islands. As in
Ireland, they may be grouped in small cemeteries of from two to four tombs,
and often occupy hill-tops. Classically the chambers are oval and corbelled
but subdivided into three compartments by projecting slabs (like Fig. 17, B).

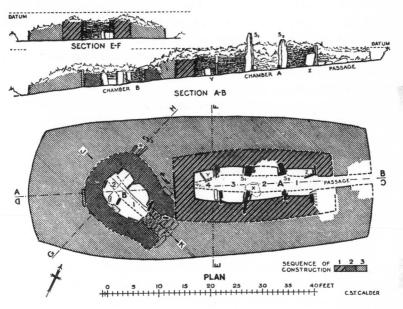

FIG. 17. Plan and section of Stalled (A) and Caithness-type (B) Chambers in
cairn on Calf of Eday. After Calder in *PSAS.*, lxxi.

But in two instances a lateral cell replaces the third compartment. While
many are contained in round cairns, some thirty are covered by long or
short double-horned cairns. Such cairns appear meaningless in Caithness,
but found a rational explanation in the development of the Carlingford
group of horned cairns (p. 56) and were amalgamated with the passage
grave on the frontier of that province at Carrowkeel (p. 67). It almost
looks as if the tradition of this Boyne–Carlingford hybrid had been trans-
planted from Sligo to Caithness and Orkney.

As many as fifty skeletons have been found in cairns of this type, the

[124] Childe, *P.S.*, 32-40.

bones in some instances having been partially burned, perhaps by accident. From short horned and round cairns we have a stone axe, leaf-shaped arrow-heads and pottery of the Windmill Hill family. But some of this is decorated with stab-and-drag lines as in the Boyne and Unstan wares, or rusticated as in the English Bronze Age. Arrow-heads, derived from the mesolithic *petit tranchet*, and narrow flint knives with polished edges would also belong to Period III in England, while a pestle-shaped mace is exactly like one from a grave of Period IV in Yorkshire. And Beakers from both long [125] and short horned cairns show that the tombs were in use until the round-headed invaders reached Caithness. As in Arran, they obtained admission into the circle of those entitled to collective burial but eventually imposed their own practice of individual burial and thus cut short the development of megalithic architecture.

Orkney was reached later by the invasion, so that the megalith-builders had time to develop very specialized Orcadian variants. In some, transversely projecting upright slabs are used as in the Caithness type, but rather to make stalls along the walls than to divide the chamber.

In the *Unstan type*, represented on Mainland, Eday and Rousay, the chamber is entered by a passage leading into the long side, the stalls being benched with flags. At Taiverso Tuick (Rousay) [126] (Fig. 18) and Hunters-quoy (Eday) [127] the chambers had been built entirely in an excavation in the hillside as in Greece and Spain. But in each case a second chamber with an independent entrance passage had been erected over the subterranean vault and covered with a round cairn. Two chambers, approximating more closely to the Caithness plan, had also been built underground on Eday.[128] An upright in one was adorned with a curved spiral providing an additional link with the Boyne culture.

In the *Long Stalled Cairns* of Rousay and Eday [129] the chamber resembles a narrow gallery, but is subdivided by paired uprights into from four to twelve benched stalls, and entered by a distinct narrow passage, generally from one end, exceptionally from the side. The skeletons reposed on the benches along one side. While stalled cairns might be regarded as merely exaggerated versions of the Caithness tripartite chambers, agreements both in plan and details with rock-hewn tombs in the Balearic Isles are at least a warning against over-simplification.[130] On the Calf of Eday the same

[125] In the long cairn of Yarrows the Beaker sherds were found with discs of a jet necklace in a secondary cist on the chamber floor.

[126] *PSAS.*, lxxiii, 155-166.   [127] *PSAS.*, lxxii, 194-204.   [128] *PSAS.*, lxxii, 209.

[129] *PSAS.*, lxviii, 320-350; lxix, 325-351; lxxi, 297-308; 115-154.

[130] Childe, *Dawn*, Figs. 104, 149.

cairn (Fig. 17) covered both a four-stalled gallery and a bipartite oval chamber of Caithness form which Calder claims was the later of the two structures.[131]

SECTIONAL ELEVATION ON A.-B

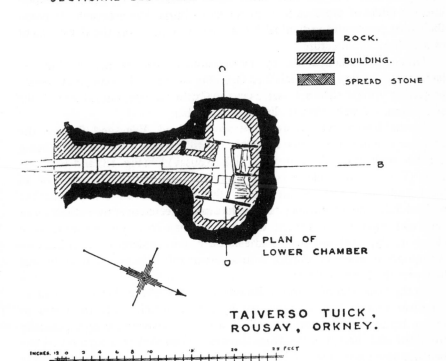

ROCK.

BUILDING.

SPREAD STONE

PLAN OF
LOWER CHAMBER

TAIVERSO TUICK,
ROUSAY, ORKNEY.

FIG. 18. Passage Grave of Unstan type. After Grant in *PSAS.*, lxxiii.

Both these Orcadian types have been found to contain up to thirty skeletons, together in some cases with cremated bones that may be intrusive, accompanied by stone axes, leaf-shaped arrow-heads and simple Windmill Hill vases of types A, D, and E. Characteristic of the Orcadian tombs,

[131] *PSAS.*, lxxi, 115.

however, are big round-bottomed bowls with broad overhanging rims, decorated with deep incisions or stab-and-drag lines often forming alternating triangles (Pl. II, 2).   The decoration of this *Unstan ware* can be matched in a potter's workshop on Eilean-an-Tighe (North Uist) and some Breton tombs and, at least technically, in the Boyne group.   But there is a club-rimmed bowl ornamented in Beacharra technique from a stalled cairn on Eday (Fig. 8, 4).[132]   So the traditions accepted in Orkney, though explicitly Atlantic, were very mixed.   Use of the tombs into some phase of the Bronze Age may be deduced from tanged-and-barbed arrow-heads found in Unstan and Yarso and disc beads of stone from the upper chamber at Taiverso Tuick.   The absence of any contact with the Skara Brae culture which was flourishing when the first and only Beaker yet found reached Orkney must be stressed.

No class of tombs in Orkney form cemeteries, but all stand isolated as do gallery graves.   But the number of tombs that survive is surprisingly large.   On Rousay there would seem to be almost as many family vaults of the Stone Age as there are farms today.   Each vault might correspond to a social and economic unit of similar size.   In that case the neolithic population would correspond to the present, less landlords, shopkeepers and artisans!

8. The Beauly Culture

On the Firth of Lorne a large round cairn at Achnacree on Loch Etive [133] covers an elongated corbelled chamber, entered by a passage 20 ft. long but only 3 ft. high, which is more like a passage grave than a segmented gallery, though it did contain a good Windmill Hill pot decorated with finger-tip fluting.   At the opposite end of the Great Glen trade route (and at Glenurquhart beside it) are cemeteries of passage graves clearly embodying the same architectural tradition as the Boyne tombs [134] (Fig. 10, F).   In such a regular degeneration could be traced if the starting-point be circular corbelled chambers in round cairns which are themselves encircled by rings of free-standing boulders.   The two monoliths opposite the passage mouth are the tallest members of such a ring, the rest diminishing progressively. In the Clava cemetery on the Nairn degeneration takes the form of the suppression of the entrance, leaving eventually a ring cairn within a stone circle, but at Croft Croy [135] produced a gallery grave just as at Carrowmore. Tombs of this class are common round the head of Beauly Firth, and a group

---

[132] *PSAS.*, lxxii, 205, 215.   [133] *PSAS.*, ix, 411.

[134] Childe, *P.S.*, 51-52.   [135] *PSAS.*, xviii, 334, Fig. 3.

round Aviemore shows that the builders spread to the Spey valley. None have yielded dateable relics, but we shall see that in the Early Bronze Age (Period III or IV) the Recumbent Stone circles of Aberdeenshire must be derived from the Beauly series, so that the latter must go back to Period III.

Achnacree and the Beauly cemeteries lie at either end of a trade route through the Great Glen, which, as we shall see, is marked by the distribution of flat axes and halberds of copper. Typologically the tombs are plainly enough connected with the Boyne series. They seem, in fact, to have been built by colonists from Central Ireland who presumably blazed this ancient trail.

9. ENTRANCE GRAVES

A small group of collective tombs in Cornwall, the Scilly Isles and south-eastern Ireland (Fig. 10, H) are generally classed as *entrance graves*.[136] In plan the chamber is just a gallery entered directly through a portal without passage (Fig. 19). But it is generally partly corbelled, sometimes swells out towards the middle, and is always covered by a very small round cairn bounded by a built retaining wall. One tomb on Scilly [137] contained a skeleton with secondary cremations; most, including the only Irish example yet excavated at Harristown,[138] yielded cremations only. The fragmentary pottery has been compared to Breton wares. An axe amulet, a widespread Mediterranean type,[139] was recovered from Harristown (Co. Waterford), and the long rubber of a true saddle quern from Samson (Scilly).[140] Despite the chamber plans, these tombs should no doubt be classed as passage graves—a few Cornish examples have a distinct passage.[141] They could theoretically be derived from the Boyne family, which did produce similar forms at Carrowmore and Croft Croy. But the distribution as known in 1940 points rather to a derivation from Brittany.

10. RELIGION AND ECONOMY

The foregoing analysis has been designed to show that 'missionaries' from various centres in Atlantic Europe brought several versions of the megalithic religion to the British Isles. What other contributions did they make to our cultural capital? As far as the adherents of the gallery grave

---

[136] See Hencken, *Arch. Corn.*, 17-38, 78-79; *Ant. J.*, xiii, 13-20.
[137] *Ant. J.*, xiii, 22.   [138] Excavated by Mrs Hawkes in 1939.
[139] Childe, *Dawn*, 222, 240, 259.   [140] *Ant. J.*, xiii, 29.   [141] *JRIC.*, vi, 211.

or long cist tradition are concerned, their contributions to material culture seem small. Apart from a few stone beads and discs from Severn tombs, the grave-goods from all kinds of English long barrows agree more closely with the relics from causewayed camps than with those from Pyrenaean or

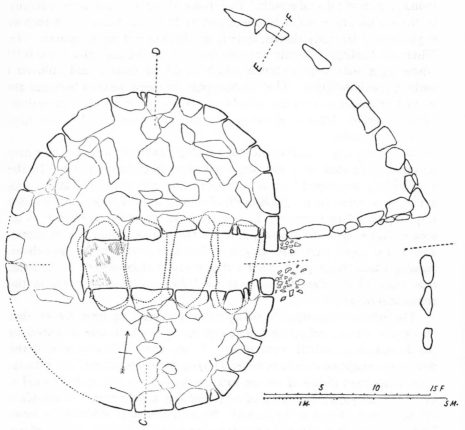

FIG. 19. Entrance Grave, Bant's Carn, Scilly. After *Ant. J.*, xiii.

Breton tombs. In the Clyde–Carlingford group Beacharra ware, and perhaps the true saddle quern, may rank as more substantial contributions. But even these innovations are associated with typically British Windmill Hill pottery and leaf-shaped arrow-heads.

The economy of all these megalithic groups seems essentially that of neolithic England as described in Chapter III. The bones of calves and lambs deposited as offerings in the tombs are products of the same inefficient pastoralism. Bones of horses from the Cotswolds and Ulster, as from Caithness, [142] might be spoils of the chase. Barley, [142a] but not wheat, was cultivated in Scotland, Man and Ulster. Gallery graves and unchambered barrows are not strung out along natural trade routes nor concentrated round sources of mineral wealth. The choice of sites was governed primarily by the availability of arable land and pasture free from heavy forest such as is guaranteed by chalk downs, limestone plateaux and recent gravels. In Ulster the Carlingford tombs are scattered over the uplands above 400 ft.[143] where light soils were available which could be cleared and cultivated without much difficulty. Their counterparts in south-western Scotland are located by preference on the raised-beach platform or beside well-drained alluvial gravels. Here as elsewhere, indeed, they often stand on the edge of modern farmlands.

Round the Clyde and in Galloway a single horned cairn or a pair may be expected in each little glen and on each strip of raised beach. In the Cotswolds a chambered barrow corresponds to each ridge of upland rising above the wooded plain. Each block of downland in Sussex boasts its own tiny cluster of long barrows. In a word, a family vault corresponds to an area of arable land and pasture, here bounded by sea, mountain or forest, and to the social unit exploiting it. Was that unit a single household, farming a lone steading, or rather a clan or group of families? In the latter case, were all the clansmen or only the 'chief' entitled to burial in the communal ossuary?

The labour of quarrying, transporting and erecting huge blocks that may weigh 4 tons, and piling a cairn containing as much stone as a modern parish church, is indeed tremendous. It was not necessarily beyond the powers of a single household who could rely on the co-operation of neighbours. Pastoralists have plenty of leisure with no cinemas to occupy it. Could it be better employed than in gradually building a permanent resting-place for the bones of potent ancestors? Nevertheless it is intrinsically more likely that the unit engaged was larger, and that the single family whose members enjoyed the privilege of burial in the vault (p. 52) was that of a clan chief, though the fate of commoners remains in this case a problem. The assumption of chiefs fits in with the suggestion made on p. 53 and the contrast between the exotic character of the funerary architecture and the essentially native character of the grave-goods.

[142] Crawford, *Long Barrows of the Cotswolds*, 26; *P.B.N.H.&P.S.* (1936-37), 40; Childe, *P.S.*, 38; *Ant. J.*, xv, 435 (general survey).   [142a] Jessen and Helbaek, 18.
[143] Evans in *Survey*, Northern Ireland, p. xii.

On a quest for Isles of the Blest or Givers of Life fanatics might brave the perils of a voyage across the Bay of Biscay to the Bristol Channel or the Firth of Clyde. Once wafted to the shores of the British Isles, such adventurers might be accepted as wizards by the local Windmill Hill peasants and installed as chiefs. And a superstitious adventurer from Spain or Brittany, thus made a British chief, might be quite ready to accept native pots and arrow-heads, provided his pious subjects would build him a tomb sufficiently like the ancestral vault to satisfy magician's logic. In response to economic needs and superstitious hopes such chiefs could lead followers on to the next ridge, the next glen or the next island. Nevertheless, on this thesis we seem forced to assume settlements of pre-megalithic farmers in Wales, Cumberland and even Galloway, for which there is not a scrap of evidence.

The foregoing account might explain in part the social organization expressed in passage graves too. But it clearly will not cover the Boyne economy. Those buried in the Boyne tombs were not furnished with the equipment of a pre-megalithic population—no such is known in Eire; the few grave-goods are as exotic as the tombs. The cemeteries imply villages, and one such is perhaps known. On a ridge at Carrowkeel (Pl. III, 2), defended on two sides by precipices, dominated on the third by cairn-crowned cliffs, Macalister surveyed the ruins of some 50 round huts.[144] One alone measures 45 ft. in diameter, 5 exceed 35 ft. and 26 are less than 25 ft. across. The site is extraordinarily like the settlement of Los Millares in Almeria, to which belonged a cemetery of 100 passage graves. Perhaps the five largest houses on Carrowkeel belonged to aristocratic families whose members were buried in the five groups of collective tombs upon the adjacent hills. A connexion between the settlement and the cemetery is in any case highly probable, and the variation in the size of huts should reflect differences in status and wealth such as might result from a more 'urban' economy. The analogy between Carrowkeel and Los Millares may go deeper than topography and suggest that the former too was already a rather distant approximation to the Mediterranean 'Copper Age' township.

A little direct evidence is in fact available for industrial specialization and trade. On a tiny islet, Eilean-an-Tighe, on a loch in North Uist, Lindsay Scott has explored what he interprets as a settlement of specialist potters.[145] The site is too small to provide pasture or even fields for tillage. But on it are remains of an habitation and of two kilns, together with a vast accumulation of sherds and wasters. Some sherds agree so closely with

[144] *PRIA.*, xxix, 331.   [145] Described before the R.A.I. in 1939.

the bowls from the stalled cairns on Rousay that, subject to confirmation by petrographic examination, it seems likely that neolithic bowls were exported from the Hebrides to Orkney. The dependence of the potters' settlement on the Boyne culture is in any case established by the pottery as well as by geography.

In any case, the distribution of Boyne tombs points explicitly to some sort of secondary industries and commerce. The numbers round Sligo might indeed be explained by the fine pasturage and tilth offered by the limestone hills, while the distribution in Ulster may be governed partly by the same factors as that of Carlingford tombs. But the concentration in Wicklow must be connected with gold. In Scotland passage graves are distributed along trade routes that are well marked also by the distribution of bronze and gold objects during the Bronze Age (Chapter VII). Passage graves were built in Denmark too, beginning later than the dolmens and in far smaller numbers.[146] Though they contain no more Britannico-Hibernian grave-goods than the dolmens, the Irish weapons and gold ornaments that are scattered about the megalithic routes in Scotland do turn up stray in Denmark [147]; conversely, beads of amber, presumably brought from Jutland, are found in the passage graves of Alcalá and Los Millares in Iberia. If the chiefs buried in Boyne tombs performed mainly sacerdotal functions, they had followers who could find a living in metallurgy and commerce as well as in farming; Chapter VII will show how the Food Vessel folk who inherited the good-will of Boyne traders adopted also their traditions of magic art. But these followers were superimposed upon, and recruited from, residual societies of hunters and fishers, still virtually unrepresented in the archaeological record.

If the foregoing account of the economy and sociology of the megalithic culture be well documented, the history of its origins is less securely based. The surviving furniture of the Boyne tombs should belong to Period IV in the British sequence. Carvings, recalling the Boyne passage grave art, recur in Britain in cists of Periods III and IV, and the Irish art itself may be older than the tombs.[148] The cremationist ritual too is appropriate to the Wessex culture of England (Chapter VIII). So in the Peninsula Bosch-Gimpera [149] has argued that the tombs of Alcalá, the closest parallels to

---

[146] Brønsted, *Danmarks Oldtid*, ii, supplement, records about 4700 *dysser* as against some 670 passage graves (*jaettestuerne*).

[147] Brønsted, i, 249, assigns these imports to the ' later passage grave period.'

[148] Many of the carvings at New Grange were executed before the decorated stones were put in position; so also at Dowth, Slieve na Caillighe, etc. See Breuil, *PSEA.*, vii (1934), 292-300.   [149] *Préhistoire*, ii, 198-229.

New Grange and Carrowkeel, were built after Beakers had gone out of fashion in Portugal. He suggests that the Copper Age economy had been brought to Ireland before the passage grave cult by Beaker folk from Brittany, represented so far only in a single cist grave at Moytirra, Co. Sligo. By thus transferring the Boyne culture to Period IV the parallelism between its funerary architecture and that of Mycenaean Greece would become significant. The Irish origin of the Northern passage graves, on the other hand, would become less likely.[150]

Our account of the British megalithic cultures is subject to a similar, if less drastic, revision. Clyde cists need not be older than Period III, even the Severn tombs might be brought down to this horizon and Period II eliminated altogether. The long barrow, and even perhaps collective burial itself, become integral traits in the original Windmill Hill culture. The whole 'megalithic religion' threatens to vanish in smoke!

[150] That Danish passage graves were still in use in what corresponds to English Period IV is highly probable; some, however, contain Beakers which, though doubtless later than the beginning of our III, ought still to fall within it. And these did not accompany the earliest interments in the vaults in question.

Addendum.—The only adult burial found under the " long barrow " at Maiden Castle was that of a male whose limbs and head had been hacked from the body shortly after death, while his brain had apparently been deliberately extracted. Near it were remains of two children. Wheeler, *Maiden Castle*, 21.

CHAPTER V

NEOLITHIC HUNTERS AND HERDSMEN

THE Windmill Hill farmers and megalith-builders had found the British Isles already sparsely populated by little groups of mesolithic food-gatherers. As such eschewed the lands most favoured as pastures by the immigrants, some could and did survive undisturbed. But before Period III new neolithic societies emerge in the archaeological record. Some may result from the acculturation of such residual food-gathering groups.

1. THE PETERBOROUGH CULTURE

A culture, that may be named after a representative site at Peterborough, was in fact recognized in England before the more classically neolithic Windmill Hill culture. Its typical pottery was regarded in southern Britain as neolithic pottery, *par excellence*, from 1910, when R. A. Smith[1] first defined it, down to 1927, when Leeds published his finds from Abingdon.

Peterborough culture, most abundantly and early represented in south-eastern England, is a distinctively lowland culture. In contrast to Windmill Hill folk, its authors lived by preference in valleys along rivers and beside marshes or on the coast, and that not only in eastern England but even in Wessex,[2] Yorkshire[3] and in Galloway. This preference seems to carry on the traditions of the North European Forest folk (p. 26). And their economy persisted too. Curved sickles of flint (Fig. 20), a type widespread in Northern Europe, may belong to Peterborough folk and prove the practice of agriculture.[4] So bones of oxen, pigs and sheep, as well as of red deer, were found in a hut at Winterbourne Dauntsey (Wilts.).[2] But on the whole Piggott[5] can plausibly argue that in its eastern homeland the Peterborough economy was essentially mesolithic. Hunting and fishing played a much more vital role than among the Windmill Hill folk.

Its domestic architecture shows no advance on that of Farnham (p. 21). The only pure Peterborough hut yet discovered was a flimsy structure

[1] *Arch.*, lxii, 335.
[2] *WAM.*, xlvi, 445.
[3] Settlement on edge of Vale of York: *PPS.*, v, 251.
[4] *PSEA.*, vii (1932), 76-79; *PPS.*, ii, 206-208.
[5] *PPS.*, iv, 55 and 91.

delimited by a ring of eight stakes with a diameter of 7 ft. 4 ins. with the central area, 4 ft. in diameter, hollowed out to a depth of 10 ins. in the chalk.[6]   Certain distinctive items of equipment too—lop-sided arrow-heads derived from the *petit tranchet* (Fig. 24, 8-10), flint knives polished along the edge in a technique that might have been suggested by bone-work, and perhaps perforated mace-heads of antler and stone [7]—may be regarded as a heritage of the Forest culture.   Finally, Peterborough pottery is extra-ordinarily like that made by the Forest folks' descendants east of the Baltic in late Atlantic and Sub-Boreal times.[8]

The vases were made of coarse clay, built up in rings and poorly fired, the common form being an ovoid bowl with a rather thick rim and hollow

FIG. 20.   Flint Sickle, Grovehurst, Kent. $\frac{1}{2}$.   (By permission of the Trustees of the British Museum.)

neck.   In the oldest specimens, represented by sherds collected by Burchell in the sunk channel of Ebbsfleet Brook (Northfleet, Kent),[9] ornament is confined to incised lattices on the rim and rounded shoulder and a row of large pits round the neck.   The better-known but later vases were covered all over with zones of ornament, the rims being heavier and the shoulders more angular than in the older style.[10]   The designs are formed by the imprint of finger-nails, of the joint of a bird's leg-bone, of a *Cardium* shell, of a coarse-toothed comb or of cords, generally whipped together or round a stiff core (Pl. IV, 1).   Crescentic or horseshoe-shaped imprints of a loop of simple or whipped cord were very popular and are suggestively termed *maggots* by archaeologists.   These motives are normally combined with a row of pits in the hollow of the neck, as already on the Ebbsfleet vases.

The agreement in technique, form and decoration between English Peterborough pottery and that of 'Dwelling Places' in Finland and Russia is so exact that in 1932 an actual immigration of Forest folk, perhaps in the

[6] Winterbourne Dauntsey: Stone, *WAM.*, xlvi, 446-447.

[7] Piggott, *PPS.*, iv, 91.   [8] Childe, *Dawn*, 193-199.   [9] *Ant. J.*, xix, 405-420.

[10] Piggott, *Arch. J.*, lxxxviii, 110-120; but some of the designs he describes should be attributed to the Skara Brae culture described on pp. 84 ff. below.

wake of the Beaker invaders, was deduced from it. Now that the extension of such a population to England even in mesolithic times is fully recognized, and the persistence of mesolithic traditions in Denmark and on the Lower Rhine has been demonstrated, the deduction seems unnecessary. The transgression of Atlantic times had not entirely interrupted the continuum that had previously embraced the whole North European plain. Parallel developments within that continuum of Forest cultures under the impact of the same Western and Megalithic societies may explain the similarity between Peterborough and Baltic wares. Peterborough folk may be descendants of the mesolithic hunters of Broxbourne and Lower Halstow (p. 28) who had adopted some neolithic arts from the immigrant Western farmers.

The faunule from Ebbsfleet suggests a date early in Period I for the formation of the new group in the Thames valley. Its products appear on the Lyonesse surface of Essex and in the Windmill Hill camp of Whitehawk in Sussex.[11] Their descendants, however, spread mainly in Period III. In Wessex, Peterborough ware appears just before Beaker sherds in the stratified silt of the ditches of Windmill Hill, Maiden Castle and Wor Barrow. Eventually Peterborough folk spread as far north as Dunbar and the Glenluce Sands, westward at least to Anglesey (where distinctive sherds occur in collective tombs,[12] as in Derbyshire and the Cotswolds). They may have reached even Ireland, since the coarse 'sandhill pottery' of Ulster is reminiscent of Peterborough ware.

The expansion from south-eastern England may have begun with hunting expeditions, imposed by their economy on food-gatherers, such as had maintained intercourse among the scattered groups of Forest folk all over the North European plain even in mesolithic times. But on such expeditions the quest for game might now profitably be combined with the transportation of raw materials that could be bartered for the farm-produce of more sedentary populations. As far away as Anglesey and Wiltshire, axes made from augite granophyre, a rock occurring only and actually worked on the slopes of Penmaen Mawr in North Wales, have been found in association with Peterborough pottery.[13] Near Avebury fragments of Niedermendig lava from the Rhineland, a stone exported in Roman times for making querns, turned up in a Peterborough settlement.[14] These may be some

---

[11] *PSEA.*, vii (1934), 375, modified by *Ant. J.*, xix, 411.

[12] *Arch.*, lxxxv, 285 (Bryn yr Hen Bobl); sherds from Gop Cave (Flints.) (*Arch. J.*, lviii, 322-341) were associated with jet sliders and a polished flint knife.

[13] Glenn in *Arch. Camb.*, xc (1935), 208.   [14] *Antiquity*, x, 422.

of the materials in which they traded. Peterborough sherds from flint-mines [15] may mean that their makers profited also from the distribution of flint. In return, as huntsmen, they could provide the miners with the antlers needed for picks. The co-operation of Peterborough groups with the presumably Windmill Hill communities mining flint at Grimes Graves must indeed have been close. Armstrong has recognized on chalk crusts naturalistic engravings the style of which has been rightly compared to the art of the Norwegian and East Baltic kinsmen of our Peterborough folk.[16] In other words, even in neolithic times Peterborough hunters were perhaps specializing as traders. We shall find reason in the sequel for believing that their descendants participated in the commerce in metal from Ireland.[17]

2. THE SKARA BRAE CULTURE

A third group which emerged during Periods I-II has been known since 1866 from the ruins exposed by a storm at Skara Brae on the Bay of Skail, Orkney (Fig. 10, 14). These became famous as a classical illustration of the neolithic economy through the conservation works carried out by H.M. Office of Works in 1928-30. Their true position in the archaeological record was, however, not settled till 1936, when Piggott [18] recognized that the grooved ware from the submerged Lyonesse surface of the Essex coast was essentially identical with the earlier pottery from Skara Brae. In the succeeding year the discovery by Grant and Yorston [19] of a Beaker in the latest occupation level of a second Skara Brae at Rinyo, Rousay, showed that the Skara Brae culture had spread to Orkney before Beakers. Apart from these extreme sites, its distinctive pottery has been recognized in low-lying occupation sites in East Anglia and the Thames valley and in Wessex, notably at the sanctuary of Woodhenge, and at Gullane on the shores of the Firth of Forth. In Wessex and at Gullane grooved ware seems to be contemporary with AC Beakers, and it is often associated with lop-sided arrow-heads in England. But only in Orkney is material available for a full picture of the culture and economy denoted by the fabric.

The Orkney villagers [20] were essentially pastoralists living by breeding

[15] Grimes Graves and Easton Down.
[16] *PSEA.*, iii, 434, 548; Kendrick and Hawkes, 76-77. Cf. Clark, *Northern Europe,* 180-188.
[17] The only certain Peterborough tomb yet published is a cist that contained two dis-articulated skeletons, pottery and an arrow-head derived from the *petit tranchet* in a rock-shelter at Church Dale, Derbyshire: *PPS.*, iv, 317.
[18] *PPS.*, ii, 201.   [19] *Ant. J.*, xviii, 402.
[20] Fully described in Childe, *Skara Brae* (1931), and *PSAS.*, lxxiii (1938-39), 8-31.

sheep and cattle. The latter belonged, like those of Windmill Hill, to a long-horned stock in contrast to the Celtic short-horn. Watson believes that some bulls were gelded. But deficiencies in rural economy made it impossible to carry many calves over the winter, so that an extravagant amount of veal was eaten. Neither grains, querns nor sickle-flints indicate the practice of any sort of agriculture. Nor do hunting-weapons and fishing-tackle demonstrate a diet of game or fish, though red deer existed and were sometimes caught. But limpets were gathered in enormous quantities. The treeless islands with their wide sandy coastal plains provide ample pastures without need of transhumance or long treks. The herdsmen could and did inhabit the same site continuously for generations; three superimposed layers of habitations exist at Skara Brae and two at Rinyo.

Substantial dwellings were needed to provide shelter against the continuous gales. But there were no trees for houses and household furniture. The Caithness flagstone that breaks easily into flat slabs provided a convenient substitute. And for us the translation into stone of articles normally made of wood has preserved a unique record. As an additional protection the huts at Skara Brae were built into hollows in sand-dunes— which, however, eventually overwhelmed and embalmed them.

The individual houses (Fig. 21 and Pl. V, 1) were parallelograms with rounded corners measuring between 20×18 ft. and 14×12 ft. internally, and partly roofed by corbelling. Each was entered through a very narrow entrance only 4 ft. high, closed by a door, presumably of stone, which could be fastened by a bar of stone or whalebone. In the centre was a square hearth on which a peat fire burned. On either side were beds, enclosed by stone slabs, once containing a mattress of heather and covered with a canopy of skins supported by stone bed-posts. Shelves in the walls above the beds served to store the personal possessions of the bed's occupants. Small boxes or cists of thin slabs with carefully luted joints, let into the floor, contained unspecified liquids. A two-shelved dresser of stone stood against the back wall. And one to three small cells open off each hut; some may have been used as storerooms, others as privies, since they are drained.

The huts were grouped into regular clusters connected together by paved alleys. In its final form Skara Brae comprised six or seven dwellings and one 'industrial hut' that lacked the usual beds and dresser but was provided with a kiln and had been used as a workshop by a chert-knapper. The alleys connecting the domestic structures were all roofed over and the whole complex buried in sand, refuse and ash. Both Rinyo and Skara Brae were drained by a system of built sewers running under the huts.

The communities sheltering in these hut-clusters were typically neolithic in self-sufficiency. No imported materials were used; the 'industrial hut' at Skara Brae is less like the dwelling of an artisan family than a communal

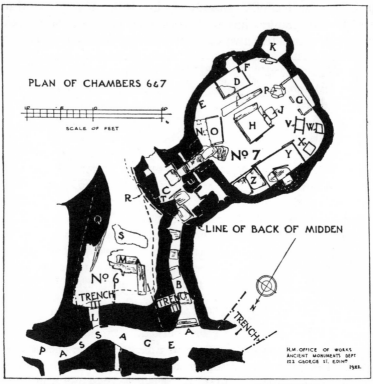

PLAN OF CHAMBERS 6&7

SCALE OF FEET

No 7

LINE OF BACK OF MIDDEN

No 6

TRENCH

PASSAGE

H.M. OFFICE OF WORKS
ANCIENT MONUMENTS DEPT
122 GEORGE ST. EDIN?
1922.

FIG. 21. PLAN OF HUT AT SKARA BRAE. After *PSAS*.
O, D, Y, ' Beds ' ; H, Hearth ; G, Dresser ; V, X, W, Boxes ; K, Cell ;
B, Roofed passage.

workroom open to all. Skins were worn as clothing; no textile appliances have been found, but a multitude of chert or flint scrapers and adze-like tools made from perforated metapodials of oxen that are suitable for leather-dressing, and bone awls and bodkins for sewing. Local rock was polished to make axe-heads which might be mounted in perforated antler hafts as in the Maglemosean culture. Socketed 'chisels' (? used for leather-dressing), made from the metapodials of cattle, also have a Maglemosean ancestry.

Simple bucket and flowerpot bowls, flat-bottomed and often quite large (Fig. 26), were built up in rings out of gritty clay and poorly fired. But many were richly decorated. True grooved ware, such as occurs in southern England, was current only in the older phases of the settlements at Skara Brae and Rinyo. In it decoration is effected by means of rather broad incisions and punctuations, generally cut into a slip of finer clay that coats the vessel. The patterns include triangles and lozenges, and at least once a true spiral. An alternative decorative device employed at all levels in

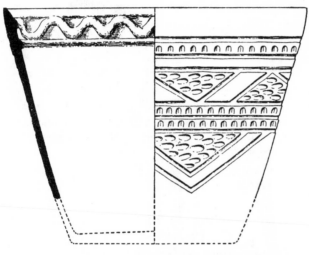

FIG. 22. Bowl of 'Grooved Ware' (restored) from Lyonesse surface, Essex. ¼. After Piggott in *PPS.*, ii.

Orkney and not unknown in England was the application of ribs and blobs of clay (held in place by the slip) to form lozenges, triangles, zigzag and wavy lines, and arcadings (Pl. XIII, 2). Bowls, mortars and paint-pots were hammered out of sandstone or the vertebrae of stranded whales.

Nodular haematite was used in place of iron pyrites in the production of fire, and was also ground up to make a red pigment. As personal finery, beads and pendants were made from the teeth of cows and killer-whales, whalebone and sheep's marrow-bones and boars' tusks. From hard stone were fashioned balls, either quite smooth or covered with symmetrical knobs or bosses (Pl. IV, 2), and other mysterious objects. A weird series of spiked and club-like implements, including a model of a double-axe with handle all carved in one piece of slatey shale, were made in soft stones.

Stones in the buildings' walls are carved or engraved with hatched triangles, lozenges, zigzags and other rectilinear devices. Two old women had been buried huddled together in a rough cist under the wall of one house at Skara Brae. Their bodies were presumably placed there not as an honour but so that their ghosts might help to hold up the walls. No regular burials of Skara Brae people are known; their characteristic relics have not yet been found in collective tombs in Orkney.

The hut-clusters with their alleys and drains can only have been built by the effective co-operation of organized societies. But there are no indications of chieftainship or class divisions, though variations in the size of dwellings may reflect gradations of wealth or status.

Spatially the East Anglian sites are linked to those of Orkney only by the settlement on the dunes at Gullane.[21] A large number of carved stone balls from the coasts of the Moray Firth and Aberdeenshire may, however, be taken as proof of a strong Skara Brae population in north-eastern Scotland. On the west a vase accompanying the latest interments in the passage grave of Unival (North Uist) [22] shows stylistic, but not technical, affinities with Skara Brae. The same may be true of some sherds from Rothesay, Bute and from Irish sand-hills.

In time the settlements on the Lyonesse surface of Essex antedate the arrival of A Beaker folk, i.e. Period III b. So a late AC Beaker was found in the latest occupation floor at Rinyo. But the Rinyo Beaker is about the most degenerate specimen from the British Isles and may be centuries later than the oldest East Anglian members of the group. The decoration of Encrusted Urns is so similar to that of the domestic vases of Rinyo and Skara Brae that these Urns must be the direct descendants of vases in the Orcadian style. But they are assigned to Period VI or VII. So the Skara Brae culture must outlast the Early and Middle Bronze Age in North Britain.

It is partly built up out of mesolithic elements; the arrow-heads in England, the perforated antler mounts and socketed bone 'chisels' of Orkney, must have been inherited from the Forest cultures. The decorative art in stone and clay, on the other hand, makes use of Atlantic patterns, and the Orcadian ribbed pottery is extraordinarily like that from 'Copper Age' caves in Catalonia.[23] The physical characters of the old women from Skara Brae are not helpful; though long-headed, they might be encountered in any mixed population. But whatever its origin, the society of pastoralists, so vividly disclosed by its Orcadian settlements, must have played no less important a part in the Bronze Age of North Britain than that assigned to Peterborough folk.

[21] *PSAS.*, xlii, 308-319.   [22] *PPS.*, iv, 337.   [23] *PSAS.*, lxiii, 273.

3. Epimesolithic Cultures in Ireland

From the relatively large population that had exploited the flint of Antrim in Atlantic times were recruited neolithic societies whose several cultures are still imperfectly defined.

(a) From above the latest raised beach at Glenarm, Movius (p. 29) recovered remains of Whelan's Campignyan. They differ from the British Windmill Hill complex most significantly in the use of the *tranchet* axe. But the pottery could most naturally be treated as a local variant on the

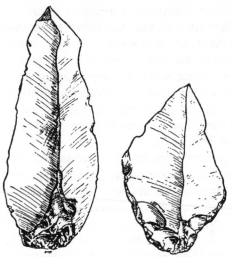

FIG. 23.   Bann Points.   ⅓.   After Movius in
in *PRIA.*, lxiii.

British style. Hence these remains can economically be attributed to a combination of neolithic immigrants who had crossed over with their stock from Great Britain and mesolithic hunters and fishers of Forest traditions (pp. 29, 44).

(b) The *Bann culture* must be similarly explained. It is best known from hearths under and in the diatomite clay deposited on its plain by the River Bann. They belong to fishers who in late Atlantic or Sub-Boreal times used to kindle fires during the dry season on the marshy flats beside the river, perhaps to smoke their fish at.[24] Their homes are so far unknown, but they were expert at working the fine local flint. While they used polished axes of basalt, their most distinctive products [25] are pointed blades narrowed

[24] Movius, *PRIA.*, xliii, C, 17-30.   [25] Knowles, *PRIA.*, xxx, C, 195-222.

by trimming at the butt ends and sometimes actually tanged (Fig. 23). They may have formed the prongs of eel-forks. In one hearth a large round-bottomed bowl with a flat lug was found. It would pass for a piece of Windmill Hill ware [26] and thus disclose the origin of the neolithic elements in the Bann culture.

A formal similarity between the distinctive Bann blades and some found in an early Boreal layer at Lyngby, Jutland, has often been noted. It is perhaps explicable by parallel developments for fishing economies of tendencies, inherited from Creswellian times, by populations dwelling round the North Sea without postulating a fresh immigration from the Baltic.[27] In any case, the fishers who frequented the lower Bann valley so regularly have left no traces on the next river, the Main. But their relatives did settle on the Isle of Man.[28]

(c) Mahr [29] has drawn attention to assemblages of odd axes and clubs made generally of clay slates that have been collected in large numbers from the lower reaches of the Bann, the Shannon and other streams. He considers these, like similar implements from Orkney and Shetland, to be manifestations of a distinct 'Riverford culture,' created by fishermen and rooted in the Maglemosean of the North Sea coast lands. None of the Irish material has been obtained under circumstances which disclosed its context; most Shetland clubs seem to be Late Bronze Age.[30] It is premature to define a people with such miscellaneous material.

[26] The rim and an applied moulding below it were embellished with notches: *PRIA.*, xliii, C, 37-40.

[27] The tanged-point tradition lasted there throughout Atlantic times, but the later points are less like the Bann ones: cf. Clark, *Northern Europe*, 70-73; *PPS.*, ii, 243.

[28] *PPS.*, i, 74.   [29] *PPS.*, iii, 283-331.

[30] Mahr includes the Bann culture in the Riverford complex, but no clubs were found in the Bann hearths nor on Man, while no Bann points are found at Riverford sites outside the Bann valley!

CHAPTER VI

THE BEAKER FOLK

1. The Invasion by Round-heads

The self-sufficiency of neolithic economy was broken down by the advent of warlike invaders imbued with domineering habits and an appreciation of metal weapons and ornaments which inspired them to impose sufficient political unity on their new domain for some economic unification to follow. The invaders, as Abercromby showed in 1901, were a branch of a race of traders and warriors who had spread over the Continent from the Atlantic coasts to the Vistula and from the Straits of Gibraltar to the North Sea. Because of the easily recognized type of drinking cup that was regularly buried with them, they are known as the Beaker folk.[1] The Beakers may really have held a sort of beer and thus denoted one source of spirituous authority by which their users maintained their dominion. In that case the name would not be just a conventional label. The people themselves nearly always conform to a single physical type, notably brachycranial and probably of the Dinaric variety. But in Britain, while generally round-headed in contrast to the megalith-builders, the Beaker population as a whole diverges from the continental, exhibiting peculiarities which suggest to Coon[2] an admixture of tall long-headed 'Battle-axe' folk. The archaeological evidence confirms the deductions of anthropology in so far as the anatomical and cultural data can be correlated.

On the Continent, Beaker folk, starting, it is believed, from the Iberian Peninsula, spread to Sardinia, Sicily, Upper Italy and Central Europe, South France, Brittany and the Channel Islands. In Central Europe they joined forces with the equally adventurous Battle-axe folk, producing a mixed race with a mixed culture. The British Isles were affected by two quite distinct waves of invaders, in each of which several bands can be distinguished.[3] All Beaker folk were armed with daggers and bows and

[1] For details see Childe, *Dawn*, 213-219, 157-159, 163-166, 335.

[2] Coon, *Races*, 159; in Yorkshire some Beaker men were actually long-headed, but quite tall (5 ft. 10 ins. to 6 ft.) in contrast to the megalith-builders: Elgee, *Arch. Yorks.*, 59.

[3] The distinction was recognized by Abercromby in his paper of 1901 (*JRAI.*, xxxii, 391), but is virtually ignored in his better-known *Bronze Age Pottery*, 1912. It was clearly restated by the present author in 1928 (*Danube in Prehistory*, 200) and demonstrated with maps in 1931 by Clark (*Antiquity*, v, 415-426) and Grimes (*PSEA.*, vi, 347). So far, anthropometrists have studied only pooled Beaker skulls without regard to this division.

arrows, all were normally buried individually in the strictly contracted attitude, often under a round barrow or cairn. But both the types of Beaker and the associated grave-goods reveal well-marked differences of tradition.

The first invaders to reach England used Beakers of the type originally classified by Thurnam [4] as B, which can now be subdivided into three or more sub-groups. All B Beakers approximate to the widely distributed continental form termed the Bell-beaker (Pl. VI, 2). The profile shows a continuous S curve and the decoration is limited to simple patterns arranged

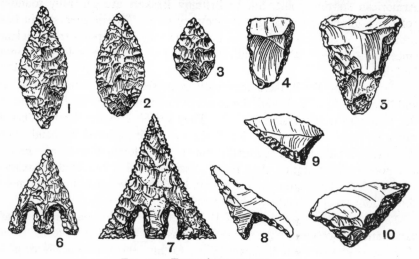

FIG. 24.   FLINT ARROW-HEADS.

1. Rhomboid ; 2, 3. Leaf-shaped ; 4, 5. Transverse (*petits tranchets*) ; 8, 9. Lop-sided (derivatives of *petit tranchet*) ; 6. Tanged-and-barbed ; 7. Breton type.   ¼.
7. Breach Farm, Glam. ; the rest Essex coast. After Mrs Burkitt in *PPS.*, ii.

in horizontal zones round the vase. In Beakers of class B I [5] the zoned patterns are executed by simple incisions, or by the imprint of a fine square-toothed comb which yielded an almost continuous *hyphenated line.* Their users were armed with West European daggers of copper (such as accompany Beakers everywhere on the Continent (Fig. 25, 1), and arrows tipped with barbed-and-tanged flint points (Fig. 24, 6). Against the recoil of the bow-string the archer wore as a wrist-guard a stone plaque, concave on one side and perforated at the four corners (Fig. 25, 4) just as in Central Europe and Holland.

Two gold discs about the size of a halfpenny and ornamented with a

[4] *Arch.*, xliii, 391-394.   [5] Abercromby, *BAP.*, i, 22-23.

traced cross were worn by a Beaker man buried at Mere (Wilts.). The graves may be simple pits under a bowl-shaped barrow or, in rocky country, stone cists under a cairn which may cover a masked ring of stones round the grave.[6] Such Beaker graves are commonest in south-western England from Dartmoor to western Sussex, but not in the Isle of Wight,[7] as if their makers had landed somewhere near Christchurch and overrun the chalk downs. As far as the pottery is concerned, the B1 invaders might have come either from the Rhineland or from Brittany. Piggott[8] and Grimes[9] favour an Armorican starting-point, but in Brittany Beakers are generally found in collective tombs and wrist-guards are very rare. The invaders might have brought their daggers with them, but these may be imports from Ireland, since such daggers were manufactured there,[10] and the gold discs must be Irish.

People using B2 Beakers admittedly came from the mouth of the Rhine and landed in Kent and along the coasts of Essex and Suffolk, arriving before the Lyonesse transgression (p. 11). They spread into the Upper Thames valley in Oxfordshire, where B1 Beakers were introduced by bands from Wessex.[11] B2 Beakers are generally more squat in form, inferior in technique and poorer in decoration than those classified as B1, but cord impression was popular. They are more often found in flat graves than under barrows, and seldom accompanied by other grave-goods.

Farther north, other bands of B Beaker folk landed on the Yorkshire coasts and in Scotland, both in the Lothians and beyond the Forth. Some of these—e.g. two from Bathgate (West Lothian)—are technically as good as any continental Beaker. A group decorated simply with cord impressions arranged in zones (B3) or wrapped round the vase in a continuous spiral (B3a) may be specially mentioned (Pl. VII, 1). Both variants are found in northern Holland, as on the Rhine, but also in Brittany and South France. A B3a Beaker comes from the segmented gallery grave of La Halliade (Hautes Pyrénées). In Great Britain cord-ornamented Beakers have been found on the old land surface under the long barrow at Skendleby (Lincs.) (p. 64), and in passage graves in Caithness. Westward they spread across Yorkshire as far as Grassington in Wharfedale,[12] and from the Lothians via the Biggar Gap to Glenluce in Galloway, and thence or from Yorkshire to Cumberland.[13]

---

[6] e.g. Nun's Cross, Princetown: *TDA.*, xxix (1897), 68.
[7] Dunning, *P.I.O.W.N.H. & A.S.* (1933), 296.   [8] *PPS.*, iv, 56.   [9] *Guide*, 49.
[10] A mould for casting one: *PPS.*, iv, 291, n. 1.
[11] Leeds, *Oxoniensia*, iii, 14-17; Pl. III, D, is obviously B2.
[12] *YAJ.*, xxix, 361, Fig. 8, d.   [13] *T.C. & W.A. & A.S.*, xxxvii, 104.

In Wessex, Oxfordshire, Yorkshire and Scotland 'hybrid' vases suggest that B and A Beaker folk intermingled and blended their ceramic traditions. On the other hand, many B Beakers preserve their form very consistently, however far their makers may have moved from their original east or south coast landing-points.   This fact may indicate that the B invaders spread very rapidly, or, as Leeds hints,[14] it may just reflect a rigid conservatism. The groups concerned were perhaps numerically small.   Piggott could enumerate only 47 B 1 and 23 B 2 Beakers in southern England in 1938.

The A Beaker folk seem to have absorbed a relatively large proportion of the traditions of the Battle-axe folk with whom the pure, Dinaric Beaker folk had mingled in Central Europe.   The typical A Beaker itself has a globular body separated by a constriction from a straight neck (Pl. VI, 3), and thus resembles in form the corded beakers from barrows in Bohemia and West and Central Germany.   A Beakers are, however, never decorated with cord impressions, but with hyphenated lines, imprints of a hollow reed, finger-nail impressions and other devices.   The patterns are not arranged exclusively horizontally, but often vertically too.   The motives include triangles, pendant and erect, lozenges, saltires, which were also used to decorate Bell-beakers in Bohemia and Germany but never in Western Europe, while the panelling in Britain may owe something to the basketry pottery of North-West Germany and Holland.[15]   In at least four graves A Beakers were accompanied by stone battle-axes, a weapon which gives its name to an extensive cultural group in Northern and Eastern Europe. But the Beaker battle-axes in Britain are less elaborate than those wielded by the Continental Battle-axe folk, and indeed approximate to the simplest possible stone copy of a copper shaft-hole axe.   Flint daggers (Fig. 25, 3) which, together with arrows, complete the armament of the A Beaker folk would be as appropriate to Beaker folk as Battle-axe folk on the Continent, and the buttons with V perforation used for fastening their clothing were regularly used by Beaker folk in Atlantic as in Central Europe, and belong ultimately to Mediterranean–Atlantic costume rather than Anatolian–Danubian, for which pins were preferred.

In Wessex, Derbyshire, Yorkshire and Scotland round-heeled riveted knife-daggers (Fig. 25, 2) may take the place of flint ones.   Such daggers were occasionally used by Bell-beaker folk in Czechoslovakia and the Rhineland.[16]   But the British examples were probably not brought from those countries by the invaders, but imported from Ireland;   for bronze

---

[14] *Oxoniensia*, iii, 13.   [15] Childe, *Dawn*, 181.
[16] Childe, *Danube*, 190; *Dawn*, 219.

daggers are conspicuously rare in East Anglia, on the coasts of which one main body of Beaker folk had landed.[17]

Within the A Beaker family it has been usual since Thurnam to distinguish a group of C Beakers in which the neck is relatively shorter than the body, whereas in A Beakers the neck was longer (Pl. VII, 2). Abercromby believed that C Beakers result from the degeneration of A Beakers, noticing

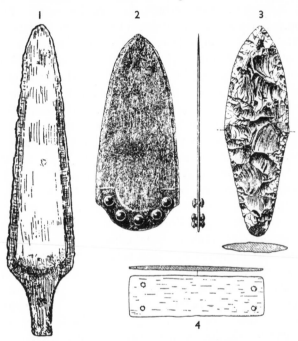

FIG. 25. DAGGERS AND STONE WRIST-GUARD. ⅓.
1. West European, Roundway ; 2. Round-heeled, Homington ;
3. Flint, Lambourne ; 4. Roundway.

that they grow more common the farther one proceeds from the assumed east coast landing-places, and are absolutely predominant in Scotland. But while it is true that some Beakers classed as C are just degenerations of A Beakers, others seem to be due to hybridization between As and Bs, others to degeneration of Bs and yet others to separate invasions from the Continent. We can, in fact, no longer believe in a single A Beaker invasion, the gradual spread of which produced the AC Beakers of the North and West. AC Beakers must have been introduced by several distinct bands

[17] *PPS.*, iv, 59.

of immigrants landing at various points on the North Sea coasts. In Yorkshire,[18] where tall, long-headed skeletons in Beaker graves indicate the presence of a strong Battle-axe contingent, two Beakers are decorated only on the neck in a manner appropriate to Battle-axe vases rather than Bell-beakers. In Aberdeenshire AC Beakers are associated with wrist-guards, and on Mull with wrist-guards and round-heeled daggers.[19]

With the English A Beakers must be classified some handled mugs decorated in Beaker style and technique (Pl. VIII, 1). Some true Bell-beakers in the Rhineland and Central Europe are also provided with handles, so that the idea was familiar to the invaders before they embarked. But Piggott[20] has noted that many English handled Beakers are copies of wooden mugs; they are often decorated on the base with patterns inspired by the grain of a section of tree-stem. In southern England Beakers are connected also with *rusticated ware*,[21] in which the whole surface of the vase is roughened by jabbing or pinching up. In Holland, too, rusticated ware is associated with Beakers. It may symbolize a fusion of the Beaker traditions with those of older Forest hunters. It is not, however, clear whether the fusion took place in Holland before the invasion or whether it did not take place independently on both sides of the Channel, Forest folk being established in England before the invasion.

The AC Beaker folk seem to have arrived in larger numbers and to have colonized Britain both more intensively and more extensively than their precursors who used B Beakers; for they eventually reached Man, Ireland, the Hebrides and Orkney. From landing-places round the Wash the Upper Thames valley and then the Cotswolds and the chalk lands of Wessex were colonized, the invaders spreading as far west as Somerset, Devon and even Cornwall. South Wales was colonized both from the Upper Thames–Cotswold area across the Severn and by sea from Somerset [22] across the Bristol Channel. A group of the latter maritime contingent must have pushed on to Ireland, since Ó Riordáin found sherds of a Beaker precisely like one from Somerset in Co. Limerick during 1939.

The limestone plateau of Derbyshire and Staffordshire was thickly populated, perhaps from Yorkshire where there were landings, as well as from the Wash. Cumberland was reached from Durham and Northumberland via the Tyne Gap, and thence some Beaker folk may have advanced

---

[18] Elgee, *Arch. Yorks.*, 59; Abercromby, i, No. 157.
[19] Mitchell, *PSAS.*, lxviii, Nos. 8, 91, 174; *PSAS.*, lxx, 328.
[20] *Antiquity*, ix, 348; cf. *Ant. J.*, xv, 280.
[21] *PPS.*, ii, 20; *PBUSS.*, v, 38.   [22] *Arch. Camb.*, xci (1936), 106-109.

to Man and Galloway. But Galloway was also settled by colonists from the Lothians. It apparently formed the starting-point for an invasion of Northern Ireland; the Beakers from the collective tombs of Largantea and Loughash are explicitly North British in character, the most freakish vessel from Loughash having a close parallel in East Lothian.[23]

Beaker folk were not colonizing a desert unexplored by man, and there are indications that they may have deliberately hastened to seize strategically and economically important areas. Many of the A Beakers from Wessex are typologically very early. Not even the Limerick Beaker with its Somerset relative can be accounted particularly late. On the other hand, it is certain that the Beaker culture lasted for several generations in Oxfordshire and Yorkshire, while the C Beakers from North Britain generally look late. Their lateness is not only a typological appearance. Some Scottish Beakers are demonstrably contemporary with Food Vessels,[24] which in Yorkshire are subsequent to Beakers. Davies indeed believes that the Beakers from Loughash in Ulster are contemporary with an Encrusted Urn which would be generally assigned to Period VI. Many Beakers in the North and West must, in fact, be assigned to Period IV as defined in southern England. Hence pre-Beaker need not mean Period II in terms of general chronology.

The Beaker folk imposed themselves as overlords on older stocks and mingled with or absorbed these. Beaker sherds are found in neolithic camps like Windmill Hill and in the family vaults of megalith-builders. In settlements and sanctuaries Beaker pottery is associated with Peterborough and Skara Brae wares[25] in southern England, in Somerset with the microliths of the mesolithic hunters.[26] In Great Britain the invaders were generally able to impose their material culture and burial rites to the virtual extinction of the Windmill Hill culture and the practice of collective burial. But in some Yorkshire Beakers the technical tradition of Windmill Hill potting is still in evidence,[27] and in Yorkshire and Oxfordshire skeletons of 'neolithic' type are accompanied by Beakers. But on the whole very little survives of the Windmill Hill tradition on the British mainland. The less agricultural peoples represented by Peterborough ware and by microliths did not compete for land with the invaders and so were better able to adjust themselves to the new conditions. We shall find the traditions of Peterborough reasserting themselves in the sequel. In Ireland and the northern

[23] Grimes, *UJA.*, ii, 264 ; Stevenson, *UJA*, iii, 79 ; *PSAS.*, xlii, 313.

[24] Childe, *P.S.*, 84, 88, 89.   [25] *PPS.*, ii, 198-200.

[26] At Gorsey Bigbury: *PBUSS.*, v (1938), 3-50.   [27] *PPS.*, iii, 197.

isles of Scotland the intrusive culture itself seems to have been absorbed so thoroughly by those of established communities that the very existence of a Beaker invasion of Ireland or Orkney was doubtful till 1937.

Though grains of barley and wheat have been detected on Beaker sherds,[28] the Beaker folk seem to have been even more pastoral than their precursors. They certainly relied for a living largely on breeding cattle, pigs and sheep and on hunting. They may have brought some kine with them from the Continent, since bones of Celtic short-horn (*Bos longifrons*) have been recognized in Beaker food-refuse both in Lincolnshire and in Wiltshire.[29]

Settlement sites are hardly known, and their virtual absence enhances the impression of pastoral nomadism. Beaker sherds have indeed been found in the neolithic camps of Maiden Castle, Windmill Hill and White-hawk, but always in such a position as to show that the ditches were already partially silted up and grass-grown and the ramparts presumably in decay before the invaders made, possibly quite transitory, encampments on the old village sites. Round the flint-mines on Easton Down (Wilts.) Stone [30] has located pits in which some Beaker folk encamped. Some were sub-rectangular like the 'neolithic' pit-dwellings and measured 10 ft. long by 4 ft. wide; others were nearly round, with a diameter of only 5 ft. All were bordered by stake-holes and cut into the chalk to a depth of 6 to 18 ins. And in Hampshire Clay [31] recovered a Beaker from a pit $6\frac{1}{2}$ ft. deep and 5 ft. across entered by a sloping ramp. In Ayrshire, on the limestone hills near Muirkirk, Fairbairn [32] found Beaker sherds in two hut-circles. One, 18 ft. across, had a paved floor and partly kerbed hearth. In the other, twice the size, there was a central post-hole, and a hearth near-by with a cooking-hole beside it. Whether the banks of earth and stones which at present define the hut-circles were foundations for walls, perhaps of turfs built round a cone of poles, or designed to protect a tent standing within them, is still uncertain. Other hut-circles, notably those on Dartmoor which often have solid stone walls, may be likewise of Beaker age, but proof is lacking.

Otherwise the only domestic remains left by Beaker folk are middens (generally near the shore) on old land surfaces beneath sand-dunes.[33] These

---

[28] Jessen and Helbaek, 19 (42 cases of barley, 9 of emmer, 2 of bread wheat).

[29] *Arch.*, lxxxv, 104; *WAM.*, xlv, 368. The pigs belong to the variety termed *Sus scrofa palustris*: *PBUSS.*, v, 53.

[30] *WAM.*, xlv, 367; xlvi, 229.   [31] *Ant. J.*, viii, 95.

[32] *PSAS.*, xlviii, 374; liv, 210.

[33] e.g. Tentsmuir (Fife), Gullane (East Lothian), Hedderwick (near Dunbar), Scunthorpe (Lincs.), Spritsal Tor (Gower).

mark where the invaders had encamped in shelters so temporary and flimsy as to leave no other trace. Round the margin of Mildenhall Fen (Cambs.) Leaf and Lethbridge [34] found a series of such middens. Among the refuse was the jaw of a human being who had suffered from caries and pyorrhoea—perhaps a slave, if not the remains of a cannibal feast.

Beaker burials, generally occurring in isolation, again suggest a nomadic life. But in southern England barrows may cluster to form cemeteries, while in Yorkshire the same mound may cover several Beaker burials. Thus Mortimer's [35] barrow 116 at Aldro covered three graves and six skeletons accompanied by Beakers of types A, B 2, B 3 and a handled mug. In Wales, too, a barrow at Merthyr Mawr (Glam.) [36] covered six skeletons, in cists, accompanied by Beakers. Still larger or more stable units must have used the cemeteries of eleven and eighteen flat graves explored by Leeds at Cassington [37] and Eynsham (Oxon) [38] respectively. In these latter a relatively high proportion of dolichocranial and mesaticranial males and females may illustrate fusion between the invaders and older 'neolithic' stocks. As we do not know how long such cemeteries were in use, they provide no data for estimating the size of the social unit.

Neither the cemeteries nor the general run of barrows demonstrate any sharp class-division within Beaker society itself. On the whole, the funerary monuments do not indicate such an extravagant elaboration of funerary ritual as do the collective tombs of the previous age. Nevertheless, enormous labour was expended on the due performance of the last rites, and many barrows are so imposing that they must have been heaped to honour persons of outstanding wealth or power, if not hereditary rank. At Kelleythorpe near Driffield (Yorks.) a tall long-headed man lay under a large barrow in a cist of slabs that must have been transported at least eighteen miles. He had been swathed in a linen shroud, wore amber beads and carried a bronze dagger, while his wrist-guard had been fastened by gold nails to the leather wristlet.[39] At Cartington (Northumberland) a man had been buried in a coffin 4 ft. long hollowed out of an oak trunk with a (?) Beaker now lost.[40] A few barrows in the Lowland Zone are surrounded by an external fosse just like the Bell-barrow of the Wessex culture of Period IV.[41] An annular or penannular ditch under the barrow has more often been recorded in

---

[34] *PCAS.*, xxxv, 126.
[36] *Arch. Camb.* (1919), 336-339.
[38] *Oxoniensia*, iii, 10-20.
[40] *A History of Northumberland*, xv, 20.
[41] Grinsell, *PSEA.*, vii (1933), 215: Woodyates 9, Amesbury 15, Winterslow.

[35] Mortimer, *Forty Years*, 54.
[37] *Ant. J.*, xiv, 272.
[39] Elgee, *Arch. Yorks.*, 54.

Wales,[42] Yorkshire [43] and elsewhere. On rocky ground, e.g. on Dartmoor [44] and also in Yorkshire,[43] the trench was replaced by a stone ring. Wick Barrow in Somerset [45] covered a circular enclosure 29 to 31 ft. in diameter and girt with a built stone wall standing over 3 ft. high. The central area had been robbed in antiquity, but eccentric cists contained Beakers of B 1 and A types (Pl. VI).

In Wessex Beaker burials, apparently without any covering mound, have been found surrounded by fosses and banks.[46] In Argyll near Kilmartin a double-causewayed fosse with external bank surrounded a low stony mound covering two cist graves of the period.[47] This monument approximates to a class of stone circles, only a small proportion of which are demonstrably sepulchral, and of these still fewer have yielded relics of Beaker folk. One class, however, can already be recognized as constituting one of the most impressive manifestations of Beaker folks' piety. These are the so-called Recumbent Stone circles confined to the counties of Banffshire, Aberdeenshire and Kincardineshire in north-eastern Scotland.

They take their name from a huge monolith (at Kirkton of Bourtie, 17 ft. long by 5½ ft. high by 4½ ft. broad) that lies prostrate on the circumference of an irregular circle of megalithic uprights. The two pillars which flank the Recumbent immediately on either side are the tallest stones in the ring; the rest diminish in height progressively to the opposite end of the diameter through the Recumbent. Cup-marks are often carved on Recumbent or orthostats. The megalithic 'circle' always surrounds some sort of cairn, which in well-preserved examples appears as a ring of boulders bordered inside and out by a kerb of big set stones. Traces of a passage leading through this ring to the central space and extending outwards even to the kerb may sometimes be recognized.[48]

Recent excavations at the Recumbent Stone circles of Old Keig [49] and Loanhead of Daviot [50] have disclosed in the central area a patch of earth burnt red by the fire of the pyre and a burial pit containing cremated human bone. In both circles Iron Age pottery occurred abundantly, but in each case scattered sherds of Beaker ware suggest that the original cremations were of Beaker chiefs while the Iron Age burials are secondary intrusions. Such stupendous monuments, if primarily sepulchral—the Recumbent Stone with its straight upper edge would form an admirable artificial horizon for

[42] *Arch. Camb.*, lxxxi (1926), 63.
[43] *Arch. J.*, xciv, 61, n. 1.
[44] *TDA.*, xxix, 68.
[45] *T.Som.A.S.*, liv (1908), 8-77.
[46] e.g. Cunnington, *Woodhenge*, 52.
[47] Childe, *P.S.*, 110.
[48] Keiller, *The Megalithic Monuments of North-East Scotland* (1934).
[49] *PSAS.*, lxviii, 387.
[50] *PSAS.*, lxix, 170.

observing heliacal risings of stars for calendrical regulation—can only belong to chiefs. Yet Keiller enumerates 71 in Aberdeenshire alone. In any case, these Beaker chiefs were heirs to a tradition derived from the Boyne culture of Ireland. The central ring cairn traversed by a passage, the outer circle of uprights, diminishing progressively, the cup-marked stones, are all directly derivable from the Beauly group of Passage Graves; and cremation was a regular Boyne rite. In Aberdeenshire Beaker folk have supplanted megalith-builders, as in Caithness and Arran, and adapted their sepulchral architecture and ritual.

Callander [51] has constructed a theoretical series to demonstrate the evolution of ritual stone circles in general from the functional kerbs round megalithic tombs. And Crawford [52] has suggested that the fosse in England might be just a substitute in the stoneless Lowlands for the stone ring of the Highlands. Such generalizations cannot be accepted as explanations of all stone circles. Grimes [53] has noted how in Wales stone circles form a distributional pattern quite different from that of collective tombs. On the other hand, in Holland, Central Germany, Galicia and the Caucasus the graves of Battle-axe or Beaker folk are sometimes surrounded with ditches or rings of posts or of stones, buried under the barrow.[54] So the Beaker folk may perfectly well have brought this item of burial ritual with them to Britain. There are, however, other, non-sepulchral circles that were apparently developed after the invasion and that illustrate, better than the tombs, the political consequences thereof.

2. RELIGIOUS AND POLITICAL UNIFICATION

The Beaker invaders eventually established throughout the occupied territories of Great Britain and even Ireland a degree of cultural uniformity never previously achieved and not repeated till Roman times. It would, of course, be absurd to claim that such uniformity reflected a political unification, a Beaker State. On the other hand, to the invaders is generally attributed the erection of 'Sanctuaries' that imply not only substantial concentration of resources, but the co-operation for religious purposes of populations all over southern England and Wales. Avebury and Stonehenge are among the most astonishing prehistoric monuments, not only in the British Isles but in the Old World. Each might be fairly compared to a cathedral and contrasted with smaller local sanctuaries, presumably filling

[51] *Arch.*, lxxvii, 97. [52] *Antiquity*, i, 428.
[53] *PPS.*, ii, 106. [54] Childe, *Dawn*, 146, 156, 165, 190.

the role of parish churches. At the time of their erection the Wessex Downs did effectively play the part of a metropolitan area, for which their situation at the nodal point of natural routes from the east, north-east, north-west, west and south fit them.

The most imposing of these monuments is Avebury in North Wiltshire. Keiller's excavations, still in progress in 1940, have already established that this is a composite monument in the construction of which two periods can be distinguished. Avebury I consisted probably of a row of three circular settings of huge stones together with an avenue. Of these the southern comprised two concentric rings, 336 and 154 ft. in diameter with a central monolith; the central, also double and slightly smaller, enclosed the horseshoe-shaped 'cove,' open to the east, one stone of which is 17 ft. high. From this group a sinuous avenue led southward to the Kennet and thence to a smaller complex, 'The Sanctuary,' on Overton Hill. The stones bordering the avenue as far as it has been traced [55] are sarsen blocks roughly dressed to two main types—the one tall and narrow, the other broad and lozenge-shaped—and arranged in pairs so that representatives of each type face one another on either side of the way. They are clearly male and female symbols, and two are carved with cup-and-ring marks, indirectly inspired by the funerary art of the Boyne (pp. 66 f.).

The Sanctuary [56] consisted of two concentric rings of stones 130 and 45 ft. in diameter. The stones of the inner circle alternated with stout wooden posts, not demonstrably of the same age. It was surrounded by a fence ring, 65 ft. in diameter, formed of close-set stakes with gate-posts opposite the end of the avenue. Within the stone-and-post ring were smaller rings of posts with diameters of $34\frac{1}{2}$, 21, 15 and 13 ft. respectively, and a central post 10 ins. thick. Piggott has recently suggested that the wooden structure may have been roofed over.

Burials accompanied by B 1 Beakers were found against two stones of the Avebury–Kennet Avenue, and one with a B 2 Beaker against a stone of the inner Sanctuary ring, while a Peterborough habitation seems to antedate the construction of the Avenue if only by a year or so. Thus the monuments were in existence while B Beaker folk lived in Wessex, and these were buried within their hallowed precincts like Christians in a church.

Subsequently Avebury was remodelled on a far more ambitious plan.

[55] *Antiquity*, x, 417-427.
[56] It was described by Aubrey in the seventeenth century, but had been completely demolished and lost till excavation by Mr and Mrs Cunnington recovered the sockets for the stones: *WAM.*, xlv, 300-335.

The northernmost of the three aligned circles was apparently demolished,[57] but the rest were incorporated in a gigantic work.[58] Round them ran a fosse, 18 to 30 ft. deep, 30 ft. wide at the top and 15 ft. wide at the base, but interrupted by at least three causeways. The upcast from the fosse was piled on its outer verge to form an imposing vallum. Its height from the floor of the ditch is estimated by Gray as 55 ft. and its circumference at 4442 ft. The diameter of the circle was 1400 ft., so that it enclosed an area of no less than 28½ acres! and now accommodates the greater part of the modern village. A very irregular ring of megalithic uprights was planted along the inner margin of the fosse. Peterborough ware from the old turf line beneath the vallum gives a *terminus post quem* for Avebury II; a Beaker sherd found in the ditch, though only 6½ ft. from the surface, is held to prove the existence of the remodelled sanctuary in Beaker times.

With some phase of the Avebury complex must surely be connected Silbury Hill, a huge tumulus, 130 ft. high, encircled by a wide fosse 20 ft. deep. It looks like a barrow, but shafts and tunnels have failed to disclose a burial. If really sepulchral and of Beaker age, the monument would be worthy of a king ruling over southern Britain, just as the Avebury circle might be taken as the cathedral of a metropolitan see. But Avebury was primarily the sanctuary of the populous and prosperous pastoral tribes grazing the North Wiltshire Downs, however much pilgrims from remoter areas may have contributed to its erection. For it had rivals that primarily constituted religious centres for the cognate tribes of Salisbury Plain. North of Amesbury are remains of what Crawford [59] believes to have been a fossed circle, like Avebury II, but with two entrances, measuring no less than 1300 ft. and 1160 ft. in its diameters.

The actual rival, destined to outstrip Avebury in renown and sanctity, was, however, Stonehenge, a little to the west (Fig. 26). The sanctuary began [60] modestly as a fossed circle with a single entrance, a bank *inside* the ditch and a ring of posts within. Only the sockets for the posts survive; as they were noted by John Aubrey in 1666, they are generally termed the Aubrey holes, and the monument to which they belong is conveniently described as the Aubrey Circle. Its diameter was 288 ft. A sherd of Skara

[57] It would have run across the fosse, and one of its stone-sockets lies across the entrance causeway: *Antiquity*, xiii, 227.

[58] *Arch.*, lxxxiv, 110 ff.

[59] *Antiquity*, iii, 49-50.

[60] I follow the account given by Newall, *Antiquity*, iii, 75-97, almost slavishly; opposing views are well summarized by Kendrick, *A.E.W.*, 90-91.

Brae ware from the primary silting of the ditch [61] and general probabilities are cited as establishing the Beaker age of this circle.

After the decay of the Aubrey posts, but while the site still retained

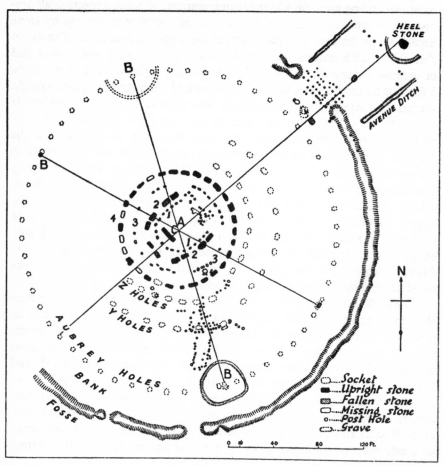

FIG. 26. PLAN OF STONEHENGE. Based on plans by Newall and by Kendrick.

its sanctity, a new and more imposing sanctuary, Stonehenge, was erected within the fosse-ringed area. The centre of Stonehenge (Fig. 26, C), differing by 2 ft. from that of the Aubrey Circle, was fixed by the so-called four station-stones, the southernmost encircled by a ditch cutting one post-hole

[61] *Antiquity*, x, 221; the faunule from the ditch is regarded by Kennard as post-Beaker though pre-Iron Age: *Ant. J.*, xv, 433-434.

and the bank of the older Circle. From this centre the strictly circular Sarsen Ring (*ib*. 4) must have been laid out with the aid of a string. Later a horseshoe of five 'trilithons' was set up within it (*ib*. 2). These are the two most astounding structures in the monument, and in some respects in all pre-historic Europe; for the uprights are joined together at the top by stone lintels—in the horseshoe in pairs only, in the circle continuously. The stones themselves are local sarsens, but beautifully dressed with stone mauls and of enormous size—the tallest upright in the horseshoe is 29 ft. 8 ins. high, 8 ft. of its length being embedded in the ground. On the top of each upright are carved projecting tenons which fit into mortise holes on the underside of the lintels. The latter are carefully cut to a curve on both sides so as to fit the circle's circumference, and are, moreover, 6 ins. wider at the top than at the bottom so that they do not seem to taper when viewed from the ground. Such compensation for perspective foreshortening has generally been regarded as a discovery of the Greeks. The so-called Altar Stone, a block of micaceous sandstone now lying prostrate just south-west of the centre, fulfilled an unknown function in the sanctuary. To it led an avenue bordered by a ditch, the axis of which passes through the centre of Stone-henge, but not through the middle of the causeway that gave access to the Aubrey Circle. In its line stands the so-called Heel Stone and perhaps once stood the fancifully named Slaughter Stone.

After the erection of the Trilithon Horseshoe another of blue stones (Fig. 26, 1) was added within it, and a circle of blue stones (*ib*. 3), 70 ft. in diameter, inserted between the horseshoe and Sarsen Circle. Though unim-pressive to look at, these additions are hardly less remarkable than the sarsen trilithons which overshadow them. For they are of spotted dolerite [62] and must have been brought from the Presely Mountains in South Wales. Two stones in the Blue Stone Circle show mortise holes on one face. Though now serving as uprights, they must once have been lintels in an older structure of trilithons. In other words, Stonehenge must once have had a forerunner so sacred that its stones had to be transported and re-erected in the existing sanctuary.

Finally, after the erection of the blue stone [63] structures the Y and Z holes were dug along the circumferences of very irregular circles with diameters of 130 and 180 ft. approximately outside the Sarsen Circle. They look as if they had been designed to hold orthostats, but actually late Iron Age pottery was found in them.

[62] *Ant. J.*, iii, 239, Thomas.
[63] Because chips from the dressing of the blue stones were found in these holes.

Like the fabric of an English cathedral, the stones of Stonehenge mirror the fortunes of a community. Neither the construction of the Aubrey Circle nor even the erection of Lintel Circle and Horseshoe of Stonehenge surpass the tasks of building and covering a megalithic tomb like New Grange or Yarrows. They would not be beyond the power of a prosperous pastoral tribe profiting from the grazing of Salisbury Plain and the products of its flint-mines. But the transportation of roughly dressed blue stone monoliths from the Pembrokeshire mountains to Wessex involved quite other problems. Though the direct distance be only 145 miles, the Bristol Channel, the Cotswolds and minor but very formidable barriers of hill, marsh and forest intervene. It is much more likely that the stones were brought by sea round Land's End and up the Channel to Christchurch or Southampton Water and thence dragged up overland. But even that must rank as an astonishing feat of seamanship. Its execution bears witness on the one hand to the economic and political power of the responsible society in Wessex and to its authority in the west, on the other to the spiritual dominion of the Highland Zone over Lowland tradition.

Now a spiritual dominion of the west has already been seen in the megalithic culture. And in fact chips of blue stone are said to have been incorporated in the structure of Bowl's Long Barrow (Heylesbury, Wilts.).[64] Hence it has been deduced that at least the hypothetical lintel circle of blue stones had been erected in Wessex in megalithic times. It would in that case have been due to the people of the Severn culture who had apparently spread in from just the right direction. These societies must, then, be credited with a degree of coherence, wealth and authority that had not been suspected from a consideration of their tombs alone, and all arguments for connecting non-sepulchral circles and lintelled monuments in particular with the Beaker complex must go by the board.

Alternatively, 'Blue Stonehenge' might have stood first in South Wales and only after having acquired a reputation for sanctity have been translated to Salisbury Plain when Wessex society rose to a position of economic supremacy in southern Britain. Such supremacy was finally achieved by the Wessex culture of Period IV, and blue stone chips were found in a barrow near Stonehenge apparently of just that age, while the snail-shells from the fosse too point to this dry period. On the other hand, the A Beaker folk themselves attained to no mean prosperity in Wessex; they had early occupied South Wales; and they were the first people in Wales to evince a special interest for spotted dolerite by using it for axes.[65]

[64] *WAM.*, xlii, 432: cf. *Ant. J.*, xii, 17-22,   [65] *Arch. Camb.*, xc, 278.

So both the original erection of Blue Stonehenge and its transportation to Salisbury Plain might be attributed to the Beaker folk, the second event being at the same time a measure of the political unification they had achieved. But in that case it might be necessary to assume that long barrows were still being erected in Wiltshire, as they were in Lincolnshire, during Period III.

There are in fact other arguments for connecting the lintelled monuments, which alone can legitimately be termed 'henges,' [66] with the Beaker complex. It is obvious that the mortise and tenon construction exemplified in Stonehenge has been taken over by the stonemason from the carpenter. One of the most dramatic triumphs of air-photography has been to reveal timber monuments of which Stonehenge might be a more elaborate and more permanent version. Photographs taken from the air by Wing-Commander Insall disclosed the post-sockets and fosses of sanctuaries, Arminghall near Norwich and Woodhenge near Stonehenge, where no indications were noticeable from the ground. In each case the details revealed on his pictures were fully confirmed by excavation.

The Arminghall monument, as excavated by Clark,[67] was an oval or horseshoe of oak posts, each perhaps 3 ft. in diameter and sunk 7 ft. into virgin soil. They may have been joined together by lintels, but naturally no positive evidence could survive. The horseshoe was surrounded by two penannular ditches with a bank between them, the over-all diameter of the work approaching 270 ft. Rusticated pottery established the age of the monument and its connexion with the Beaker invasion from Holland. Situated well outside the megalithic province, in wooded country where timber-work is appropriate, Arminghall strengthens the claim of the Beaker folk to be the bearers of the 'henge' idea.

Woodhenge (Fig. 27), excavated by the Cunningtons,[68] was rather more complicated. Within a bank and ditch, interrupted by a single causeway, had stood six concentric oval rings of posts, the major diameters of the outermost and innermost being respectively 144 and 38 ft. But only the posts of the fourth ring from the centre were of any great size. Between two of these posts on the south is the socket for a stone that has been compared to the Recumbent of the Aberdeenshire circles. The monument's axis as determined by the major diameter of the ovals does not point north and south but towards the midsummer sunrise, like the axis of Stonehenge.

---

[66] The word contains the same Anglo-Saxon root as 'hang,' so that the extension of the term to cover monuments without lintels is quite indefensible.

[67] *PPS.*, ii, 1-13.   [68] Cunnington, *Woodhenge*, Devizes, 1929.

Right on the axis in the central area (at G), an infant had been buried. As its skull had been cleft, the infant must be considered a dedicatory sacrifice and not a ceremonial burial.

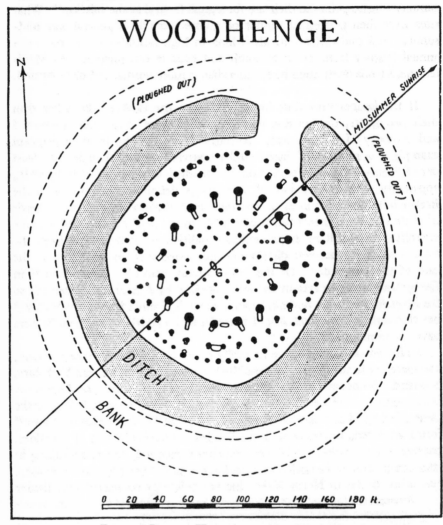

FIG. 27. PLAN OF WOODHENGE. After Cunnington.

These wooden structures may have been roofed over [68a] and may exemplify the sort of temple on which Stonehenge is modelled. They are more appropriate to the inhabitants of forested plains, like the Beaker folk in East

[68a] Piggott, *Arch. J.*, xcvi, 193 ff.

Anglia and their Battle-axe ancestors in Northern Europe, than to the megalith-builders of the rock-bound Atlantic coasts. And the orientation of Woodhenge and Stonehenge (not, however, of Arminghall) to the midsummer sunrise points to their use for a great festival at the solstice.[69] What rites were then performed cannot be guessed, but in a general way midsummer and midwinter festivals belong to high latitudes where the sun's annual journey from north to south and back is conspicuous; in Mediterranean lands orientation by the meridian is more normal and more natural.

If the henges may thus be attributed to the Beaker folk rather than their precursors, the position of the possibly older circles like Avebury I and Avebury II is less clear. Avebury II is just the most magnificent example of a number of fossed circles scattered all over Britain. At least one of these—Gorsey Bigbury [70] on the Mendips, an oval area 63 ft. by 78 ft., apparently without any sort of upright—is definitely attributable to the Beaker folk; for remains of no less than 47 A Beakers together with sherds of rusticated ware, arrow-heads derived from the *petit tranchet* and genuine microliths in the local epipalaeolithic tradition were recovered from the fosse. Neither relics nor distribution guarantee such an attribution in the case of the remainder. Of the most famous examples, Arbor Low [71] in Derbyshire lies in an area intensively colonized by A Beaker folk, but not so the Stripple Stones on Bodmin Moor, Cornwall,[72] while Stennis in Orkney [73] lies close to the Boyne tumulus of Maes Howe on an island where no Beakers have yet been found.

Unfossed stone circles are naturally much commoner on rocky ground, and therefore in the Highland Zone [74]—Dartmoor, Wales, western Yorkshire, Scotland. Some, associated with avenues of standing stones, on Dartmoor, in Somerset,[75] in Wales [76] and in Sutherland,[77] would seem to belong to the same ideological complex as Avebury I. But that at Callernish on Lewis [78] forms an external tangent to a small cairn containing a sort of cruciform passage grave. Other circles are explicitly sepulchral, and many belong to later complexes, as we shall see. Finally, Grimes [79] has suggested that some embanked circles in North Wales that are definitely connected with Beaker

[69] Attempts like Lockyer's to date Stonehenge by the precession of the equinoxes involve too many unknown factors to be reliable; see *Antiquity*, i, 31-53.

[70] *PBUSS.*, v (1938), 3-56. [71] *Arch.*, lviii, 464 ff.

[72] *Arch.*, lxi, 4-24. [73] *Arch.*, xxxiv, 98-106 (bank very doubtful).

[74] Piggott has suggested that unfossed circles may have been introduced by B Beaker folk from Brittany where such circles also occur sometimes associated with stone rows.

[75] Dobson, *Arch. Som.*, 60. [76] *PPS.*, ii, 108.

[77] RC. *Suth.*, No. 379. [78] RC. *Hebrides*, No. 89. [79] *PPS.*, ii, 110.

folk may really be settlements or kraals, comparable to the Dartmoor 'pounds.'

In Ireland the only site in the south that can definitely be attributed to Beaker folk is a curious circle at Lough Gur (Co. Limerick), excavated by Ó Riordáin in 1939. The circle, 155 ft. in diameter, was demarcated by upright stones (the largest 14 ft. high) backed up against an earthen bank 30 to 40 ft. wide. The entrance passage on the east was faced with flat slabs and ended in two big portal stones. Sherds of an A Beaker, similar to one from Wick Barrow (Pl. VI, 1), many Food Vessels and some sherds probably belonging to the North Irish variety of Windmill Hill ware were found beneath a filling by which the interior had been raised 2 ft. above the level of the surrounding country. A circle of similar structure existed in Wales at Meini Gwyr near the Presely Mountains, but cannot be dated.[80]

Like the corbelled tomb and the round barrow, the circular temple and sanctuary—very likely the circular kraal too—have at least one root in the round house. But the round house could belong equally to the Mediterranean–African heritage of Beaker folk and megalith-builders. Which party first thought of enlarging the round house to a temple or a temenos cannot be decided in 1940. But Beaker folk certainly worshipped in, if they did not build, such sanctuaries in various parts of the British Isles and even in Ireland. And no circle is demonstrably older than the Beaker invasion. The smaller sanctuaries may well stand to Avebury in the relation of parish churches to a cathedral. Their use by Beaker folk demonstrates once more the cultural uniformity these established throughout the British Isles. The history of Avebury and Stonehenge gives at least a hint of a corresponding political uniformity. And the scale of these works in any case betokens a more substantial population than can be inferred for neolithic times. In this the invaders presumably formed only a small ruling class, replacing the megalithic aristocracy and exploiting the labours of Windmill Hill peasants, Peterborough and microlithic hunters.

3. THE BRONZE AGE ECONOMY

As a ruling class the Beaker folk would be in a position to accumulate surplus wealth above the immediate needs of mere subsistence. They did not expend that surplus entirely on sepulchral monuments and sanctuaries. The furniture of Beaker graves shows that their occupants had a higher

[80] Grimes in *BBCS.*, ix (1939), 373-374.

standard of life on earth than those buried in princely megalithic vaults; they demanded more efficient equipment and more refinements and could make their demands effective. The political unification of which religious monuments give ambiguous indications had at least proceeded far enough to allow commerce to be conducted more regularly and freely. The relative isolation and self-sufficiency proper to neolithic communities was so far broken down that the Beaker period can legitimately be termed the Early Bronze Age. Beaker graves contain imported luxury articles on a scale never observed in collective tombs before the round-headed invaders had arrived.

Of course flint knives, scrapers and arrow-heads and stone axes were

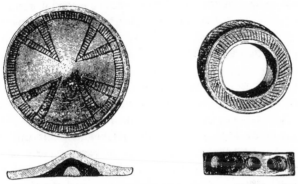

FIG. 28. V-perforated Button (Rudstone) and Pulley-ring (Thwing) of Jet. ⅓. By permission of the Trustees of the British Museum.

still the commonest tools. Flint-mines were still worked in Beaker times. It was at this period that Peterborough folk brought axes of Graig Llwydd rock to Wessex (p. 83). Thin greenstone axes with pointed butts were probably imported from Brittany for the Beaker folk.[81]

But the jet of Whitby in Yorkshire [82] was certainly used by the Beaker colonists of the Wolds for making the V-perforated buttons with which, in true Mediterranean fashion, they fastened their clothing (Fig. 28, 1), and pulley-rings perhaps for belts (Fig. 28, 2). Similar pulley-rings—i.e. broad rings about an inch in diameter and perforated on the circumference with holes converging to a V—were worn by Beaker folk buried in the West Riding, Wessex and Devonshire [83]; in Aberdeenshire, bone substitutes were accepted.[84] Similarly, 'jet necklaces' were found in five Beaker graves

[81] PPS., iv, 58.   [82] Elgee, Arch. Yorks., 59.
[83] YAJ., xxxi, 41.   [84] Childe, P.S., 88.

in Scotland, but the type was taken over by these belated Beaker ladies from the Food Vessel folk (p. 123). Amber was used for beads in one Yorkshire grave and in one in Aberdeenshire, but in each case the material might have been brought by the waves and not by trade from the Baltic.[85]

The most permanent and significant step in raising the general standard of life was the Beaker folk's demand for metal. As warriors they appreciated the superiority of metal weapons, and as conquerors they could make their demand effective. The oldest metal objects found in any context in Britain—quadrangular awls or tattooing needles, flat triangular knife-daggers and flat axes of copper or bronze—come from Beaker graves. So do the oldest dated gold objects—the small discs from Mere and the rivets from Kelley-thorpe. It used to be thought that the Beaker folk introduced the knowledge of metallurgy into the British Isles, but it is now admitted that the Beaker folk were just the first purchasers in Great Britain of the products of Irish smiths; all the objects mentioned can be regarded as imports from Ireland.

Admittedly the oldest metal axes were cast in an open mould. They were therefore flat, or at best strengthened by low flanges formed by hammering along the sides. A distribution map prepared by Miss L. Chitty[86] shows graphically the Irish origin of such flat and hammer-flanged axes. The find spots are densely concentrated in Ireland, particularly in Ulster and round the ore-bearing mountains of Wicklow, Cork and Kerry, and cluster quite thickly in Galloway and Cornwall. In none of these areas do numerous Beaker burials attest intensive colonization or effective domination by the invaders. On the other hand, there are no flat axes at all in Suffolk to correspond to a dense concentration of Beakers, and their rarity in Wessex is in striking contrast to the number of Beakers.

A number of these simple axes are decorated. The simplest of these, adorned on the sides with hammered lozenges or oblique flutings and on the faces with punched or incised dots, herring-bones and other simple all-over patterns (Fig. 29), are represented by 58 examples from Ireland as against 15 from the whole of Great Britain.[87] But four axes of this class were found in a Yorkshire barrow, the latest interment in which was accompanied by a Beaker.[88] Finally, stone moulds for casting flat axes or the wax patterns for cire-perdue moulds[89] are common in Ireland.

[85] Elgee, Arch. Yorks., 54. [86] Fox, Personality, Pl. II.
[87] PPS., iv, 272-282. [88] Arch., lii, 3.
[89] S. S. Crichton Mitchell in PSAS., lxix, 426, gives technical reasons for believing that the stone moulds were used for preparing not the final casting but the wax model to be subsequently wrapped in clay.

A distribution map of the simplest type of flat, round-heeled daggers [90] tells the same tale (Figs. 30 and 31). Though normally found in Beaker graves, they are excessively rare in some areas of intensive Beaker settlement. None have been recorded from Aberdeenshire, only two from East Anglia. As noted on p. 93, even the West European dagger was made in Ireland, where a mould for casting one, combined with the mould for a flat axe, has been found.

Hence the Beaker invaders did not bring with them either the metal

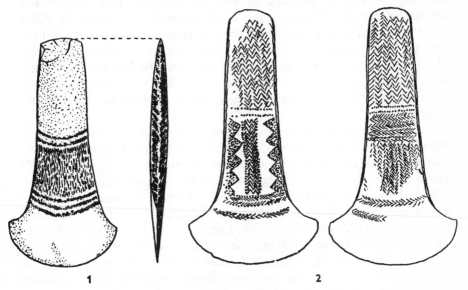

FIG. 29.   Decorated Irish Axes.   ⅓.

objects they used or the craftsmen who made them. The Beaker folk were enabled to overrun Britain not by virtue of superior metal armament but only by brute strength combined with practical traditions of organization and social cohesion. But they did purchase the products of smiths already established in Ireland. Presumably the expeditions to Ireland revealed by the Beakers from double-portalled gallery graves in Ulster and the stone circle at Lough Gur were undertaken to ensure supplies. The invaders soon lost their identity in the Atlantic island, but they had at least established channels of communication. And it may have been under their auspices that Irish copper was linked up with Cornish tin. Though Beakers are rare

[90] Piggott, *PPS.*, iv, 59, correcting Fox and Grimes, *Arch. Camb.*, lxxxiii (1928), 145.

in Cornwall, they are as well represented there as the Boyne culture of the alternative claimants.

FIG. 30. DISTRIBUTION OF BEAKERS IN SOUTHERN BRITAIN.
Based on maps of Chitty, Fox, Grimes and Mitchell. The broken line marks
the boundary of the Highland Zone.

The Irish smiths in addition to axes and daggers produced halberds—
a dagger hafted at right angles to the shaft. Such were exported both to
Great Britain and the Continent, but no exported specimen is older than

Period IV and the corresponding phase of the Continental Bronze Age. Yet Ó Riordáin [91] has shown that the exported Irish halberds are a late

FIG. 31. DISTRIBUTION OF FLAT KNIFE-DAGGERS IN SOUTHERN BRITAIN.
Based on map by Fox and Grimes.

development in a series the earlier stages of which can be found in Ireland alone (Fig. 32). They must, then, be referred to Period III.

[91] *Arch.*, lxxxvi, 305.

There was, therefore, a flourishing metallurgical industry established in Ireland by the time of the Beaker domination in southern England. Its origins are fairly plain. Metallurgy, like other arts, was, of course, cradled in the Near East between the Nile and the Indus. The method adopted for mounting the round-heeled daggers in a hilt that overlapped the blade leaving a crescentic aperture in its base proves that the tradition inspiring Irish metallurgy was Egyptian rather than Asiatic.[92] But immediately that tradition reached Ireland from the Iberian Peninsula. In the metalliferous regions of southern Spain and Portugal copper was mined and worked by communities who buried their dead in corbelled passage graves. They used flint halberds, which in the succeeding El Argar phase of Spain were

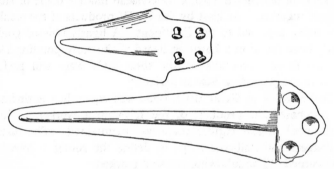

FIG. 32. Irish halberds, types 2 and 4. ¼. After Ó Riordáin.

translated into metal. On schist plaque idols they engraved geometric patterns recalling those on Irish decorated axes.[93]

Miners and smiths from the Iberian school must have settled in Ireland, discovered and exploited its ores and developed their traditions on insular lines—Ó Riordáin believes that the Irish halberds are not directly derivable from the Spanish types of El Argar, but a parallel translation into metal of an ancestral flint form. Presumably the metal-workers came in the wake of the megalith-builders responsible for the Boyne passage graves (p. 79). But the relation of metal-workers and megalith-builders is not yet clear, and there is no guarantee that they arrived simultaneously.

Of their mining and smelting no traces have been detected, but we have the moulds in which copper tools and weapons may have been cast. They are blocks of sandstone on the flat surfaces of which the form for the desired object was hammered out. (But perhaps only wax models were cast in these stone moulds; the models would then be coated in clay and baked in the

[92] Childe, *Bronze Age*, 78.   [93] Childe, *Dawn*, 255-263.

fire, when the wax would run out so that metal could be poured into the cavity thus left.) The casting would in any case have to be finished off and sharpened by hammering.

The same metallurgists must have discovered the alluvial gold in the streams from the Wicklow Mountains. The earliest gold objects have been made by beating out ingots of gold into thin sheets, cutting these up and decorating them by twisting or by incising the surface. But the nuggets were first cast into bars, matrices for which are sometimes juxtaposed to moulds for flat axes on the same sandstone slab.[94] These bars were generally D-shaped in section, but by hammering can easily be made rectangular. By twisting rectangular bars the Irish goldsmith later learned to produce very handsome ornaments, imitating Mycenaean models made of ribbons of gold soldered together. At least by Period IV products of the resultant bar style were being exported to the Continent. A lightly twisted gold armlet has recently been found in a Bavarian hoard of the corresponding Danubian period.[95] In Britain products of the sheet style were still preferred at that date as in the preceding Beaker period.[96]

The Beaker lords in Great Britain and subsequently Continental communities purchased the products of the Irish metal-workers. To supply their needs more or less regular trade was maintained. The distribution of axes, daggers and halberds helps to define the routes followed by the traders concerned. The following are well marked:

1. To the Firth of Clyde, up Loch Fyne to the Firth of Lorne and thence up the Great Glen to the Moray Firth (well marked by axes, halberds, jet necklaces, etc., see p. 122 below).

2. From Galloway through the Biggar Gap to the Lothians—or from the Clyde along the Midland Valley (rather vague).

3. From the Solway through the Tyne Gap (vague at this date).

4. Coastwise or via Man to Lancashire, thence up the Ribble Valley, across the Pennines by the Aire Gap and so down Airedale or along the ridge between the Aire and the Wharfe to the York or Escrick moraine that provided a bridge across the swampy Vale to the Wolds.[97]

5. From ports in North Wales, perhaps mainly by ridgeways west of the Severn, to Wessex and southern England.

[94] Maryon, *PRIA.*, xliv, C, 206. [95] *Germania*, xxii (1938), 7-11.
[96] For the distinction see Piggott, *PPS.*, iv, 78.
[97] Raistrick, *YAJ.*, xxix (1929), 365.

These routes may have been followed by regular caravans. Hoards of flat axes have been found on the coast of Galloway and in north-east Scotland on route 1, in Lancashire and Yorkshire on route 4, in Cornwall on the way to Brittany, and on other routes. Such are supposed to represent the stock-in-trade of travelling merchants that had been buried in a moment of danger and never recovered.

Not all the products of Irish metallurgy found in Great Britain had been imported ready-made. Moulds for casting flat axes are not uncommon in north-eastern Scotland and in Northumberland. Presumably the metal trade was in the hands of itinerant artificers, like tinkers, who not only transported and sold finished goods, but also cast them to the order of customers. Some of these artificers may have settled in Scotland, and in England too. The Beaker folk were the first customers of this trade, which they doubtless protected. It was not they who extended it to the Continent or profited from it as middlemen, but another group distinguished by new funerary pottery and burial rites.

Addendum (1946). Three discoveries, published since 1940, substantially enlarge our knowledge of the Beaker culture. A man, buried with a B1 Beaker on Crichel Down (Dorset) (*PPS.*, vi, 112–132), had been trepanned and probably died as a result. This delicate operation used to be performed with flint knives for clinical or ritual reasons in several parts of Europe at different prehistoric periods as well as by many recent barbarians, notably in South America and the Pacific. While there are some early examples of such surgery, mostly by the technique of scraping away the bone, from Central and Northern Europe, true trepanning, involving the excision of a roundel from the braincase, had become almost a cult in France and the Iberian Peninsula, and most Central European cases belong to a period after contact with the West had been established through the Beaker-folk's wanderings. The use of this technique in Dorset is thus fresh evidence of the western connexions of our B1 Beaker group, though the operation, performed *post mortem* on the man buried under the Maiden Castle " long barrow " (p. 80), should be earlier than their arrival.

Eastern connexions are illustrated by the other new finds. At Stanton Harcourt (Oxon.) Grimes (*Oxon.*, viii/ix, 1944, 34–44) found at the centre of a ring ditch a young man buried in a wood-lined pit or coffin with a debased B Beaker, arrow-heads and a bone ring pendant. This ring ditch cut one surrounding an earlier burial accompanied by a jet slider and a polished flint knife. The latter articles are appropriate to the Food Vessel complex, and the ring pendant can be best matched in Sweden in the Stone Cist phase which is contemporary with our Wessex culture. So B Beakers were still fashionable in Period IV. But the wood coffin reproduces features repeatedly found in " Battle-axe graves " even in Jutland, Finland, Central and South Russia (Childe, *Dawn*, 1946, chap. IX).

Finally, under two barrows on Beaulieu Heath, New Forest (*PPS.*, ix, 1943, 7–9, 17–19, 24–25), the grave-pit contained a mortuary house or tent, framed with stakes. These constructions can be exactly matched in graves of the earliest, *yamno*, phase of the South Russian " Battle-axe culture " and, less exactly, under Dutch barrows. In funerary practices at least the British Beaker culture is just the westernmost of a series extending across the Eurasian plain to the Black Sea, the Volga and beyond.

CHAPTER VII

THE RESULTS OF FUSION

THE Beaker folk must have formed a relatively thin governing class, dominating and organizing older alien societies. In Period IV the Beaker aristocracy in Wessex was displaced by a new ruling group; elsewhere it was absorbed and older constituents re-emerge. At the same time the relatively moist 'Atlantic' conditions, still attested in southern England by the faunule from Beaker sites, were giving place to a drier regime, corresponding presumably to the Sub-Boreal phase in the Baltic area. No settlements whatsoever are known from this dry phase, so that we have to rely more than ever on grave-finds.

In the funerary record so-called Food Vessels replace Beakers in Britain, north of the Thames, and in Ireland take the place of Beakers in succession to Windmill Hill and Beacharra wares. The societies these sepulchral vases typify, while perpetuating many traits of the Beaker culture and organization, inherited the metallurgical and commercial traditions associated with the Boyne and Peterborough cultures, the ritual art of the Boyne megalith-builders and the basketry tradition of Peterborough ceramics; they adopted the rite of cremation, presumably from the Boyne, the sepulchral circle from Battle-axe folk or megalith-builders; they created original implements and ornaments—the plano-convex flint knife and the crescentic jet necklace with its derivative the gold lunula. But they are best defined by their pottery. Its distribution [1] shows two main areas of settlement—north-eastern Britain (Derbyshire, Yorkshire, Northumberland, the Lothians, Fife and Strathmore) and Ireland together with south-west Scotland and Man. In each province different ceramic styles and forms were preferred.

All Food Vessels are shallower than the Beakers that precede them and the Urns that replace them; all are poorly fired; the majority are richly decorated. One rare variety, equally common in England and Ireland and found in explicitly early contexts,[2] is a bowl decorated

[1] See Miss Chitty's map in Fox, *Personality*, Pl. V.
[2] Fargo Plantation (Wilts.) with a Beaker (*WAM.*, xlviii, 363); cairn on Lyle's Hill (Antrim) with primary interment (*Belfast Museum Quarterly Notes*, lxiv (1940), 8); cf. Simondston (Glam.) (*Arch.*, lxxxvii, 13) and Needham (Norfolk) (*Ant. J.*, xx, 272–4).

with horizontal ribs embellished with notches (Fig. 33). The rest fall into two series, best represented in north-eastern Britain and Ireland respectively.

The so-called 'British' or Yorkshire Vase consists of two distinct members —the body, shaped like an inverted truncated cone, and the neck, normally concave (cavetto) (Pl. XII). The rim is usually broad and bevelled internally. In the simplest form—Abercromby's type 3—the neck is superimposed directly on the body, with which it makes a sharp shoulder. More often

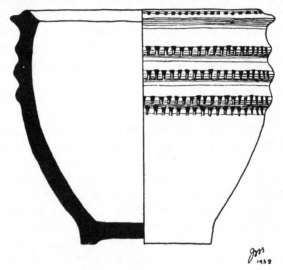

FIG. 33. Food Vessel from Fargo Plantation
(Wilts.). ½. After Stone in *WAM*.

there is a groove on the shoulder (type 2), which in type 1 is spanned by perforated or unperforated lugs or '*stop-ridges*' (Pl. VIII, 2). In types 2a and 1b the groove is duplicated with or without stop-ridges. Decoration, concentrated on the rim, neck and shoulder, may be executed with a point, with a cord or with a comb-stamp, more rarely with a shell edge or a hollow bone. Simple motives like herring-bones and maggots arranged in continuous zones were preferred, but pendant and alternating triangles (as in Unstan ware) or panels of vertical and horizontal lines (as at Beacharra) might be executed in cord technique.

Of the Irish Bowls, Abercromby's type A (Pl. IX, 1) is a lotus-shaped vessel the smooth curve of whose profile may be interrupted by a constriction.

Type B approximates to British type 2 save that the shoulder is lower down and the 'groove' broad, shallow and decorated. Type C is a bowl rather like A, but with two or three deep grooves—or three or four raised mouldings —round the body (Pl. X, 1). Type D is another bowl, but provided with an everted rim. Finally, type E (Pl. IX, 2) has an inverted cone-shaped body with a rounded shoulder surmounted by a straight funnel-like neck. In none of these Irish types is the rim normally thickened as in the British series. The decoration, composed mainly horizontally but sometimes in panels, covers the whole vessel. For executing the patterns engraved lozenge-shaped, hexagonal and octagonal dies or stamps[3] of baked clay, a broad-toothed comb, whipped cords and a triangular point were employed. The point, impressed alternately upwards and downwards into the soft clay, left a zigzag band that seems to stand out in relief—a very popular motive termed *false relief* (Pl. IX, 1).

Food Vessels of both series are often decorated on the bases like the handled Beaker-mugs. This basal decoration, the form and even the surface texture of many vessels, and such devices as false-relief, are probably copied from wooden models. The wooden model is even more conspicuous in the case of some Yorkshire Food Vessels with feet.[4] It may indeed be said that Food Vessels in general are cheap substitutes for wooden vessels. And these may sometimes have been encased in, or inlaid with, sheet gold. A gold casing for, or copy of, a bowl of type A has turned up in North Germany.[5] A carved wooden bowl, found in a bog near Caergwrle Castle[6] (Flints.), though of later date than most Food Vessels, illustrates the sort of thing imitated by the clay Food Vessels. And the boat and tree-trunk coffins, as well as the sockets of posts,[7] to be described later, provide concrete proof that Food Vessel societies included competent carpenters. Since the pottery vessels are substitutes—and presumably cheap substitutes—for perishable wooden vases, Food Vessels may not be found in all graves actually belonging to that culture.

Finally, while we speak of 'Yorkshire' and 'Irish' types and decorative styles, no type is confined exclusively to the province after which it has been named. So we have perfectly good 'Irish' Food Vessels in Yorkshire and Aberdeenshire, though much less often than in Ireland. Similarly, the 'Irish' technique of false relief was applied, though exceptionally, to vases

---

[3] Abercromby, i, No. 281 bis.   [4] Abercromby, Nos. 222-223; Elgee, *N.E.Y.*, 76.
[5] *Amer. Anthrop.*, xxxix, 13.   [6] Grimes, *Guide*, 83-84.
[7] Both Greenwell, *B.B.*, 170, and Mortimer, *Forty Years*, 181, insist how skilfully the posts round Yorkshire graves had been sharpened.

of purely British form in Yorkshire and Lincolnshire.[8]　Conversely, English forms with English decoration occur all over Ireland.

The makers of Food Vessels practised some agriculture, since casts of barley have been observed on many Food Vessels in Britain and Ireland and of wheat too in England.[9]　But judging by the prominence of bones of sheep and game in their graves, they must have relied even more than the Beaker folk on pastoralism and hunting.　And Food Vessel graves spread onto upland areas in Northumberland suitable for pasture and hunting-grounds, while the Beaker folk selected more easily cultivated territory near the coast.[10]　The same phenomenon is observable in Yorkshire,[11] but the Food Vessel people occupied the Wolds as intensively as the Beaker folk, so that here it looks like a case of an expanding population spreading onto inferior land.　For the population was apparently greater than before. Elgee reports twice as many Food Vessels as Beakers in Yorkshire, and Raistrick finds a similar ratio in Northumberland, in Durham and in Derbyshire.

But another factor helped to determine the distribution of Food Vessels— trade.　For the makers of these vases had taken over the role of the Peterborough folk and Boyne megalith-builders in the distribution of metal and other materials.　Their graves are strung out along the great trade routes defined by the distributions of flat axes and halberds.[12]　On route 1 (p. 117 above) an extraordinary concentration of Food Vessels between Lochgilphead and Oban, where there was a porterage from Loch Fyne to the Firth of Lorne, and at the northern end of the Great Glen, proves that their makers were following in the steps of the Boyne peoples.　Routes 2, 3 and 4 are also sprinkled with Food Vessels.　Their makers had other aims besides hunting-grounds, pastures and arable land, and some could find a livelihood in industry and trade.

The grave-goods confirm this.　The equipment buried with Food Vessels is indeed still largely lithic.　Stone axes have been found so buried in Argyll and Ireland.[13]　One Yorkshire grave contained a battle-axe, differing from the Beaker form in that the profile expands from the perforation to the blade and to the butt.[14]　And the plano-convex knife—a

[8] *BBCS.*, ix (1938), 277; cf. *PPS.*, i, 83.
[9] Jessen and Helbaek, 20.
[10] Raistrick, *Arch. Ael.*, 4, viii (1931), 157.
[11] Elgee, *Arch. Yorks.*, 63; *N.E.Y.*, 78; Raistrick, *l.c.*
[12] Cf. Pls. II and V in Fox, *Personality.*　[13] *PSAS.*, lxx, 396; Abercromby, i, 143.
[14] Thus resembling the stone battle-axes from Danish passage graves, but perhaps inspired by Aegean metal axes like that allegedly found at Whitby: Elgee, *N.E.Y.*, 62.

broad flint flake, smooth on the bulbar face but beautifully trimmed by pressure-flaking on the upper surface (Fig. 34)—is almost as distinctive of the culture as the Food Vessel itself.[15]

Bronze knife-daggers are indeed less common with Food Vessels than with Beakers, and most belong to the narrow types current in Periods IV and V.[16] A grooved dagger with a gold-bound pommel found with a skeleton and a bowl of type E under a large cairn on Topped Mountain (Fermanagh)[17] and a similar blade associated with a bowl decorated in false relief at Croghan Eirin (West Meath),[18] are in fact typical products of the Wessex culture. The only halberds found in graves[19] may likewise be assigned to the Food Vessel people, despite the absence of pottery. Finally, the only flat axe ever found with sepulchral pottery in Britain—it was of bronze containing 10 per cent. tin—accompanied a Food Vessel at Butterwick (Yorks.).[20]

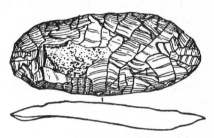

FIG. 34.   Plano-convex flint Knife. ¾.   After Clark.

Ornaments, presumably belonging to ladies, give a better idea of the wealth Food Vessel people derived from trade, and of its direction. They include jet necklaces, metal earrings and bracelets. The first-named are the most spectacular. Simple necklaces composed of disc beads may have been adopted by Food Vessel folk from megalithic or Beaker predecessors; four have been found with Food Vessels and three with Beakers in Scotland. But the Food Vessel folk created, perhaps as substitutes for gold collars, a handsome new variant consisting of several strands of long barrel-shaped or fusiform beads, held together by flat spacers and fastened at the back with a triangular toggle (Fig. 35). The spacers are embellished with punctured geometric patterns comparable to those adorning Irish axes.

These crescentic necklaces are very common round the Firth of Tay (ten), where they may first have been made, the Moray Firth (ten or eleven examples) and in Argyll. But they were exported or copied all over the

---

[15] Clark, *Ant. J.*, xii, 158-162.

[16] e.g., like Fig. 41, 2, with two rivet-holes, Abercromby, i, O. 33, O. 47—(Yorks., Antrim) *Arch. Camb.* lxxvi (1921), 265-285 (Flints.).

[17] *PRIA.* (1898), 651-658.   [18] *PRIA.*, iv, 388; *JRSAI.*, lxx, 61.

[19] Bishopmill (Elgin), in cist with contracted skeleton; Moylough (Sligo), with cremation in cist with decorated coverstone (*JRSAI.*, lix (1929), 113).

[20] Greenwell, *B.B.*, 186; Abercromby, i, O. 32a.

Food Vessel area—Northumberland, Yorkshire, Derbyshire, East Anglia and Northern Ireland. In Ireland, or even Scotland, the crescentic necklace

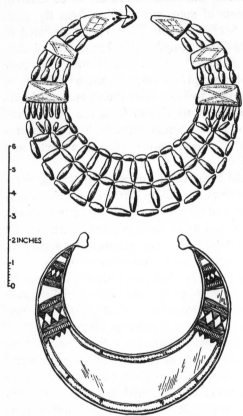

was translated into a crescentic collar, cut out of a sheet of native gold and relieved with designs in panels, imitating the spacer-plates of the necklaces [21]; these collars or *lunulae* (Fig. 35) were in their turn exported to the Continent. Not only have crescentic jet necklaces been found with Food Vessels in fourteen instances, but the combined distribution of such necklaces and of lunulae coincides remarkably with that of Food Vessels.[22] Outside the Food Vessel province the type was adopted by the invaders of Wessex who, however, were rich enough to replace jet by the more costly amber.

Jet or lignite was used also for the V-perforated buttons with which Food Vessel folk used, like the Beaker invaders, to fasten their clothing, and for sliders to serve as clasps for men's belts.[23] But for the hooks of scabbards bone was used.[24]

FIG. 35.   Jet necklace from Poltalloch (Argyll) and gold lunula from Co. Cavan. After Wheeler in Eyre, *European Civilization*. By permission of the Oxford University Press.

Irish gold was imported for ornaments even into north-east Scotland and Northumberland. Women

[21] Craw, *PSAS.*, lxiii, 164, who first established the connexion, believed that the translation took place in Scotland and that Scottish gold was used for the oldest lunulae. Hawkes (*Foundations*, 324) thinks, on the contrary, that the lunulae inspired the necklaces.

[22] Clark, *Man*, xxxii, No. 46, who also shows that the distributions of lunulae and crescentic necklaces are complementary.

[23] Never actually found with Food Vessels, but occur in cists with no pottery in Yorkshire and in the segmented gallery of Beacharra.

[24] Killicarney (Cavan): *JRSAI.*, xv, 189.

wore basket-shaped earrings of this material[25] or of bronze.[26] Earrings of this form are well known in Ireland, but seem ultimately to be derived, probably via Spain, from ornaments of gold wire familiar from the great hoard of jewelry uncovered by Schliemann in Troy II but depicted in Egyptian paintings as late as the New Kingdom.[27] From Ireland they were exported to Belgium and Poland.[28] Food Vessel folk may have worn also *ribbon torques* made by simply twisting a narrow ribbon of gold. More than three dozen are said to have been found on Law Farm, Urquhart (Elgins.), and other specimens are known from the Food Vessel provinces of Ross and Fife, but also from Aberdeenshire.[29] Such ornaments are common in Ireland, and may have been associated with a lunula in a hoard from Largatreany (Donegal).[30]

A proportion of the trade in which the Food Vessel population of North Britain engaged must have gone on from the Moray Firth and the Yorkshire–Northumberland coasts to Denmark and North Germany; for Irish halberds, decorated axes and lunulae have turned up in those regions.[31] Amber, the most likely Northern export to have been received in exchange, was apparently diverted southward to satisfy the rich Wessex chieftains, as hardly any is found with Food Vessels. On the other hand, a pin, probably of Aunjetitz type from Central Europe, was found in 1937 in a secondary burial at Loose Howe, excavated by Elgee but still unpublished. Cuff armlets of sheet bronze like one found with a jet necklace in a grave at Melfort (Argyll),[32] and the massive bronze armlets like those worn by a Food Vessel dame buried near Kinneff Castle (Kincardine), though certainly not imported thence, may have been inspired by the bangles, popular among the Aunjetitz population of Bohemia. Finally, proof of continued intercourse with the South-West by the megalithic route is afforded by Irish lunulae from western France and derivatives (or prototypes) from Galicia and Portugal,[33] by a ribbed cylinder pin-head of Iberian 'Copper Age' type found with an (English!) Food Vase in a cremation grave near Galway,[34] as well as by rock-engravings.

[25] *Arch. Ael.*, 4, xiii (1936), 210—Kirkhaugh (Northum.), with Food Vessel; Childe, *P.S.*, 102—Orton (Morays.), with no pottery.

[26] Mortimer, *Forty Years*, 218—Garton Slack (Yorks.).

[27] Childe, *Dawn*, 43 and Fig. 22, 1. Maryon reports a parallel from Merida, Spain.

[28] *Mat.* (1885), 318; Šturms, *Bronzezeit im Ostbaltikum*, 194.

[29] *PSAS.*, lvii, 165. [30] Armstrong, *Catalogue*, 23–24; cf. *Man*, xxxii (1932), No. 222, but cf. Fox, *Personality*, 1943, 49. [31] Childe, *Dawn*, 178 and 189.

[32] Childe, *P.S.*, 102; cf. the armlet from Normanton (Wilts.): *Arch.*, xliii, 469.

[33] *Préhistoire*, ii, 229, Figs. 40 and 42.

[34] *J. Galway H.&A.S.*, xvi, 65-66; 125-132; cf. Childe, *Dawn*, 259.

Food Vessel people seem to have adopted from the Boyne societies their magico-religious art or symbolism, but carried still further the conventionalization noted in the Boyne tombs. Chalk cylinders, like drums, found in a fosse-ringed inhumation grave under a barrow at Folkton (Yorks.),[35] do indeed reproduce more faithfully than any other carvings in the British Isles the lineaments of the divinity so often represented on schist plaques and phalange bones in the Iberian Copper Age (Fig. 36). But on the monuments spirals and cognate figures were reduced to mere circles or circles surrounding cup-like depressions, termed *cup-and-ring marks*. Very similar marks are carved on the rocks of the metalliferous region of Galicia.[36] Concentric circles adorn the capstone of a cist at Ballinvally (Co. Meath).[37] Cup-and-ring marks had been pecked out on the coverstone of a cist containing a Food Vessel at Tillicoultry (Clackmannan) (Fig. 37).[38] Even in Yorkshire [39] and in Dorset such occur on stones in and under barrows covering Food Vessel interments. More often they are carved on natural rock surfaces. Inscribed rocks are particularly common between Lochgilphead and Loch Crinan in Argyll, in Galloway, round the Coquet in Northumberland [40] and between the Aire and Wharfe in western Yorkshire,[41] all regions colonized by Food Vessel communities or traversed by their traders.

These carvings are doubtless the symbols of some aniconic cult which we cannot interpret, the inscribed rocks scenes of periodic ceremonies which may have continued to be performed for generations right down into the Iron Age, since among the carvings near Ilkley is a whirligig in La Tène style.[42] But to the same group of carvings belong sepulchral representations of metal objects. Daggers and axes as well as cup-marks were pecked out on a stone built into the wall of a cairn at Badbury (Dorset) that covered several interments, one accompanied by a Food Vessel.[43] Representations of flat axes were carved also on the sides of two cists in the Crinan district of Argyll [44] where so many Food Vessels have been found. These sepulchral carvings are not moulds, tools of the smith's craft, such as have been found under a barrow in South Russia. But they show not only interest in, but also veneration for, his products. Perhaps, then, the producer too was

---

[35] *Arch.*, lii, 14.   [36] Childe, *Bronze Age*, 150.   [37] Nat. Museum, Dublin.
[38] *PSAS.*, lxxii, 144.   [39] *YAJ.*, xxiv (1917), 267.
[40] *Arch. Ael.*, 4, ix (1932), 50; x, 206.
[41] *YAJ.*, xxxii, 33-44. On Ilkley Moor, as in Galloway (*PSAS.*, xxxii, 144) and Midlothian (*PSAS.*, lxxiii, 316), in addition to concentric circles true spirals are carved on some rocks, as also on the stones of two cairns covering Beakers in Scotland (Childe, *P.S.*, 116) and on the orthostats of circles and cairn peristaliths in Cumberland (*T.C. & W.A. & A.S.* (1895), Pl. X; n.s., i, 298).
[42] Jacobsthal, *JRS.*, xxviii, 69.   [43] *Ant. J.*, xix, 291-296.   [44] *PSAS.*, lxiv, 131-134.

accorded fuller recognition by this society than by those which preceded
and replaced it.

FIG. 36. Figurine in the form of a Drum
of Chalk from Folkton. ¼. By permission
of the Trustees of the British Museum.

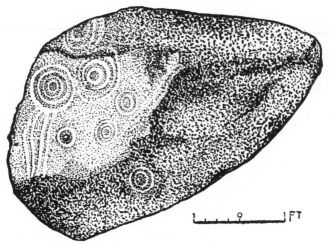

FIG. 37. Capstone of a cist at Tillicoultry (Clackmannan).
After *PSAS*.

Food Vessels normally accompany contracted skeletons, but in all areas
cases of cremation occur. In the East Riding of Yorkshire cremation was
the rite in 20 per cent. of the Food Vessel graves examined by Mortimer;

in Wales, where Food Vessels are absolutely rare, it was the normal practice.[45] The rite and the beliefs it implies may perfectly well have been inherited from the Boyne megalith-builders, so that there is no reason to assume that cremation burials are late in the Food Vessel period or are due to influence from the Wessex culture (unless the rite in collective tombs too be derived from that quarter, cf. p. 79). In the composite society denoted by Food Vessels some families adhered to inhumation while others practised cremation.

Cremations were occasionally deposited in small shallow pits under barrows. But normally Food Vessel people, whether burned or unburned, were buried in cists of slabs or, where the soil conditions permitted, in pit graves. In Scotland and Ireland the slabs walling some cists, and still more the capstones, seem unnecessarily big, as if memories of the megalithic tomb still haunted their builders. And in fact, as already noted, Food Vessel people did gain admission to the ranks of those entitled to burial in family vaults, not only in Ireland, but also in the Clyde province on Arran. Nevertheless, in Ireland the Food Vessel, like the Beaker in Britain, 'brings a break in burial rite with the megalithic past—the abandonment of collective for single burial.' [46]

The graves may be covered with cairns or barrows. Some of the cairns are so large that they might be regarded as monuments of chiefs; those on Kilmartin glebe measure over 100 ft. in diameter. But they are small in comparison with some 'neolithic' tumuli. Some barrows conceal stone circles in Argyll and Yorkshire,[47] circular trenches (Yorkshire) or rings of wooden posts or stakes.[48] Still more often a crescentic or D setting of boulders was arranged to guard the central burial, as in Ross,[49] Fife,[50] Berwickshire [49] and Eire.[51] On the other hand, flat graves with Food Vessels occur at the centres of stone circles in Ross, Clackmannanshire and Arran.[52] Though the uprights are truly megalithic, the circles in question do not exceed 45 ft. in diameter. Similarly, in Wiltshire a fosse interrupted by two broad causeways bounded an area 12 ft. by 19 ft. in diameter with a central grave containing a Beaker inhumation and a Food Vessel cremation.[53] Small cemeteries of flat graves containing Food Vessels are not uncommon

[45] *Arch. Camb.* (1919), 329.   [46] Hawkes, *Foundations*, 322.
[47] Childe, *P.S.*, 109; Bateman, *Ten Years*, 207.
[48] Bateman, *l.c.*, 154, 181.
[49] *PSAS.*, lviii, 114; lvii, 65; xlviii, 318.
[50] *PSAS.*, xii, 441: primary interment accompanied by a Beaker.
[51] *J. Cork H.&A.S.*, xxxviii, 81.   [52] Childe, *P.S.*, 112.
[53] *WAM.*, xlviii, 360; contained Fig. 33.

in Scotland.[54] They presumably belong to small communities, settled in hamlets, like the Beaker cemeteries in Oxfordshire, but none comprised more than twelve graves. A much larger number of graves were apparently destroyed on Ballon Hill (Co. Carlow), but only twelve Food Bowls survive.[55]

So, too, a single cairn often covers several burials with Food Vessels. In Yorkshire [56] Elgee records 34 cases of three graves under a barrow, four interments thrice, and five twice. A cairn near the mouth of the Coquet in Northumberland is said to have covered twenty cists,[57] while four Food Vessels were found on virgin soil beside an empty cist under a cairn at Balmerino (Fife).[58] Instances of four to eight cists under a cairn have been reported from Counties Dublin, Tyrone and Fermanagh, and a famous cairn at Mount Stewart (Co. Down) covered no less than fourteen small cists, each apparently containing a Food Vessel.[59] Here the small cists were all grouped in the southern quadrant of the cairn, at the centre of which stood a larger cist measuring internally $5\frac{2}{3}$ ft. by $2\frac{1}{2}$ ft.

Such multiple interments have been variously interpreted as parallels to the cemeteries of flat graves, as survivals of the megalithic tradition of communal burial, as evidences for the sacrifice of retainers at the burial of a chief (who would occupy the central cist) or as secondary intrusions into a pre-existing cairn. As noted already, the megalith-builders in Derbyshire, Galloway and Ulster tended to multiply the number of ossuaries under a cairn. On the other hand, the concentration of the burials in one quadrant recalls the arrangement of Deverel–Rimbury secondaries in south English barrows (p. 188). And in Yorkshire the same barrow may cover Neolithic, Beaker, Food Vessel and Urn burials. Even in this case continuity of settlement may be deduced from the re-use of the barrow.

Burials in coffins hollowed out of tree-trunks must be attributed to the Food Vessel period, and in some cases to that culture. Such have been reported from Aberdeenshire, Fife, Midlothian and Northumberland; there are seven undoubted instances in Yorkshire, at least one in Wales and others in the south of England. The Welsh example and one from West Tanfield on the Yore in Yorkshire contained Food Vessels. As burials in tree-trunk coffins were characteristic of the Middle Bronze Age in Denmark, North Germany and Holland, Elgee [60] writes: 'Our coffins were the work of settlers from Denmark.' In some cases the agreement between

[54] *PSAS.*, xl, 204 (Elgins.); RC. *Fife*, xxix; RC. *Berwicks.*, xxxii; *PSAS.*, lxix, 352-370 (Dumbartons.).

[55] *JRSAI.*, ii (1853), 296; iii, 375; ix (1867), 209. [56] *Arch. Yorks.*, 63.

[57] *Arch.*, lii, 67. [58] *PSAS.*, xxxvi, 635.

[59] *PPS.*, iii, 30-39; cf. Pls. IX and X here. [60] *N.E.Y.*, 74.

the English and Northern coffins is quite close; an oak trunk was split horizontally, one half being hollowed out to receive the extended body while the other served as a lid.[61] The burials in question might in fact belong to Bronze Age precursors of the Vikings who established themselves as overlords among the Food Vessel population to capture the profits from the metal trade. But, after all, the Beaker burial in an oak-tree coffin from Northumberland is older than any Danish or Dutch examples.

But the same Elgee suggests elsewhere that 'the coffins represent the dug-out canoes in which their makers voyaged across the North Sea and up our rivers.' They would be boat burials such as were accorded to early Saxon and Norse princes. In fact, some of our tree-trunk coffins are not just square-ended sections of logs like the Danish, but have their ends hewn round to form canoes. Forde [62] recently found two such 'canoe-coffins,' one 8 ft. long, with a Food Vessel of the Irish series, under a round barrow at Disgwylfa Fawr (Plynlimon), 1660 ft. above sea-level. The coffin from Rylston (West Riding) also had 'partially rounded ends,' [63] while Elgee himself excavated an undoubted dug-out canoe used as a coffin and older than a secondary burial of the Wessex culture, at Loose Howe in eastern Yorkshire.[64] There seems no reason to accuse those buried in these canoe-coffins of being Nordics. They were more likely the boat-chiefs [65] of the Food Vessel population who guided their trading expeditions. But Hawkes [66] more plausibly connects these boat burials with the idea (probably Egyptian) of a voyage by water to the next world. These burials, in any case, give concrete proof of navigation in the Bronze Age. They also confirm the impression given by the larger Scottish and Irish cairns that, among some Food Vessel communities, at least, the capital needed for their commercial enterprises was concentrated in the hands of chiefs, not necessarily hereditary.

Physically, no single racial type is associated with Food Vessels. In Yorkshire, long-heads and round-heads occur in about equal proportions, but intermediate, mesaticranial skulls predominate. The measurable skeletons from oak-tree coffins in that county belonged to tall but brachy-

[61] Note that the oak coffin at Hove, Sussex, contained a cup of Baltic amber resembling in form a wooden cup from a Danish Bronze Age barrow (Curwen, *Arch. Sus.*, 162-164).

[62] *Ant. J.*, xix, 90; on the Food Vessel see Chitty, *BBCS.*, ix, 278-282.

[63] Greenwell, *B.B.*, 375.

[64] In B.M. unpublished; the secondary burial was furnished with a midrib dagger, a stone 'double axe,' an incense cup and a local copy of an Aunjetitz pin.

[65] For such today see Malinowski, *Argonauts of the Western Pacific.*

[66] Hawkes, *Foundations*, 366.

cranial men. The few skulls actually associated with Food Vessels in Scotland and a larger series from Ireland are all brachycranial, one Scottish individual standing over 6 ft. high. Martin [67] takes these round-heads in Ireland to belong to Beaker men from Britain. Coon,[68] however, finds that the round-heads of Ireland diverge substantially from the English Beaker folk and resemble rather the Dinaric population of the Mediterranean Bronze Age, one branch of which appears as the Continental Bell-beaker folk. He believes that these Irishmen came from Spain by the Atlantic route independent of Britain's invaders from the Rhineland—a hypothesis which should logically be extended to the Dinaric Beaker folk in Scotland.[69]

The chronological position to be assigned to the Food Vessel culture must be determined by the following considerations:

(1) In Wessex Food Vessels must immediately succeed Beakers, the burial at Fargo Plantation [70] suggesting an overlap. In Yorkshire, 'wherever it is possible to decide on the evidence, the Food Vessel is secondary to the Beaker.' [71] In Scotland, however, a partial synchronism may be deduced, (i) from the exclusive distributions of the two cultures in areas like Aberdeenshire and Strathmore, (ii) from Beakers with bevelled rims and other features copied from Food Vessels, and (iii) from the association with both Beakers and Food Vessels of identical ornaments like massive bronze armlets.[72] Finally, in the west of Scotland and in Ireland Food Vessels occur in collective tombs. Abercromby [73] indeed argued that 'certain Food Vessels in North Britain are anterior to its invasion by the Brachycephals' (Beaker folk). But this argument depended upon undemonstrable assumptions as to the typology of Food Vessels and the unity of the Beaker invasion, and on mistaking a Food Vessel from Mount Stewart for a Beaker.[74] The reliable evidence cited warrants only the statement that the Food Vessel culture may have begun during Period III.

(2) The stone battle-axes and bronze knife-daggers associated with Food Vessels are typologically more developed than those found with Beakers and would be appropriate rather to the Wessex culture of Period IV. But only two grooved daggers, distinctive of the Wessex culture, have actually been found with Food Vessels (p. 123). So, too, crescentic amber necklaces, characteristic of the Wessex culture, must be the counterparts of the jet

[67] *JRSAI.*, lxv, 190-199.   [68] *Races*, 161.
[69] P. 91 above; these ' Short Cist ' skulls may include Food Vessel as well as Beaker men.
[70] P. 119 above; Stone could not determine which burial was the earlier, but insists that no long interval is likely to separate the two.
[71] Kitson Clark, *Arch. J.*, xciv, 50.   [72] Childe, *P.S.*, 94.
[73] *BAP.*, i, 131.   [74] Evans and Megaw, *PPS.*, iii, 40.

necklaces farther north. But of course lignite beads associated with a B 2 Beaker at Beggar's Haven (Brighton) must be earlier.[75]

(3) True Food Vessels are very rare south of the Thames, presumably because the early establishment of the intrusive Wessex culture cut short the development of native traditions. In South Wales 'new-comers brought the Collared Urn into an area where the Food Vessel culture was in a late stage of its prolonged evolution.'[76] The same seems true of Derbyshire, Yorkshire and North Britain generally. Now, in southern England Collared Urns form part of the Wessex culture of Period IV. Still, their range extends beyond that period, and time must be allowed for 'new-comers' to bring them even to Glamorgan and Yorkshire. Yet segmented fayence beads are never associated with true Food Vessels in South Wales, Derbyshire or Yorkshire, but only with Urns. These imported beads must define a clear-cut horizon about 1400 B.C. If we say they are peculiar to Period V, we could assert that the Food Vessel culture does not outlast Period IV in the areas mentioned. The statement could be extended to Scotland only with the reservation that the fayence beads, found with Urns but not Food Vessels[77] there, differ technically, and perhaps also chronologically, from the English.

(4) On the other hand, a bead of English type was found with an Urn and a Food Vessel in a cist at Llangwm (Denbigh).[78] And in Ireland an overlap between Food Vessels and Urns seems almost certain. One and the same cist at Kilskeery (Tyrone) contained two cremated bodies, an Encrusted Urn, a Pygmy Vessel, a Food Vessel—debased type E ornamented with roughly scratched patterns—and another vase.[79] So at Burgage (Co. Wicklow) a large type 3 Food Vase not only lay in the same cist but was decorated with the same implement as an Encrusted Urn (Pl. XII).[80] As Encrusted Urns are assignable to Period VI, these cists seems to indicate that Food Vessels in Ireland lasted to that late date. Hencken[81] draws the same conclusion from a cairn covering forty interments at Knockast (West Meath). The gold Food Vessel from North Germany—a bowl of type A (p. 121)—likewise belongs to our Period VI (Montelius' Period IIIA of the Northern Bronze Age). Finally, even in Cambridgeshire a crescentic jet necklace is

[75] Curwen, *Arch. Sus.*, Pl. XI; *Ant. J.*, xx, 45.   [76] Fox, *Arch.*, lxxxvii, 164.

[77] In the Knappers cemetery near Glasgow, while several burials were accompanied by Food Vessels, that furnished with segmented fayence beads contained plain ware (*PSAS.*, lxix, 362).   [78] *Arch*, lxxxv, 235.   [79] *UJA.*, ii, 65.

[80] *Report Irish National Museum* (1933-34), Pls. 6 and 7.

[81] *PRIA.*, xli, C, 238 ff.; an ornate Food Vessel in a cist was obviously primary, late Urns presumably secondaries.

said to have been associated with a socketed chisel of Period VI at Soham Fen, though Clark admits that the association is dubious.[82]

A survival of Irish Food Bowls as late as Period VI is thus quite likely. Gogan has gone much further, establishing comparisons between some bowls of type E and the Marnian 'flowerpots' appropriate to Period VIII—comparisons endorsed by Favret, Hawkes, Kendrick and R. A. Smith.[83] If accepted, they would mean that the Food Vessel culture was still prominent in Eire in the third century B.C. when La Tène invaders raided the British Isles. The possibility cannot be dismissed altogether, but it is odd that it was a Food Bowl of just this type E that was associated with the most explicitly Middle Bronze Age 1 grooved dagger ever found in an Irish grave (p. 123)!

The origin of the Food Vessel culture is generally deduced from an analysis of the distinctive vase, though the chronological facts just recited must always be remembered. In 1912 R. A. Smith [84] showed how many features of the Food Vase could be derived from Peterborough ware. His view, shared by Abercromby, that the Irish type A Bowl could serve as an intermediary between the 'neolithic bowl' and the British vase is hardly compatible with the known chronology of this type. And formally type D is nearer the Peterborough bowl. Miss Kitson Clark can find 'no proof of the existence in (eastern Yorkshire) of Neolithic B before Food Vessel ceramics.' [85] Moreover, what seems the earliest type of all, the ribbed bowl common to England and Ireland (p. 119), is clearly related to Irish variants on Windmill Hill ware like that from the Bann (p. 90); for these are also decorated with notched ribs.

On the other hand, Åberg, Scott and the author have sought South-Western inspiration, pointing to analogies between the radial decoration of type A and the bowls associated with Bell-beakers in the Peninsula, between the A form and footed bowls of the Pyrenaean megalithic culture, and seeking in Sardinia rather than in Central Germany the models for the Yorkshire, footed Food Vessels.[86] A 'twin vase,' two Food Vessels of English type 2 joined together at the shoulder,[87] is the sole British representative of a popular Mediterranean ritual vessel; but the idea might have come through

[82] Clark, *VCH. Camb.*, i, 271.

[83] *J. Cork H.&A.S.*, xxxiv (1929), 65-70.   [84] *Arch.*, lxii, 351.

[85] *Arch. J.*, xciv, 62; Peterborough ware has since been found abundantly on the western edge of the Vale of York, where it would be expected rather than on the Wolds (*PPS.*, v, 251).

[86] Cf. Childe, *P.S.*, 93-94; in *Man*, xxxii, 299, Gogan illustrates a Food Vessel of type 1 with eye-decoration that might be regarded as Iberian.

[87] Preserved in Aqualate Hall (Staffs.); Chitty, *Ant.J.*, ix, 137-139.

Central Europe as well as through the Peninsula since the type is known in both areas. Finally, Elgee, Gogan and Kitson Clark have suspected Northern elements. Besides some doubtful ceramic parallels, the tree-trunk coffins are cited. The tall skeleton buried extended under barrow 139 at Towthorpe (East Riding) (p. 144) is also relevant, since the rite is very ancient in Northern Europe. But though a few Northerners may have settled in northern Britain, Northern products are so very rare [88] that no colonization such as took place in the Dark Ages can be admitted.

In 1937 Mahr emphasized the contribution of the Beaker folk in the formation of the Food Vessel culture, and the subsequent discoveries in Ireland have abundantly justified him. But while the Boyne culture remain so nearly unknown, it is premature to try to give greater precision to the statements at the beginning of this chapter as to the place of origin and components of the Food Vessel culture beyond remarking that the admission of a Beaker element and the adoption of separate as against collective burial align the Food Vessel complex with North Central, rather than Atlantic, Europe.

[88] Cf. e.g. Piggott's map in *PPS.*, iv, 81.

CHAPTER VIII

THE WESSEX CULTURE AND THE URN FOLK

1. THE WESSEX CHIEFTAINS

FOOD Vessels are very rare in southern England. In effect, their place is taken by the Cinerary Urn (p. 146). But on the rich downlands of Wessex a hundred barrows of exceptional construction and furniture belong to a new ruling class who had there replaced the Beaker overlords. These barrows and their contents define what Piggott [1] terms the Wessex culture of Middle Bronze Age 1—our Period IV.

The Wessex culture evidently belongs to 'a small ruling class expending their accumulated surplus wealth on luxury trade with far-flung connexions.' The basis of that wealth was presumably the farming and gathering activities of subject populations, including perhaps the makers of Overhanging Rim Urns, and the industry of the flint-miners, who were demonstrably still at work. But no settlements of the Wessex culture are known; their chieftains have left no remains on the causewayed hill-top camps which their Beaker predecessors had still frequented. That may be due to increasing dryness; the land molluscs of this period are species that prefer open grassland, no longer the moisture-loving woodland species found in the neolithic camps. The change of flora may be due to the Sub-Boreal climate as well as the activities of man and his stock. In any case, the new chiefs could extort a surplus to barter for metals, amber and even Mediterranean beads and to support skilled artisans to work these imports. The smiths they employed were familiar with the technique of casting metal in a valve mould consisting of two or more pieces, and so could turn out among other novelties axes strengthened with cast flanges down both sides in contrast to the flat or hammer-flanged axes produced by the Irish smiths in a simpler mould. The new technique is undoubtedly derived from Central Europe; its exponents, if not actually immigrants, must have served an apprenticeship there or in some secondary centre of the school like Brittany. Goldsmiths could overlay boxes, sceptre-staves, scabbard-mounts and conical buttons with sheet-gold, and adorned the sheet-metal with incised rectilinear patterns.

[1] *PPS.*, iv, 60-106.

They ingeniously decorated wooden dagger hilts with tiny gold nails to make geometric patterns (Fig. 38, 1). Amber was imported from the Baltic, but in the raw condition; for the beads and ornaments from Wessex graves are

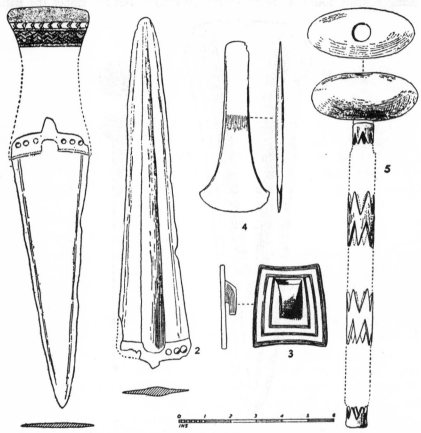

FIG. 38. 1. Dagger with gold-studded pommel; 2. Tanged dagger; 3. Gold scabbard hook; 4. Axe; 5. Shale-headed sceptre: from Bush Barrow (Normanton, Wilts.). After Piggott in *PPS.*, iv.

all of British, none of Danish types. Carpenters must have been acquainted with a pole-lathe, and with its aid cups of shale were neatly turned.[2]

The trade of Wessex extended from Ireland to the Baltic and southward perhaps to Crete. The gold at least is of Irish origin, while pendants of amber and shale[3] accurately copy the stone pendants from the Boyne

[2] Newall, *WAM.*, xliv, 111.

[3] *Devizes Museum Cat.*, 188c, 223; cf. Gogan, *J. Cork H.&A.S.*, xxxv, 95.

passage graves. The favourite type of necklace in Wessex was a translation into amber of the crescentic jet necklaces associated with Scottish Food Vessels. Tin was naturally brought from Cornwall, beads of that metal being actually found at Sutton Veny (Wilts.).[4] Besides amber the Baltic

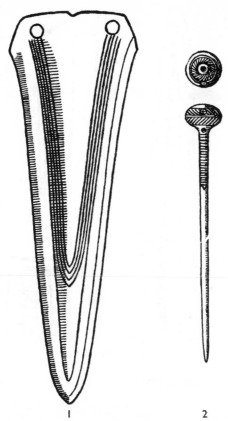

1   2

FIG. 39. Grooved ogival dagger and bulb-
headed pin from a grave (with Plate X, 2) at
Camerton (Somerset). ½. Bristol Museum.

sent double-axe beads such as had been common in the Danish passage graves, and perhaps ring-pendants appropriate to the long cists of the last phase of the Baltic Stone Age; but these imports are known only from local copies made in England. From Central Europe came at least one pin with a perforated globular head (Fig. 39, 2), while others—crutch-headed or

[4] Colt Hoare, *Ancient Wilts.*, i, 103.

surmounted by two or three rings—if not imports, are at least copies of Central European forms. Miniature halberds with gold-bound amber shafts and bronze blades (Fig. 41, 11) are amulets modelled on the bronze-cased halberds that the Saxo-Thuringian smiths had developed out of the Irish weapons.[5] As a counterpart to these imports English axes of the period, as well as Irish flat axes and halberds, have been found in the Saale–Elbe region.

Finally, segmented beads of bluish fayence (Fig. 40), the oldest actual imports from the Mediterranean found in Britain, were worn by persons buried in some 25 Wessex graves.[6] A counterpart to these imports is perhaps an amber disc bound with gold from a Late Minoan II tomb near Knossos in Crete, to which an exact parallel is provided in a similar disc from a barrow at Manton (Wilts.) [7] (Fig. 41, 10).

FIG. 40. Segmented fayence beads from Lake, Wilts. ¼. By permission of the Trustees of the British Museum.

The chieftains who amassed the capital to support such commerce were warriors armed with daggers and bows. The favourite type of dagger is often ogival in plan and regularly adorned with grooves running parallel to the edges (Fig. 39, 1). In some specimens there is a rudimentary tang projecting from the butt (Fig. 38, 2). Two were mounted in wood or amber hilts decorated with a pointillé pattern of tiny gold nails. The rich Bush Barrow contained also a hooked scabbard-mount of gold (Fig. 38, 3), just as in the contemporary Perjamos graves of southern Hungary hooked mounts of bronze or bone are common. Whetstones were carried for sharpening the weapons.

The arrows were still tipped with flint points, tanged and barbed, the barbs being generally trimmed square with consummate skill (Fig. 24, 7). To straighten the shafts the archer used a pair of stones each bearing a groove on the flat face [8] (Fig. 42). This device, an innovation in England, was popular about the same time in Scandinavia and Mycenaean Greece, but had been known even earlier in the Danube basin.[9]

The Wessex dagger might be developed into a spear-head with rhomboid blade by elongating the rudimentary tang to fit into the shaft (Fig. 51, 3). Shaft and tang were both enveloped in a metal ferrule or collar (Fig. 52, 1).

[5] Piggott, l.c., 84; Childe, Dawn, 191; Danube, 242.
[6] Arch., lxxxv, 203-244.   [7] Ant. J., v, 68-70; Arch., lxv, 42.
[8] WAM., xlv, 439-457.   [9] Childe, Dawn, 69, 102, 166.

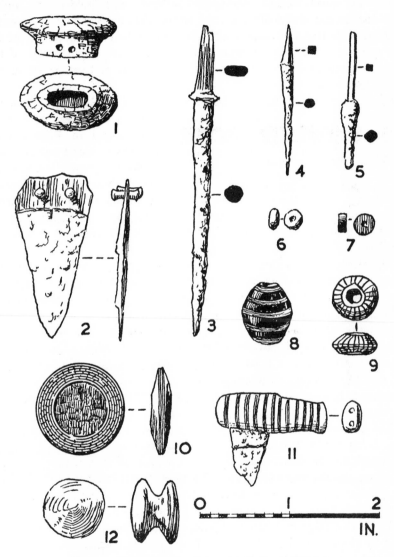

FIG. 41. FURNITURE OF GRAVE AT MANTON (WILTS.).

1. Amber pommel ;   2-5. Bronze ;   10. Amber bound with gold ;
11. Amber, gold and bronze (blade) ; 12. Clay. ⅓. After Piggott.

So the Central European socketed spear-head could be translated into a British form which looks as if it were a tanged spear-head with collar and blade cast in one piece and the tang suppressed [10] (Fig. 51, 4). But the chiefs sometimes still wielded stone battle-axes which expand in profile from the shaft-hole to the blade and butt like those found with Food

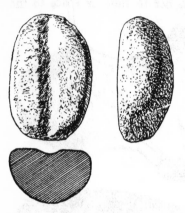

FIG. 42. Stone 'Arrow-straightener' from Normanton, Wilts. ½. By permission of the Trustees of the British Museum.

Vessels farther north (Fig. 43, 1). As symbols of authority others carried sceptres—globes or ovoids of stone or shale, studded with gold, mounted on wooden staves about a foot long.

In only 13 instances were Wessex burials accompanied by native Cinerary Urns; in 23 barrows the funerary vessels were *pygmy vessels* or *incense cups* which have no roots in British tradition. All are perforated with two small holes, doubtless symbolic, but several varieties can be recognized. Obviously foreign and confined strictly to Wessex are *grape cups*—minute bowls decorated with knobs (Fig. 44, 2). Equally foreign and restricted are shallow bowls with expanding rims of fine hard ware decorated with incised triangles and ribbons, filled with punctuations and termed *Aldbourne cups* (Pl. X, 2). In technique and ornament both carry on the traditions of the Chassey ware of Normandy and Brittany.[11] Another variety of incense cup with triangular slits through its walls forming a lattice has been compared to the *vases supports* that belong to the same Chassey context. Others, decorated with finely incised lines including radial patterns on the base or with cord impressions, are not confined to Wessex. But in the Wessex culture the handled cups of shale and amber, already mentioned, may sometimes take the place of the small clay vessels.

The aristocrats of Wessex were buried with peculiar pomp. In 23 instances the bodies had been interred contracted, but 63 had been cremated. Both rites might be observed for presumably contemporary burials in the same grave.[12] Burnt and unburnt remains might be enclosed in wooden coffins [13] either hollowed out of tree-trunks or made of planks, or else laid on planks.[14] Many classic burials of this group come from bell and disc barrows, characterized by a continuous fosse surrounding them. In the bell barrow

[10] *Arch.*, lxi, 440-446.   [11] *Arch. J.*, lxxxviii, 52.   [12] *WAM.*, xlv, 432.
[13] *WAM.*, xliv, 103.   [14] *Arch.*, lii, 50.

the fosse encircles 'a large mound the slope of which is concave or which is surrounded by a well-defined berm (i.e. flat platform).'[15]   The disc barrow, on the contrary,[16] 'consists of a ditch, nearly always strictly circular, with a bank generally on its outer side, surrounding a platform of bare level ground.   In its centre is a small low mound covering a deposit of burnt bones.' Neither type is rigidly restricted either in time or space to the

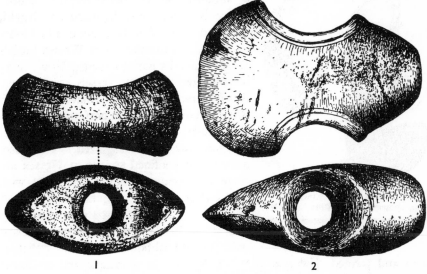

FIG. 43. STONE BATTLE-AXES. ½.

1. Double-axe form, from barrow on Windmill Hill (Devizes Museum); 2. Bann type, Eire (National Museum of Ireland).

Wessex culture; Beakers accompanied primary interments in two bell barrows, Food Vessel and Urn folk used disc barrows for interments, for instance in Berkshire.[17]   Both types cluster significantly round the great sanctuaries of fossed circles at Stonehenge and Avebury as if the one inspired the other.   At the same time a genetic relationship to the stone-walled barrows and stone circles of the Highland Zone cannot be ignored.   Barrows and sanctuaries, cairns and circles may in the long run be alike modelled on the hut-circle which the living inhabited.

Piggott suggests that the chieftains who had succeeded to the domain of the Beaker folk in Wessex were invaders from Brittany.   There indeed

[15] Grinsell, *PSEA.*, vii, 204.   [16] Crawford, *Antiquity*, i, 425.
[17] *Oxoniensia*, iii, 33.

may be found on the one hand the closest parallels to our exotic pygmy vases in 'neolithic' camps, megalithic tombs and stone circles, on the other rich burials, by cremation or inhumation, laid as in Wessex on wooden planks, and enclosed in stone chambers designed to hold only a single person. These Breton graves are furnished with grooved daggers—no less than eight fitted with gold-studded hilts, as in Wessex—flanged axes and arrow-heads with squared barbs. They agree, in fact, so closely with those

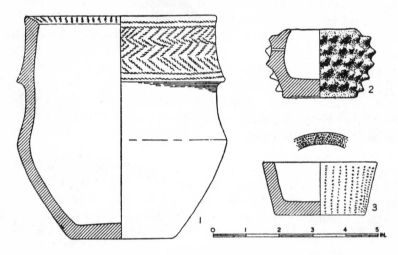

FIG. 44. FUNERARY VASES FROM BARROW AT MANTON (WILTS.). The grape cup (2) was found with objects shown in Fig. 41. After Piggott.

of Wessex that we are evidently dealing with two aspects of the same culture. Nevertheless, the dagger graves in Brittany do not contain Chassey pottery, but handled biconical urns, unknown in Wessex. The counterparts of the English grape cups and Aldbourne cups are associated with the megalithic culture partly older than the dagger graves and restricted to the southern coasts, while the separate graves of the 'Bronze Age' are concentrated rather in the interior and north of the peninsula. Moreover, the origin of the Breton culture is itself uncertain. Its authors would be somehow connected with the warlike Bell-beaker–Battle-axe population of west Central Europe, another branch of which reached England as the Beaker folk [18]; their daggers would be derived from the bronze culture of the Rhone. But the links connecting either region with Brittany are at present slight. The

[18] Hawkes, *Foundations*, 312-314.

possibility that Piggott's invasion should be reversed and that the Bronze Age intruders in Armorica came from the British Isles must not be overlooked. Relations between Britain and Armorica were certainly not one-sided; for the spacer-plate of a jet necklace was found in one dagger grave in Finistère.[19] The British relatives of the Wessex culture must therefore be examined.

That culture in its classic form is found on the chalk downs of Berkshire, Hampshire, Wiltshire and Dorset. A famous burial in an oak-tree coffin accompanied by an amber cup (in form rather different from the shale and amber cups from Wessex) (Pl. XI, 1) and a grooved dagger from Hove in Sussex might be attributed to a stray Wessex chief.[20] So perhaps might a couple of very rich barrows in Essex and Norfolk.[21]

But in Cornwall we meet a parallel culture rather than a provincial outpost of Wessex society. The relevant burials must have been very rich, but most had been plundered rather than excavated in the eighteenth and early nineteenth centuries.[22] Some had been contained in extravagantly large stone cists—one measured 7 ft.×3½ ft.×2¾ ft.—covered by enormous round cairns and were accompanied by daggers, stone double-axes and segmented beads as in Wessex. But instead of pygmy cups, the funerary vases are generally biconical urns with ring handles. They resemble the vases from the Armorican cairns, but not exactly; they are decorated with cord impressions, a device seemingly foreign to the Breton school. In one grave the shale and amber cups of Wessex were replaced by a corrugated gold mug,[23] in shape recalling a handled Beaker (Pl. XI, 2) but comparable technically to gold cups from the Shaft Graves of Mycenae.[24]

If the furniture of the Cornish graves recall Wessex, the cairns and cists are no less reminiscent of the Irish West. And at least a strong purely British substratum must be admitted.[25] And the kistvaens and stone-walled cairns of Devon and Somerset [26] are structurally connected with Cornwall as much as Wessex, though the furniture at Camerton and Priddy No. 2 in Somerset, as at Hambledon in Devon, is quite appropriate to the latter area. So, too, beyond the Bristol Channel a barrow on Breach Farm near Cowbridge (Glam.) contained with a cremation an incense cup, a grooved dagger, square-barbed arrow-heads and arrow-shaft straighteners, but in

[19] *PPS.*, v, 193.   [20] Curwen, *Arch. Sus.*, 162.
[21] *PPS.*, iv, 92.   [22] Hencken, *Arch. Corn.*, 73-76.
[23] *BMQ.*, xi, 1.   [24] Karo, *Schachtgräber*, Pl. CIV, Nos. 392-393.
[25] It is more obvious in the sequel when early examples of the Cornish two-handled urns (Abercromby, ii, Nos. 357-358) show the grooved shoulder of the Food Vessel!
[26] Dobson, pp. 71-74; note the bark coffin from Gristhorpe, Sigwell.

its structure conformed to the more western pattern—'a composite barrow with a mound of earth containing or enclosed by a stone ring.' [27]

Farther afield, barrow 139 at Towthorpe (Yorks.) [28] covered the burial of a tall man lying *extended* with a grooved dagger, a pestle-shaped mace-head and a plano-convex knife appropriate to the Food Vessel culture. So again on a peak of the Sidlaws at Westermains of Auchterhouse (Angus) an enormous composite cairn covered a cremation burial in a double cist, accompanied by a long dagger, strengthened by a stout midrib and mounted in an ox-horn hilt.[29] The core of the cairn was a mound of fine black earth, 20 ft. across and delimited by a ring of large boulders. Over it was piled a pyramidal cairn, in its turn bounded by a kerb 62 ft. in diameter. Warriors were buried extended with daggers also at Gilchorn (Arbroath), Bishopsmill (Elgin) and Craigscorrie (Beauly), while a cist at Blackwaterfoot (Arran) contained a dagger strengthened by three converging midribs with a ribbed gold band binding the hilt.[30] And we have already met a similarly gold-mounted dagger of true Wessex type associated with a type E Food Bowl at Topped Mount (Fermanagh) (p. 123).

Such princely 'dagger graves' in the Food Vessel province may, like the coffin burials,[31] belong to foreign chiefs, but hardly to Armorican invaders. But though they may thus denote further enrichments of British culture by exotic traditions, they may just as well reflect merely a concentration of wealth and power within the bosom of the Food Vessel societies themselves. If so, a similar concentration in the largest and most prosperous single province in the British Isles might suffice to explain the rise of the Wessex culture.

In any case, such a concentration did occur, and the Wessex chiefs were its beneficiaries. It produced a fitting political and economic background for the crowning achievement of Bronze Age architecture, Stonehenge itself. The Breach Farm barrow could indeed be hailed as evidence for an extension of the Wessex domain towards the Presely Mountains whence the blue stones came. Despite arguments to the contrary adduced on p. 106, Stonehenge should perhaps be regarded as a monument to the piety and power of the new plutocracy of Period IV.

Be that as it may, the wealth of the new upper class in Cornwall and

[27] Grimes, *PPS.*, iv, 106-120; cf. Fox, *Arch.*, lxxxvii, 164.
[28] Mortimer, *Forty Years*, 6.
[29] Childe, *P.S.*, 109; *PSAS.*, xxxii, 205.   [30] Childe, *Scotland Before Scots*, 119.
[31] P. 129 above; note that, as at Howe Hill, Old Brotton (Yorks.) (*YAJ.*, xxiv (1917), 266), coffin-burials are sometimes covered by ' composite cairns ' as defined by Grimes and Fox.

Wessex attracted to their tents the most skilled artificers and supported trade with Ireland, North Britain, Scandinavia, Central Europe, the Rhone valley and even the Aegean. The connexions thus established provide for the first time a reliable basis for a guess at the absolute antiquity in terms of our calendar reckoning of any phase of social development in the British Isles. The segmented fayence beads, all of a uniform type, are the most reliable indicators of Period IV as a chronological horizon. Beck and Stone [32] have proved that they were imported ready-made from the East Mediterranean. There segmented fayence beads were quite common from about 3000 B.C. onwards.[33] But the only exact parallels to the Wessex beads came from an Egyptian grave reliably dated round about 1400 B.C. While, therefore, 1400 B.C. may provisionally be accepted as falling within the life of the Wessex culture, that date might be nearer its end than its beginning, and may in fact be taken as marking the beginning of Period V. The gold-mounted amber disc from Knossos should be dated 1450 B.C. or earlier. Parallels to the Rillaton gold Beaker and Wessex types in the Shaft Graves at Mycenae should go back before 1500 B.C. British and Irish imports in Central European Aunjetitz graves and Aunjetitz imports in Wessex prove that our Period IV ran on the whole parallel to my Danubian IV period in the Danube, Elbe and Saale valleys. While segmented fayence beads do occur in some Aunjetitz graves, the consensus of opinion at present is that in Hungary and Bohemia Danubian IV should begin by 1600 B.C. or even a century earlier.[34] Admittedly the round-heeled triangular daggers, here associated with A Beakers, are proper to Danubian IV also. So that period may overlap a little with our III. But the overlap cannot be extensive, and Period IV may well begin as early as 1500 B.C. On the other hand, the sequel will show that Periods IV and V together (they cannot be sharply distinguished in the funerary record) ought to last till nearly 700 B.C.

2. The Urn Folk

The Wessex culture had been based on the same sort of primitive subsistence-farming as its predecessors, with perhaps an increased emphasis on stock-breeding and hunting. By concentrating the beggarly surplus resulting from these pursuits and by exploiting the flint-mines and perhaps

[32] *Arch.*, lxxxv, 203-252 (1935).

[33] In 1938 Dr Mallowan found a number in the foundations of a temple dated about 3000 B.C. at Tel Brak in North Syria.

[34] *AJA.*, xliv, 22-24; *Dawn*, 320-321; Hawkes, *Foundations*, 345-348.

the piety of pilgrims to their sanctuaries, a handful of chiefs had been able to amass considerable wealth. But it was expended on unproductive weapons and luxury objects, providing insufficient employment to absorb a growing population. Yet, conditions of life being favourable, population presumably did expand. The sole outlet for the surplus was to find fresh land for pasture and tillage. So the funerary record does disclose an actual migration of population which eventually reached right to Caithness and, crossing from Galloway to Ulster, spread all over Ireland too. Finally, a few of our migrants settled even overseas on the coasts of Holland and northern France. The result was an unprecedented uniformity of culture—or at least of burial rites and funerary pottery—all over the British Isles, though this uniformity may not have embraced the whole territory simultaneously, and indeed probably did not.

The migrants who affected this astonishing unification appear in the funerary record not as 'Wessex chiefs,' characterized by foreign grape and Aldbourne cups, but as members of that probably subordinate element who had preferred the purely native Cinerary Urn. Judged by their pottery, this element was recruited from people of Peterborough traditions, modified by their Beaker lords. South of the Thames, Cinerary Urns of the Overhanging Rim family (and also those of the Cornish handled variety) are really the counterparts of the Food Vessels of Yorkshire and the Highland Zone. Indeed, the Overhanging Rim Urns are just Food Vessels of unusually tall form, early specialized as containers for cremated bones, and, in Cornwall, provided with handles.

They are made of the same coarse clay by the same method of ring-building as are Peterborough and Food Vessels. Like these, they are decorated occasionally by bird's leg-bone stamps and very commonly by the imprints of a coarse twisted cord. The latter quite often form 'maggots' or horseshoe devices too.[35] But one urn from barrow 156 at Normanton (Wilts.)[36] in its zones of hyphenated line patterns and well-smoothed red exterior is really quite like a Beaker. During the long period of the culture's life the form of the urns underwent progressive modification, providing a devolution series that may serve as a rough chronometer.

In the earliest urns, according to Grimes,[37] the profile of the Peterborough bowl is preserved in a relatively shallow vertical collar-like rim, a concave neck, and a sharp shoulder which coincides with the widest part of the vase,

---

[35] Stone, *WAM.*, xlvi, 224, gives a list; cf. Childe, *P.S.*, 125-126, and *Arch. Camb.*, xci (1936), 301.

[36] *Devizes Museum Cat.*, i, No. 280; *PPS.*, iv, 91, Fig. 21, 1. [37] *Guide*, 89.

but the lower part is always an inverted truncated cone, as also in all subsequent stages (Fig. 45, 1). Next in stages II and III the collar is widened downwards till it even overhangs the neck in a flange; the neck may grow shallower and the shoulder may be rounded off (Figs. 44, 1, 45, 2). The

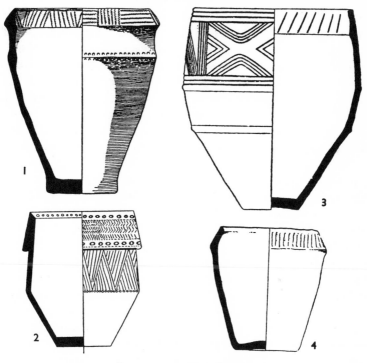

FIG. 45.   CINERARY URNS.

1. Soham (Cambs.); 2. Bleasdale (Lancs.); 3. Magdalene Bridge (Midlothian); 4. Latch Farm (Dorset); all ⅛. 1 after Clark, 2 after Varley, 4 after Piggott

devolution from this point may proceed along one of two divergent lines: in series A first the neck (stage A IV) and then (stage A V) the shoulders too are flattened out, leaving a bicone—collar and base separated only by a low moulding or a keel (Fig. 45, 4). Finally (A VI), the profile is completely smoothed out, but the place of the original collar is marked by a band of decoration. Alternatively the neck is completely flattened out, but the places of the collar-flange and the shoulder keel are taken by applied mouldings. The resultant tripartite *Cordoned Urn* is at first (stage B IV, Fig. 45, 3) biconical, later (B V) barrel-shaped. Eventually the cordons disappear, so that stage VI in both series is the same. In early stages the decoration, besides covering the collar, may spread to the neck and even onto the shoulder. Later it is restricted to the collar or its representative.

The chronological value of this series must not be over-estimated. The earliest urns of stage I are indeed practically restricted to England south of the Thames.[38] But urns of stage II-III are found practically all over Britain, from the Channel to the Moray Firth, and even in Northern Ireland. The later stages are, however, better represented in the north than the south; Cordoned Urns are virtually confined to Yorkshire, the Highland Zone and Ireland [39] (Fig. 46). But this remarkably homogeneous group of funerary vessels can only embody the traditions of a single social group. Its diffusion by recognizable steps must be connected with the actual movements of this society. Its origin south of the Thames is suggested by the typology of the urns. It is confirmed by accessory vases.

In all regions Cinerary Urns are associated with pygmy vessels. Though the grape and Aldbourne cups are never found outside Wessex, other Wessex types, including the open-work lattice variety, may be found almost anywhere in the Urn province. Other varieties have been inspired by the funerary vessels of different societies—some, for instance, are just miniature Food Vessels—but these too are perforated with the symbolic holes, alread;' noted in Wessex. These tiny ritual or symbolic vessels must represent a contribution from the 'Wessex chiefs' to the traditions of the new Urn society.

In their expansion the Urn folk occupied territories formerly inhabited by other social groups. They do not seem to have exterminated such but actually incorporated some of their traditions in their own. In Yorkshire and Derbyshire Overhanging Rim Urns succeed Food Vessels in the funerary record. But in the Urn cemeteries or burials in accordance with Urn ritual there appear *Enlarged Food Vessels*—which are just Food Vases (nearly always of the so-called 'Yorkshire' type) adapted in the light of the Urn pattern to serve as ossuaries. And these Enlarged Food Vessel Urns accompany the Overhanging Rim (and Cordoned) Urns to North Britain, Ireland and Wales. At the same time, miniature Food Vessels may accompany the larger urns. Food Vessel communities were, in fact, simply absorbed into the Urn societies.

Farther north a similar contact with, and incorporation of, Skara Brae tradi-

[38] Abercromby, *BAP.*, ii, 10-16; the arguments of Elgee (*N.E.Y.*, 82-84) for a Yorkshire origin are untenable.
[39] See map in Fox, *Personality*, Pl. VII, and Raftery, *J. Galway H.&A.S.*, xviii, 166.

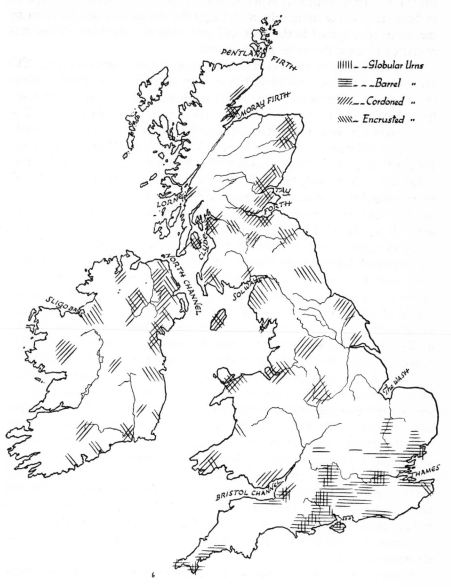

||||| _Globular Urns

≡ _ _Barrel "

/////_ _Cordoned "

_ Encrusted "

FIG. 46. DISTRIBUTION OF LATE CINERARY URNS.

tions produced what are called Encrusted Urns (Pls. XII and XIII). Fox [40] argues that these are developed out of Enlarged Food Vessels. Now several specimens from eastern Scotland and Northumberland do resemble Food Vessels both in form and decoration. But the decorative technique—applied mouldings and blobs smeared over with a thick slip enhanced with jabbed and incised patterns—is identical with that employed in the Orkney villages (p. 87). And particularly in Cumberland the designs are often similar too In Ireland and Wales they may be even more complicated; semicircular arcadings seem derived, through Food Vessels of type E, from the Beacharra repertory, while alternate ribs and knobs on some Irish urns have been compared to the corrugations and rivet-heads of bronze cauldrons. [41] The distribution of Encrusted Urns [42] coincides on the whole with that of Cordoned Urns (Fig. 46). Nevertheless, Encrusted Urns are rather commoner in Ireland and sometimes are found in apparently early contexts— e.g. in megalithic tombs (pp. 57, 68) and with Food Vessels in cists. At the moment it still seems likely that the fusion between Collared Urn and Skara Brae traditions took place in North Britain and that the composite groups spread thence to Ireland and northern Wales, much as Fox thought in 1927.

The devolution of the Collared Urn accordingly is some measure of the time taken by a wave of culture, or rather, of people, to spread over the British Isles, accumulating fresh contingents and new traditions on its way. Starting south of the Thames while the Wessex culture was still in its heyday, and reaching Yorkshire and Derbyshire while segmented fayence beads were still current, it survives in Ross-shire into La Tène times and in Co. Limerick perhaps later still. For the central cist in a cairn near Edderton contained a La Tène glass bead while a Cordoned Urn covered a secondary burial in the surrounding trench. [43] And at Cush an abandoned rath whose inhabitants had used flat rotary querns was used as a cemetery comprising burials in a Cordoned Urn and in an Enlarged Food Vessel. [44] Yet throughout this long period—approximately twelve centuries—funerary pottery and burial rites remained stable within the Urn societies.

The barrows heaped over primary Urn burials are often no less carefully constructed than those of Wessex chiefs. In southern England, indeed, some Urn burials lie at the centre of true bell barrows, and as far away as Ross and Mayo [45] more or less debased versions of this type may be recog-

---

[40] *Ant. J.*, vii, 113-134.
[42] cf. Pls. VI and VII in Fox, *Personality*.
[44] *PRIA.*, xlv, C, 104-113, 166-169, 176.
[41] *PRIA.* (1899), 344.
[43] *PSAS.*, v, 312; Childe, *P.S.*, 138.
[45] *J. Galway H.&A.S.*, xviii, 158-166.

nized. Composite barrows were heaped up too. In the Pond Cairn near
Coity (Glam.) [46] the primary burial was covered with a pile of stones above
which a turf stack had been built up, the whole being subsequently enclosed
in a ring cairn reveted on both sides with built walls. Settings of slabs and
rings of uprights are associated with Urn barrows as with others.[47]

Similarly, Urn burials are often found in stone circles, though generally
as secondaries. Near Lough Gur (Co. Limerick), a small ring of tall uprights
enclosed a flat platform-mound covering cremations in Cordoned Urns.
In Cumberland and Westmorland urns occur, not certainly as primaries, in
cairn circles the peristaliths of which include stones adorned with pecked
spirals.[48] Finally, at Bleasdale on the edge of the Pennines in Lancashire
one of the most remarkable monuments in England had been built round
an Urn chief.[49] The burials in two Collared Urns (Fig. 45, 2) lay in a pit
4 ft.$\times 2\frac{1}{2}$ ft.$\times 1\frac{1}{2}$ ft. It was encircled by a ring of eleven stout oak posts,
36 ft. in diameter, outside which ran a penannular ditch, lined with birch
poles and interrupted on the east by a causeway flanked by two gate-posts;
the upcast from the ditch had been heaped as a low mound over the central
area. The whole complex was then enclosed in a palisade of poles, close-set
between oak posts spaced at 15 ft. intervals. The palisade ring had a
diameter of 150 ft., was set eccentrically to the inner monument the ditch
of which nearly touched it at the causeway, and was entered by a gap on
the south-south-west (Fig. 47).

This exceptional monument combines features proper to the non-
sepulchral entrenched circles of Period III-IV and to the palisade circles
buried under Yorkshire and Welsh barrows of the Food Vessel complex.
But it cannot itself be earlier than Period V, while its closest analogies are
to be found in Dutch barrows which generally cover Beaker burials!

Quite often Urn burials are found unmarked by any surviving superficial
monument. Occasionally in southern England,[50] more frequently in the
Highland Zone, they are clustered in cemeteries or urnfields comprising up
to 30 interments, not all enclosed in urns, and sometimes stated to have
been laid out in circles or in rows.[51] On Pule Hill near Todmorden (Lancs.)
an earth bank, 3 ft. wide, enclosed a circular area, 90 ft. across, with an
Overhanging Rim Urn in the centre and four other urns, four pygmy vessels
and unurned cremations around it.[52] So at Loanhead of Daviot (Aberdeen-

[46] *Arch.*, lxxxvii, 143-154.
[47] e.g. Elgee, *Arch. Yorks.*, 78; Childe, *P.S.*, 128; *T.C. & W.A. & A.S.*, x, 340-350.
[48] *VCH. Cumberland*, i, 241; *T.C. & W.A. & A.S.*, i, 298.
[49] Varley, *Ant. J.*, xviii, 156-168.   [50] *WAM.*, xlvi, 220.
[51] Childe, *P.S.*, 130-131.   [52] *Reliquary*, ix (1903), 278.

shire) 30 cremations, only 14 inurned, had been deposited in a circular area, 35 ft. in diameter and surrounded by a narrow trench interrupted at

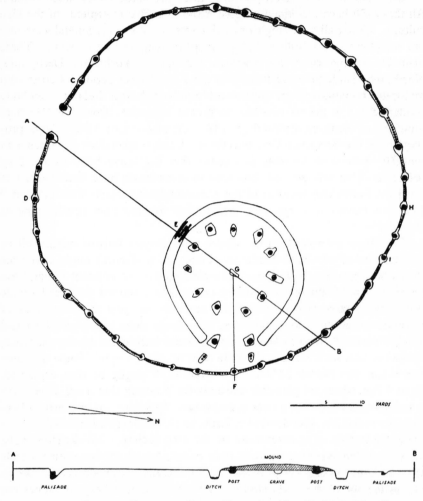

FIG. 47. PLAN OF BLEASDALE CIRCLE (LANCS.). After Varley in *Ant. J.*

two points and abutting on a Recumbent Stone Circle.[53] Often, too, Urn burials and unurned cremations under a single barrow are so numerous as to deserve the name cemeteries or, as Elgee says,[54] 'family mausolea.' One

[53] *PSAS.*, lxx, 278-310.   [54] *N.E.Y.*, 95-96; *Arch. Yorks.*, 78.

barrow in north-east Yorkshire covered 17 vessels and 3 cremations without urns.

On Stanton Moor (Derbyshire) [55] there are some thirty small tumuli. All that have been examined covered three to twelve interments of the Urn culture. Under all were single or double settings of stones, generally circular but sometimes rectangular; T. 13 was 40 ft. long and 22 ft. wide. These mausolea simply carry on practices familiar in Yorkshire, Derbyshire, Northumberland, Fife and Ireland in the Food Vessel period. Cairns with multiple cremations from south-west Scotland [56] and Ireland [57] embody similar ideas; it seems needless to invoke influences from the 'Urnfield invaders' of southern England (p. 188) to explain them. But a large proportion of the recorded Urn burials are frankly secondary interments in round or even long barrows and cairns that may have been erected long before the Urn folk arrived, but may in some cases have been heaped to cover the immediate ancestor of the persons whose remains were inurned.[58] The Urn burials in megalithic chambers in Ireland may equally rank as secondaries.[59]

The single interments at the centre of a complex barrow might well be the remains of chiefs or headmen; Pond Cairn (Glam.) might cover the chief whose retainers were buried as secondaries in the adjacent Simondston Cairn (p. 157). But the secondary cremations intruded into ready-made cairns, the family mausolea and the urnfields are just the cemeteries of communities all of whose members, not chiefs alone, were cremated and ritually buried. Nevertheless, there are some indications of the existence, within the Urn societies, of a class too poor to afford a pyre. Some skeletons interred in the Barton Mill Barrow (Suffolk) [60] might be thus explained. Elgee [61] has advanced plausible grounds for thinking that *small cairns* such as are so common on the moors of north-east Yorkshire—as in Northumberland, Berwickshire, Aberdeenshire, Sutherland, Cumberland and Galloway—cover the burials of a lower class in the Urn society. No skeletons have indeed been recovered from such little cairns, but in the lime-hungry soils unburnt bone would be consumed. Nevertheless, the sepulchral use as well as the age of the small cairns is doubtful. Similar heaps of stones are

---

[55] *DAJ.* (1930), 1-44; (1936), 21-35; (1939), 105-115.

[56] e.g. Ardeer, 19 interments: *PSAS.*, xl, 378.

[57] *PRIA.*, xli, 254-257; *PPS.*, iii, 380.

[58] Childe, *P.S.*, 129; so in Ireland five cremations had been intruded into the cairn covering an entrance grave at Harristown, Co. Waterford (p. 75).

[59] Cf. pp. 57, 68.

[60] *PCAS.*, xxvi, 28-56.   [61] *N.E.Y.*, 97-100; *Arch. Yorks.*, 81.

associated with remains of prehistoric, Iron Age cultivations on the heaths of western Norway and are taken by Pedersen[62] to be mere dumps of stones gathered from the fields.

Despite the large composite barrows and hill-top cairns which cover

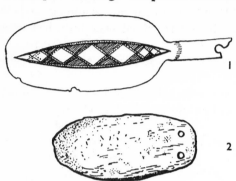

some Urn burials, the general furniture is poor in contrast to the wealth of the chieftain's burials in Wessex. This poverty may, however, be due to the eschatological ideas associated with cremation. A very few burials were accompanied by small, narrow knife-daggers, hardly suited for use as weapons.[63] Flint arrow-heads are slightly commoner; they are usually rather rough and tanged-and-barbed, but at least one urn at

FIG. 48. 'RAZORS.'—1. Pollacorragune; 2. Carrowjames (Galway). ½.

Crooks near Sheffield contained a leaf-shaped head of 'neolithic' type.[64] Finally, in North Britain and Ireland some Urn men carried battle-axes or mace-heads (Fig. 43, 2) derived from the stone 'double-axes' proper to Period IV.[65] A moulding is generally developed along the sides. The blade is splayed, the butt lengthened into a truncated cone.[66] Transported to Northern Ireland this variant became so popular along the Bann that it is termed the Bann type. Alternatively both blades of the double-axe are blunted till the weapon becomes a mace-head of the Crichie type most popular in north-eastern Scotland and there associated with Cordoned Urns.[67]

In Scotland and Ireland, razors, doubtless ritual, are associated with Cordoned Urns.[68] The earliest (Fig. 48, 1) are thin oval blades with a flat perforated tang and a wide midrib which is decorated with finely incised patterns of triangles and lozenges in the old Bronze Age style. In a derivative form confined to Eire (Fig. 48, 2) the tang is abbreviated or

[62] *Gamle Gardsanlag i Rogaland.*
[63] e.g. Wilmslow, Ches.: *JBAA.,* xvi (1860), Pl. 25; Tomen y Muer, Merion.: *Arch. J.,* xxiv (1867), 16; Creggan, Antrim: *PRIA.,* xxxiii, C, 1; list, *Arch. Camb.,* lxxxiii (1928), 145.
[64] *Trans. Hunter Arch. Soc.* (Dec. 1928). [65] *Arch.,* lxxv, 90-105.
[66] *Arch.,* lxxv, 99-103; Childe, *P.S.,* Fig. 32; *PSAS.,* lxxii, 241-247.
[67] Childe, *P.S.,* 132-134.
[68] Childe, *P.S.,* 136-137; *J. Galway H.&A.S.,* xvii (1936), 48; xviii (1939), 167; *N. Munster Ant. J.* (1936), 34.

suppressed, the rivet-hole transferred to the base of the blade and the decoration omitted. Similar tanged oval blades, but undecorated, are associated with the Deverel–Rimbury culture of southern England, and the device may have been borrowed from these invaders (p. 193) by the native Urn folk who would have added decoration in their own traditional style.[69] In addition, one Scottish and one Irish Urn burial were furnished with small narrow blades with notches, instead of rivet-holes, at the base,[70] which agree curiously with blades assigned to the Copper Age in southern Spain and Portugal.[71]

A few distinctive ornaments are associated with Urns. Segmented fayence beads of Egyptian type and/or quoit-shaped beads of the same

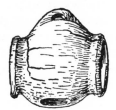

FIG. 49.   Bone toggle or bead from Over-Migvie (Angus). ¼.
After *PSAS*.

material are found with urns not only in Wessex but also in Sussex, Derbyshire and Wales. In Ayrshire, on Clydeside, and in Strathmore too, segmented and even star-shaped beads of vitreous material have been found in Cordoned Urns, but these differ in texture and form from the southern specimens and cannot be dated.[72] In several Scottish burials bone toggles in the shape of cylinders transversely and longitudinally perforated with carved mouldings at the ends (Fig. 49) had been worn. They agree in every detail with bone toggles, dated by Broholm [73] 700-650 B.C., in Denmark, but are also comparable to a gold toggle from a Wessex grave. An Urn burial discovered in 1939 at Breckmont Mill near Leuchars [73'] contained in addition to a toggle a hooked scabbard-mount of bone that is an accurate copy of the gold one (Fig. 38, 3) from the Wessex burial in Bush

[69] For a possible Italian prototype see *BPI.*, xxxv, Pl. X; cf. Sumerian razors, Childe, *New Light on the Most Ancient East*, Fig. 65, 5.

[70] Gilchorn, Arbroath: Childe, *P.S.*, 137; Harristown, Co. Waterford, unpublished.

[71] Childe, *Dawn*, Fig. 128.

[72] Childe, *P.S.*, 135-136; *Arch.*, lxxxv, 206; star-shaped beads occur also in Derbyshire, *DAJ.* (1939), 120.

[73] *Studier øver den yngre Bronsålder*, 109, 250.   [73'] *PSAS.*, lxxvi, 88.

Barrow (Wilts.). Like the segmented beads and some other ornaments,[74] it shows how tenaciously the Urn folk clung even in Scotland to the fashions popularized by the prestige of the southern chieftains.

Urns of the families here described are quite the commonest sort of funerary vessel in England and Wales, exceeding in number Beakers and Food Vessels combined. For the north of England Raistrick[75] has enumerated 666 Cinerary Urns as against 126 Beakers and 256 Food Vessels. His figures are incomplete but probably give the correct proportion of surviving vases. Yet Cinerary Urns, being particularly friable, rarely enclosed in cists and usually exposed by casual ploughing or sand-digging, have very much less chance of being preserved and recorded than the smaller and finer vases from barrows of Periods III and IV. Moreover, there are the unurned cremations belonging to the same societies that are ignored save by the most careful excavators. Even without Elgee's small cairns the burials of Urn folk in Great Britain may be reckoned safely as four times as numerous as those of Food Vessel and Beaker folks combined; in Ireland Food Vessel interments may exceed those accompanied by Cinerary Urns.

Since Cinerary Urns were current for some 1200 years the above figures cannot be taken as proving growth in population. But the area of settlement was extended. The Urn folk occupied not only the areas of easy settlement as defined on p. 33, but spread also onto less attractive lands, too marshy or too barren to have been colonized by the less congested Beaker and Food Vessel populations. So they settled on sandstone knolls and ridges and on patches of heath-clad gravel in the marshy and heavily wooded Cheshire plain[76]; they advanced beyond the Cleveland Hills onto the black moorlands of north-east Yorkshire,[77] onto the fells of the Lake District[78] and onto the gritstone moors of the Pennines, deserted since mesolithic times.[79] This expansion of Urn peoples into regions unoccupied by their immediate predecessors who made Food Vessels must be due to a growth in population just as much as the occupation of those predecessors' lands had been—a growth not offset by any improvements in rural economy.

Indeed, Varley has noted that the newly colonized territories are better adapted to pigs and goats than to cattle and sheep. Their occupation may have been made possible by an intensification of swine-breeding at the

---

[74] e.g. crutch-head pin: *PSAS.*, l, 303; clay button-toggles like Fig. 41, 12: *DAJ.* (1936), 29.

[75] *Arch. Ael.*, 4, viii (1931), 157.

[76] Varley, *J. Ches. A.&H.S.*, xxix, 59.

[77] Elgee, *N.E.Y.*, 88.

[78] RC. *Westmorland*, p. xxx.

[79] *Ant. J.*, xviii, 165.

expense of mixed farming. Nevertheless, the role of agriculture must not be unduly minimized on the strength of the unfertile situations of many urnfields and urn barrows. The usual evidences for a cereal diet—querns— are not to be anticipated in poorly furnished cremation graves. But grains of wheat, barley and even flax [80] have been detected in the clay of Cinerary Urns. Indeed, the oldest deposit of authenticated barley grains in the British Isles comes from an urn barrow (the Pond Cairn in Glamorgan), [80a] as did the earliest recorded instance in the world of the use of coal for fuel.[81] In fact, though stock-breeding—and of course hunting—outweighed corn-growing, the Urn folk need have been little more nomadic and exclusively pastoral than the mediaeval Welsh as described by Giraldus Cambrensis or the Highlanders before the Forty-Five. We have, in fact, some fields probably belonging to the Urn folk on the moors of Yorkshire and Devon. On the Cleveland Moors are irregular curvilinear enclosures—measuring in one case 108 ft. by 60 ft.—round which stones have been carelessly heaped up. They are lyncheted across the slope (p. 190), but the lynchets are so low that the fields cannot have been tilled for long. And while the small stones have been picked off, heavier stones have been left cumbering their surfaces so that they cannot have been tilled with a plough but only with a digging stick or a caschróm.[82] On Dartmoor small enclosures are connected with some clusters of hut-circles; at Trowlesworthy the eight patches of cultivated fields connected with no less than 40 hut-circles make up only 4 acres in all. On Standon Down 5 acres, divided among 15 plots, go to 60 hut-circles.[83]

Apart from these rural pursuits there were naturally domestic industries, including weaving; a piece of woollen fabric found in an Urn near Coniston had 33 threads to the inch in the weave—an exceptionally fine textile product.[84] Flint was doubtless still mined and exported, but probably on a smaller scale than hitherto, as bronze must have been becoming more common. But the bronze-smiths and traders seem to have been excluded from the ranks of those entitled to inurnment. We can identify no grave as a smith's by the tools of his craft. And the distribution of types of tool and weapon distinctive of the several phases of the bronze industry's development at no time coincides with that of any variety of Cinerary Urn. Metal-workers, in fact, seem to have been 'detribalized,' or rather to have formed

[80] Jessen and Helback, 55.   [80a] Arch., lxxxvii, 150.

[81] Arch., lxxxvii, 137, with secondary at Simondston (Glam.).   [82] Elgee, N.E.Y., 146.

[83] Curwen, PPS., iv, 37; it is by no means certain that all circles were dwellings or that all were inhabited contemporaneously.

[84] T.C. & W.A. & A.S., x, 350.

a society of their own. Though our Urn folk must have been the principal purchasers for their products in Great Britain, these products and their makers are more conveniently treated apart. We may, however, mention here some settlements, plausibly but not with absolute certainty, attributed to the Urn folk.

In the Upper Thames valley all that survives are ring ditches enclosing areas 30 to 66 ft. in diameter,[85] presenting, as Leeds notes,[86] a significant resemblance to disc barrows. They may mark the emplacements for tents or even farmyards in which stood a tent or other equally perishable dwelling. In Yorkshire the dwellings proper are equally absent, but Elgee[87] has recognized some settlement sites. That on Danby Rigg, a spur some 1000 ft. above sea-level, is cut off from the main massif on the south by a double dyke of stone walls with a ditch between them, and down-hill is protected on the north by a single wall. These defences isolate a stony area some 400 yds. wide and 700 yds. long, outside which is a 'cemetery' of 800 small cairns and a stone circle which contained a late Collared Urn.

Finally, on the high moors of south-western England the absence of intensive modern agriculture has preserved the remains of numerous settlements as well as cairns, stone circles and alignments. Only those on Dartmoor have been at all seriously explored, and even here the relics recovered and the plans published do not suffice for a classification of the monuments into chronological or cultural groups. While it is plain that not all are of the same age, it is much less plain to what extent the occupation of any site was confined to a single period. Most sites lie above the 500 ft. contour on moorlands that may already have been stripped of forest by the gales.

The dwellings are the familiar hut-circles, but mostly of specialized form.[88] The walls are generally faced with stone and sometimes still stand $3\frac{1}{2}$ or 4 ft. high; at that level a stone lintel spanning the entrance gap or passage shows that the masonry can hardly have been carried higher. The roof resting on the walls may have been conical and supported by a central post the socket for which survives in the hut floor. Near the centre or against the wall behind it was a simple slab hearth on which a peat fire had burned, and beside it a 'cooking-hole,' a depression 1 ft. 9 ins. by 1 ft. 4 ins. at the mouth and some 1 ft. 3 ins. deep. The rear segment or one side was raised to form a built daïs. Some huts occur in isolation, but often they are clustered to form hamlets of various types.

[85] *Arch.*, lxxvi, 60.
[87] *N.E.Y.*, 134-136.

[86] *Oxoniensia*, iii, 38.
[88] *TDA.*, xxviii, 175.

Pounds are circular enclosures bounded by stone walls which contain from 3 to 20 hut-circles. They are often situated on improved pastures or arable land, sometimes near modern farms, never on naturally defended hill-tops or ridges. Nor do the stone walls look like formidable military works. Grimspound,[89] the best preserved, was girt with a double wall, the over-all width of which was about 10 ft. though it can hardly have stood more than 5½ ft. high. Within were 20 circles, from 9½ to 15 ft. in diameter. But at least 8 of these lacked hearth, daïs and other domestic fixtures and have been interpreted as cattle-stalls in view of their wide entrances. A stream runs through the enclosure, but this feature is exceptional. Most pounds are a hundred yards or more from water.

These circular enclosures might be the secular counterparts of the round sanctuaries wherein Bronze Age societies expressed their religious unity. They are not fenced villages—near Postbridge there are remains of some fifteen pounds in an area of little more than a square mile [90]—but rather steadings in which members of a joint family or clan might find refuge for themselves and their beasts against marauding wolves and bears. Judging from the absence of querns their occupants should have been almost exclusively pastoral.

But there are also on the moor groups of from 5 to 60 hut-circles connected with low walls or baulks that seem to demarcate corn plots. The circles here are relatively large—15 to 25 ft. in diameter—and the plots normally small and irregular.[91] But a few clusters, as at Foales Arishes and Kestor, are connected with large rectangular enclosures comparable to the Celtic fields described in Chapter X. These latter are not earlier than the Deverel–Rimbury invasion.[92] The rest have been attributed to anything from neolithic and Beaker times onwards, but circles at Smallacombe Rocks and perhaps Raddick and Grimspound had been occupied by Urn folk using Cinerary Urns of the Cornish type.[93]

Finally, the hill-top camp on Whit Tor, girt with two stone walls, each 10 ft. thick and enclosing an area of 1½ acres, has been regarded as a tribal refuge for the inhabitants of the circles and pounds in the valley below.[94] But to what extent Whit Tor and the corresponding Cornish fort at Rough Tor [95] can be termed Bronze Age is uncertain.

The very numerous ring forts of Ireland may be compared to some

[89] *TDA.*, xxvi, 113 ff.; xxvii, 82 ff.
[90] *TDA.*, xxvi, 187.
[92] *TDA.*, xxix, 153; Radford, *CISPP.*, 139.
[94] *TDA.*, xxxi, 147.

[91] *TDA.*, xxviii, 183, 184; *supra*, p. 157.
[93] *TDA.*, xxix, 157, 191.
[95] Hencken, *Arch. Corn.*, 100-101.

extent to the Dartmoor pounds both in form and function, and some at least seem to have been built under the auspices of the Urn folk who invaded that island from Britain. All are circular, most quite small, and few situated in naturally defensible positions. On drift and clay country the ring appears as an earthen bank with a ditch outside it; such is technically termed a *rath*. On rocky ground the earthen bank and ditch are replaced by a built masonry wall, some 10 ft. thick, giving what is known as a *cashel* (castellum) or *caher* (castra). Within there is room for one or two houses to which is usually connected a subterranean chamber or cellar termed a *souterrain*. This in its simplest form is just a gallery with walls of undressed boulders built in a wide trench dug in the soil or cut in the rock, and roofed with stone lintels or less often with wooden beams. There are, however, many variations in plan and in size.

In a general way a rath seems to have been the fortified steading of a farmer, or a local chief sometimes with accommodation for fellow-clansmen or retainers. Even the largest may be more aptly compared to the 'compound' of an African chief than to a Mediterranean city. The souterrain again may be just a cellar but is generally taken to be also a refuge against the weather and against human foes. A souterrain could not withstand a siege any more than a ring fort, but it would offer a relatively safe asylum for women and children in case of sudden attack by cattle-reevers, agents of a blood-feud, or head-hunters.

Souterrains were used as refuges even in the days of Cromwell, but most excavated examples, like many raths, show evidences of occupation in the Dark Ages between A.D. 500 and 1100. But at Cush (Co. Limerick; Fig. 83, 21), Ó Riordáin [96] has recently excavated a group of six small raths, 60 to 75 ft. in internal diameter, of considerably higher antiquity (Fig. 50). For rath 5 had been used as a cemetery for cremation burials, one in an Enlarged Food Vessel and another in a Cordoned Urn. According to the excavator its use as a place of burial began only after its abandonment as an habitation and after the collapse of the roof of its souterrain (this consisted of two chambers respectively 10 and 12 ft. long and 3½ and 5 ft. wide, connected by a short passage only 2 ft. high). Now two or more successive round houses had been built and demolished in this rath before its abandonment, and rath 4 was built before rath 5. All these events must be earlier than the burial in a Cordoned Urn, provided the excavator's deductions be correct. On the other hand, all the forts, including 5, yielded iron objects or slag and numerous flat-faced rotary querns of a type unknown

[96] *PRIA.*, xlv, C, 83-181.

in England before 50 B.C., while in rath 5 was also part of a composite bone comb such as occur in Britain first in the Roman period.

It is thus unlikely that the Urn burials in rath 5 took place before the

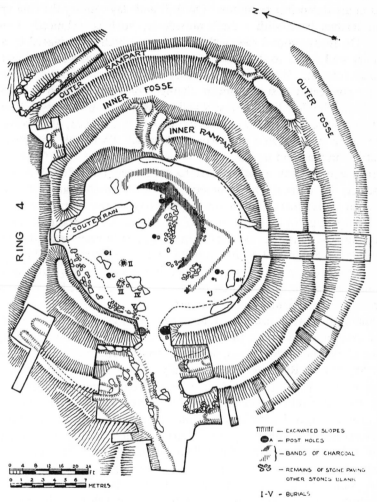

FIG. 50. PLAN OF RATH 5 AT CUSH.
After Ó Riordáin in *PRIA*.

first century B.C. at earliest. None the less the tradition of the Cinerary Urn was still alive at that date, and the oldest ring fort yet found in Ireland belonged to members of the Urn societies. Of course these had adopted technical processes and other cultural elements from groups to be considered later, and it is too soon to decide to what extent the idea of the souterrain and the intensified agriculture, implied by the numerous querns, had been similarly inspired. The funerary practice, in any case, is based on the Bronze Age tradition, and in the light of the Dartmoor pounds it is not too rash to ascribe to it the ring fort itself and the social structure associated therewith. In other words, the dominant social group in south-western Ireland at the beginning of our era was just the Urn folk whose spread over Britain and thence to Ireland we have traced in the funerary record. However much they may have been modified by older populations whom they absorbed in Ireland as previously in Britain [97] and by the small groups of La Tène invaders to be mentioned below, the Urn folk should still be strong enough to determine the linguistic complexion of the island as they still dominated its funerary ritual. That is to say, the Urn folk spoke Goidelic, unless—or even if—the Food Vessel people, whom they superseded but did not exterminate, had already spoken Goidelic.[98]

[97] We should again insist that in Ireland, as in England, native Food Vessels may occur in the same grave as Cinerary Urns, and Irish Food Bowls might be diminished to serve as pygmy vessels, showing, as in England, a fusion between the two groups.

[98] Nevertheless, the complete absence of any reference to cremation in the later Irish literature of the Heroic Age might denote a complete break in the dominant population; cf. Gogan, *J. Cork H.&A.S.*, xxxiv, 68.

CHAPTER IX

THE OLDEST INDUSTRY AND TRADE OF BRITAIN

1. THE MIDDLE BRONZE AGE

POSSESSION of copper and tin and geographical advantages made the British Isles manufacturing countries, producing for a world market when bronze was the principal industrial metal. Yet this oldest industry is very imperfectly represented in the funerary record; the cemeteries tell us even less of the smiths and miners who won for the British Isles a leading position in prehistoric trade than they do of the humble artisans of the nineteenth century. Perhaps metal-workers formed a class apart, a distinct society excluded from the ranks of those entitled to ceremonial burial. But if they were thus 'detribalized,' they were *ipso facto* liberated from the bonds of local custom and enjoyed freedom to travel and settle where they could find markets for their products and their skill, not only in the British Isles but even abroad. Metallurgists must, then, be treated as a distinct society.

They are known only by their products—a few found in graves of Periods III and IV, the majority lost or hidden as hoards (p. 118). Thanks to the progressive improvement illustrated by these finds, the prehistory of the metal industry can be divided into several phases, each characterized by distinctive improvements in tools and weapons.

The first phase, the Early Bronze Age, is characterized by flat or hammer-flanged axes, West European and flat triangular daggers and presumably the oldest Irish halberds, as well as by gold-work in the sheet style. We saw in Chapter VI how such products were purchased by Beaker folk and thus dated to Period III, and how the industry was based on Iberian traditions, presumably introduced with the Boyne culture. The rich dagger graves of Wessex show how the Irish school was fertilized in England during our Period IV by absorbing new ideas from Central Europe (135). The second phase (Middle Bronze Age I) is thus characterized by axes with cast flanges (Fig. 51, 5), daggers strengthened with grooves or midribs and sometimes ogival in outline (Fig. 39), and tanged spear-heads. These types were at first confined to England, where we encounter them both in graves

163

and in hoards.[1] Outside Lowland England old-fashioned types of axe and dagger persisted, occurring, for instance, in a Scottish hoard with basket-shaped earrings fashionable early in Period IV.[2] Both phases are therefore sometimes grouped together as Early Bronze Age, as on the Continent. But by the second phase of this period at least the Irish smiths were exporting advanced halberds, decorated axes, gold lunulae and earrings, and even ornaments in the bar style, to Denmark, Sweden, Central Germany, Bavaria and Brittany (pp. 117, 124), arriving everywhere during the first phase of the local Bronze Ages (Montelius' I, Reinecke A) or in the North still in the Stone Age (Montelius' Neolithic IV).

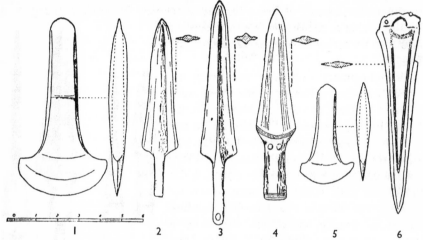

FIG. 51. PART OF A HOARD FROM ARRETON DOWN (I.O.W.).
1. Axe with cast flanges and incipient stop ridge; 2-3. Tanged spear-heads; 4. Socketed spear-head; 5. Flanged axe; 6. Dirk. After Piggott.

Naturally the innovations soon penetrated to Ireland, and before the end of Period IV we have an industry which is neither English nor Irish but Britannico–Hibernian. A flanged axe in the Westbury hoard is decorated in Irish style, though with more elaborate and carefully planned designs than adorn the flat axes of phase 1. Such decorated axes are still commoner in Ireland than in England, though the discrepancy is less marked [3]; they denote a return of the native tradition from England. The daggers of Wessex type too were made in Ireland, as the mould for an ogival

[1] Plymstock (Devon), Stoke Abbott (Dorset), Westbury (Glos.), Arreton Down (Isle of Wight): *PPS.*, iv, 88. Ebnal (Salop) (Wheeler, *Wales*, Fig. 50) belongs already to phase 3.
[2] Migdale (Sutherland): *PSAS.*, xxxv, 266; lvii, 126-133.
[3] *PPS.*, iv, 289.

dagger shows.[4]   Tanged spear-heads (Fig. 51, 3) are represented in Scotland by a single example from Ayrshire and are extremely rare in Ireland.[5] But moulds for casting such, and even for the collar that reinforces the junction of blade and shaft in the oldest Wessex type, were found at Omagh (Tyrone).[6]

By the Middle Bronze Age the rhomboid tanged spear-head with collar was being imitated by a socketed spear-head with similar blade, inspired by Aunjetitz models and cast in the Danubian technique, represented at Arreton Down (Fig. 51, 4).   This is already commoner in Ireland than in Britain.[7]   And in phase 3 Irish smiths provided it with a pair of loops on the socket instead of holes for the attachment of binding thongs [8]—a device peculiar to the British Isles and applied already to the earlier separate collar at Omagh[9] (Fig. 52, 1).

A rudimentary stop-ridge was being inserted between the flanges of axes that were exported to the Continent in Middle Bronze Age 1 (Fig. 51, 1), and led in Middle Bronze Age 2 to the true *palstave* in which the section below the stop-ridge is cast solid and often ornamented with a vertical rib (simulating the end of the shaft which had once shown up between the flanges); a loop for binding thongs is usually added on one side, a feature again distinctive of the British Isles (Fig. 53, 4).

1   2

FIG. 52.   SPEAR-HEADS.

1. From Ireland; 2. From a Wessex grave at Snow's Hill (Glos.). The tanged blade and ferrule are separate castings. By permission of the Trustees of the British Museum.

Finally, the ogival dagger might be elongated to form a dirk or even a rapier (Fig. 53, 1); one from Ireland attains a length of 2½ ft.[10]   The rapiers have a very broad square butt, the outermost rivet-holes taking the form of crescentic notches on the edge. This type too must have been inspired immediately by the similar rapiers

[4] Evans, *Bronze*, Fig. 519.   [5] *Ibid.*, p. 259.   [6] *Arch.*, lxi, 446 and Pl. LXXXI.
[7] Greenwell enumerated 15 Irish, 5 English and 5 Scottish specimens.
[8] Sprockhoff (*MZ.*, xxix (1934), 56-60) shows that Early Bronze Age spear-heads were attached by leather thongs, not pegs.
[9] The translation into bronze of the flint-javelin heads (p. 69) produced a peculiar Irish spear-head with rapier-like blade: Evans, *Arch.*, lxxxiii, 194, corrected by Mahr, *PPS.*, iii, 370.   [10] *Arch.*, lxxiii, 255.

of the Tumulus Bronze Age in South-West Germany and Bohemia, ultimately perhaps by the much longer weapons current in Mycenaean Greece from 1600 B.C.

The best diagnostic types of the Middle Bronze Age—palstaves, rapiers

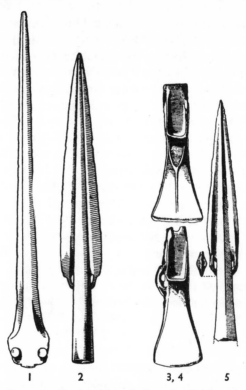

FIG. 53. Rapier (1) and Spear-head (2) with basal loops from Maentwrog hoard, ⅓; Palstaves (3, 4) and Spear-head (5) from Stibbard, ¼. By permission of the Trustees of the British Museum.

and spear-heads with looped sockets—can all be regarded as weapons. There is little evidence that metallurgy was yet being used to provide anyone save the smiths themselves with better tools; the tracer or chisel-shaped punch with two lateral projections is certainly dated to this phase,[11] the palstave chisel[12] probably. Both could be best utilized in metal-work.

[11] e.g. in the Westbury hoard; on use see Maryon, *Ant. J.*, xviii, 243-245.
[12] A narrow palstave with the blade parallel to the flanges: Evans, *Bronze*, 85, 105; Childe, *P.S.*, 147.

Ornaments suitable for warriors' wives must have still been turned out, though in the absence of grave-finds it is very uncertain what new fashions characterized the Middle Bronze Age. Funicular torques of the Tara type are generally supposed to belong here, as are earrings composed in a similar manner. In Mycenaean Greece and Cyprus, between 1500 and 1300 B.C., ladies wore earrings composed of strips of gold ribbon folded to a V section, soldered together and finally twisted. It is commonly stated that this process was employed in making earrings of similar form and the Tara torques in Ireland. But Maryon [13] has shown that the Irish goldsmiths did not employ this process in making the torques and knew nothing of solder till the Late Bronze Age. To reproduce the effect of the Mycenaean ornaments they improved on the process already employed in phase 2; in the cast gold bar grooves were cut at equal intervals along the whole length save for strips at each end to serve as terminals. The four members of the bar were then hammered flat, producing a bar of cruciform section with four flanges. The work was then annealed and twisted into a funicular or screw pattern.

The Middle Bronze Age is generally described as 'an age of peaceful development.' The distinctive metal-types—weapons of war and ornaments for a warrior's spouse—belie that description,[14] unless it mean that neither metal-work nor yet pottery and burial rites give any hint of deflection or disturbance by aggression from without.[15] But foreign trade still flourished. In Northern Europe imported Britannico–Hibernian types with stop-ridge between the flanges (Fig. 51, 1) provided the starting-point for the local series of palstaves.[16] Early forms of mature palstaves from the British Isles reached Central Germany and even Hungary.[17] A rapier from these islands like Fig. 51, 6 (or at least from Western Europe), accompanied flanged axes and a true Northern spear-head in a hoard from Virring (Jutland) that is older than the earliest Danish Bronze Age graves and so contemporary with the latest burials in long cists of Montelius' Neolithic IV.[18]

A British spear-head with loops on the socket and a leaf-shaped blade was comprised in a hoard from Danzig Heights.[19] A whole series of East European double-looped spear-heads may have started with such imports.

---

[13] PRIA., xliv, C, 207. [14] Fox, Arch., lxxxvii, 164.

[15] But a skeleton accompanied by a Danish palstave from a barrow near Driffield (Yorks.) might belong to a raider of this period: Ant. J., iii, 370.

[16] Forssander, Ostskandinavisch., 220.

[17] Böhm, Die ältere Bronzezeit Mark-Brandenburg, 49, T. 9, 13; Hampel, Altertümer der Bronzezeit in Ungarn, Pl. VIII, 8.

[18] Forssander, Ostskandinavisch., 195, Pl. XL. [19] Šturms, Ostbaltikum, 29.

In Holland and northern Gaul Britannico–Hibernian spear-heads and other imports are abundant. Trade with the South-West is illustrated by looped palstaves from northern Spain and Portugal. In the Peninsula the insular type was transformed into a double-looped palstave, a few examples of which were traded back to England, Wales and Ireland.[20] These return imports mostly belong to the Late Bronze Age, though a rather exceptional example is said to have been found with a trilobate pin, a tanged blade and Cinerary Urns under a cairn at Bryn Crûg (Caernarvon).[21] The interchange of products with the mining regions of north-western Spain admirably illustrates how metal-workers kept in touch with fellow-craftsmen even across the stormy Bay of Biscay.

The chief purchasers of rapiers and contemporary weapons in England must have been the Urn folk, though the weapons are never found in graves. But as Urn folk had hardly reached Ireland at this date, Food Vessel warriors may have brandished Middle Bronze Age arms. On the other hand, in Scotland no rapiers have been found north of the Tay, and Middle Bronze Age hoards are confined to the areas south of the Southern Uplands. In the North, then, flat axes and daggers presumably persisted throughout phase 3. Thus the Middle Bronze Age industry can be connected with no single society listed in the funerary record. The period must have been quite short; rapiers and palstaves recur in hoards with types of phase 4.

2. The Industrial Revolution of the Late Bronze Age

The Late Bronze Age is ushered in by an influx of exotic types of tools and weapons, by a technical revolution and a drastic reorganization of the distributive side of the industry. The long period of local development thus initiated can be subdivided very tentatively into three phases, principally with the help of the tools and weapons. The new items of equipment which, appearing beside modified palstaves, looped spear-heads and even rapiers, define phase 4 are socketed axes, leaf-shaped swords and pegged spear-heads with leaf-shaped blades.

The *socketed axe* is the logical outcome of the method of hafting an axe-head on a knee-shaft, but does not appear to have been evolved in the British Isles. Its ultimate inspiration is presumably an ancient Mesopotamian form of adze with folded socket, but immediately it reached us from North or Central Europe, where socketed axes belong generally to the Late Bronze Age.[22]

[20] *Ant. J.*, xix, 320.   [21] Wheeler, *Wales*, 145.
[22] In the North they certainly belong to Montelius' IIb, in Central Europe to his III, which may quite well be contemporary.

A sword serviceable for slashing as well as thrusting needs the weight concentrated in the blade, which therefore tends to be *leaf-shaped*, and a

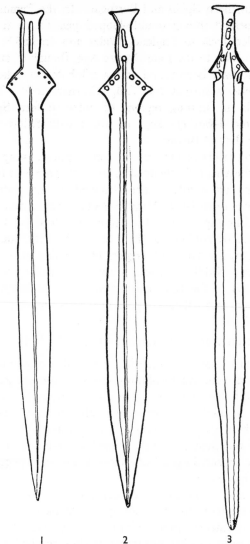

FIG. 54. Swords of U, V, and carp's tongue types. $\frac{1}{6}$. After Brewis.

stouter hilt attachment than that of our Middle Bronze Age rapiers. To secure this the hilt consists of a broad tang cast in one piece with the blade,

to which are riveted bone or wooden plates on each face, kept in place by flanges along the tang's margins. Such are therefore called flange-hilted or *tongue-grip* [23] swords. What are regarded as the earliest English specimens, virtually confined to southern England, Wales and Ireland, have rounded shoulders and are accordingly classified by Parker Brewis [24] as the *U type* (Fig. 54, 1). In a possibly later variant, popular throughout the Highland Zone, the shoulders are flat so that the term *V type* is descriptive (Fig. 54, 2). In 'degenerate' forms it had a long history in Highland Britain and Ireland (Fig. 76, 1). Both the foregoing varieties were carried in scabbards terminating in tongue-shaped chapes of bronze (Fig. 55, 1).

Despite some attempts to adapt rapiers to the new mode of fighting,[25] the cut-and-thrust tongue-grip sword denotes a complete break with native habits. The form and presumably the appropriate tactics were introduced from North or Central Europe. Now tongue-grip *rapiers* were current in the Aegean from 1500 B.C. and imported thence into Central Europe.[26] There or in the North they were adapted for slashing also. Swords rather like our U type (but without rivets in the tang) are attributed to Montelius' II in the North,[27] and to III a more widespread type, like our V, which reached even to Egypt about 1215-1210 B.C.

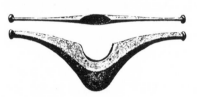

FIG. 55. Tongue-shaped and Winged Chapes. ¼.
By permission of the Trustees of the British Museum.

Leaf-shaped spear-heads, attached to the shafts by wooden pegs [28] fitted through rivet-holes in the socket, were reintroduced at the beginning of the Late Bronze Age and reacted on native types. The latter's blades became leaf-shaped—and generally small [29]—while the old method of

[23] Peake and Fleure, *The Horse and the Sword*, 87.
[24] *Arch.*, lxxiii, 253-265; Kendrick and Hawkes, 124-125.
[25] Grimes, *Guide*, 71; Evans, *Bronze*, Fig. 321; *Arch.*, lxxiii, 256.
[26] Childe, *Dawn*, Fig. 14, 2; *Danube*, 250-252.
[27] Sprockhoff (*Die german. Griffzungschwerter*) hence deduces a Northern origin for the whole series; cf. Childe, *Danube*, 251.
[28] The actual pegs have been found with the spears in Irish bogs: *PPS.*, iii, 370.
[29] *YAJ.*, xxxiv, 4.

attachment by loops was retained. Alternatively the new method of pegging was adopted, but loops were retained in a more or less vestigial form. The loops were shifted upwards to the base of the blade which forms their upper margins in the *spear-head with basal loops* (Fig. 53, 2, 5). Such are already found in hoards with rapiers and other types of phase 3,[30] oftener with early socketed celts and Late Bronze Age forms.[31] No less than 175 specimens have been found in Britain as against 80 in Ireland, where, however, a specialized and long-lived variant with square loops arose. Subsequently, perhaps not before phase 5, the now functionless loops were incorporated in the blade itself as *protected loops*. In Ireland and Highland Britain these develop into decorative *lunate openings* in the broadest part of an often lanceolate *blade* (Fig. 56).

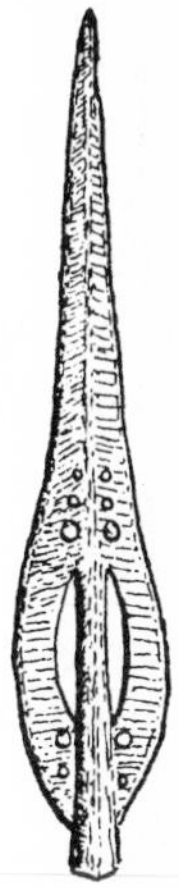

A simple pegged spear-head was found on the old ground surface beneath the urnfield of Pokesdown (Hants)[32] and is therefore older than Period VI. An imported British spear-head with basal loops formed part of the armament of a Northern warrior buried in Holstein at the very beginning of Montelius' Period II of the Northern Bronze Age[33]; and another was buried in Baden in a Late Bronze Age urnfield of Montelius' III (Reinecke D).[34] Finally, a perfectly good Britannico–Hibernian spear-head with lunate openings in the blade was dredged up from Huelva harbour[35] with many other bronzes, including several Sicilian safety-pins of a type which had gone out of fashion before the Greeks colonized Syracuse. Assuming that all these bronzes formed part of the cargo of a sunken merchantman, the whole evolution of the spear-head in the British Isles must have been completed by 750 B.C.

FIG. 56. Spear-head with lunate openings in the blade, Denhead (Perths.). ⅛.

In Lowland England a second phase of the Late Bronze Age (phase 5) is supposedly defined by the abrupt apparition of another group of obviously exotic bronzes. The axes typical of this phase have wings at the butt and a lateral loop, or are socketed axes with cast imitations of such wings. The new sword is the *carp's tongue* form (Fig. 54, 3)—a tongue-grip sword, but designed for thrusting, with a curiously tapered point and carried in scabbards terminating in purse-shaped chapes. Estyn Evans[36] has shown

---

[30] e.g. Maentwrog (Merioneth): Wheeler, *Wales*, Fig. 52; Glentrool (Kirkcudbright): *PSAS.*, lv, 30.

[31] *Arch.*, lxxxiii, 196.   [32] *Ant. J.*, vii, 470-471.

[33] Kersten, *Zur älteren nordischen Bronzezeit*, 65; *Amer. Anthrop.*, xxxix, 13.

[34] *MZ.*, xxix, 58.   [35] Ebert, *Real.: s.v.* Huelva.   [36] *Antiquity*, iv, 157-170.

that these types are repeatedly associated together and with other exotic forms such as bugle-shaped horse-trappings, hog-backed knives (sub-rectangular blades with a perforation near the back) and perhaps bifid razors, in a restricted area of Lowland England and again in France, and can all be traced to the Lake Dwellings of the Rhone basin. They were probably introduced by actual invaders, whom we shall later be able to identify by pottery too.

These invaders did not penetrate into Highland Britain or Ireland, where the foregoing types are virtually unknown. Hence phase 5 is not easily defined there, though a number of V-type swords must belong to it while winged palstaves may imitate the foreign winged axes. Moreover, a third phase of the Late Bronze Age has to be distinguished there parallel to the Hallstatt phase (Period VII) of the Lowlands. It should be characterized by V-type swords the hilts of which have very low or no flanges and widen out at the end to secure the pommel while the chapes are *winged* (Fig. 55, 2), and by imported objects of Hallstatt character or copies of such. While such imports occur in Welsh, Scottish and Irish hoards they are unrepresented in the great founder's hoards that illustrate the zenith of the bronze industry.

This phase must have lasted in places till the beginning of our era. A socketed bronze axe was found in the Roman camp at Ardoch under conditions which suggest that some of Agricola's adversaries in Scotland may still have used bronze weapons.[37] In Ireland a late palstave and a funicular bronze torque were apparently found together with a Roman provincial fibula at Annesborough (Armagh)![38]

New technical processes were employed for the production of the Late Bronze Age types. A notable innovation was the adoption of a clay mould formed on a pattern. This might be an actual axe or sword or a wooden copy of such.[39] It was pressed into a lump or strip of clay of suitable size until half-buried. The exposed surface of the mould was then dusted over with ash or sand and a fresh mass of clay laid on covering the rest of the pattern. When dry the two parts, or valves, kept apart by the ash layer, were separated and the pattern removed. The valves were then keyed together (a core for the socket having been inserted if needed), wrapped in a protective coating of clay and provided with a gate or funnel into which the molten metal could be poured. The mould was then baked hard, set

---

[37] J. Anderson in *PSAS.*, xxxii, 461-470.   [38] *PRIA.*, xxxii, C, 173.

[39] The grain of the wooden pattern can be discerned on clay moulds from Northern Ireland and Shetland.

upright in a casting pit filled with sand, and the metal poured in.[40] Such moulds would only produce a single casting, but they could be made much more quickly and accurately than a multiple mould could be carved in stone. They seem alone to have been used for swords, but for making socketed axes (or wax models for casting such by the *cire perdue* process)[41] stone and even bronze moulds[42] existed too.

At the same time the technique of casting on came into vogue. It involved building up, upon the object to be added to, a clay mould for the addition round a wax model or as described above.

Proficiency in hammer technique, enabling the bronzesmith to produce, shape and decorate large sheets of metal, is another characteristic of the Late Bronze Age in the British Isles, as on the Continent and even in the contemporary industries of Phoenicia and Assyria.[43] Finally, the Irish goldsmiths at last learned to use solder, which had been employed by Oriental jewellers as early as the third millennium B.C. Our Late Bronze Age goldsmiths employed alloys of gold and silver, or gold and copper, to solder together hemispheres of gold or attach the terminals to some funicular torques and 'fibulae.'[44]

To help them in their craft the smiths made themselves an enlarged kit of tools—socketed chisels, gouges and hammers, lug-adzes (trunnion celts),[45] small anvils, tongs and curved knives[46] of bronze.

On the extractive side of the industry the supplies of copper from Ireland were by now certainly being supplemented by the exploitation at least of surface lodes in Wales, northern England[47] and even Shetland. Moreover, lead, familiar even to the megalith-builders in south-east Spain, was now for the first time being demonstrably used by metallurgists in the British Isles, who made socketed celts (perhaps patterns or core-cases)[48] of that metal.

[40] Maryon, *PRIA.*, xliv, C, 213-215; Curle, *PSAS.*, lxvii, 118; p. 184 below.

[41] Götze, Ebert's, *Real.*: *s.v.* Bronzeguss.

[42] Evans, *Bronze*, 441-448; microscopic examination suggests the use of clay moulds even for early palstaves (*PSAS.*, lxix, 426).

[43] Vessels of beaten copper were of course familiar in the Orient from 3000 B.C., but the technique reaches its apogee in Assyrian works like the gates of Balawat.

[44] Maryon, *PRIA.*, xliv, C, 190-193, 208.

[45] An East Mediterranean type current in Greece by Late Mycenaean times: Frödin & Persson, *Asine*, 311; for Britain see *Ant. J.*, v, 51 f., 409 ff. Maryon, *Ant. J.*, xviii, 249, suggests that some were used as anvils in embossing.

[46] Childe, *Bronze Age*, Fig. 11, 10; found with an anvil in Calvados, Evans, *Bronze*, 209.

[47] Use of Weardale ores attested by analysis of socketed axe: *Arch.*, liv, 99.

[48] Evans, *Bronze*, 445; *Arch. J.*, xc, 143.

A reorganization of the distributive machinery is attested by the appearance of a new sort of hoard that is indeed such a novelty that Fox [49] has taken it as defining the Late Bronze Age. Such, *founders' hoards*, consist largely of old worn objects—scrap metal—sometimes accompanied by moulds, ingots and metallurgical appliances. The merchant artificers must now have travelled the country in veritable caravans collecting scrap metal, doubtless in exchange for new tools. Precisely the same organization is attested about this time by similar founders' hoards found all over Europe, including the western Mediterranean. In the British Isles the use of gold rings as a sort of currency may be connected with the reorganization of the sales department.

The result of the changes just described must have been to make bronze-work cheaper than ever before. The number of Late Bronze Age objects still surviving is enormous. The hoards of the period exceed those of all previous phases put together in the proportion of 10 to 1, and as a rule contain a larger number of castings. In the Cambridge region Fox enumerated 190 axes of Late Bronze Age character as against 108 attributed to phases 1, 2 and 3 combined. In Scotland Henderson [50] has traced 136 swords as against 25 rapiers and 26 daggers. A larger circle of consumers could accordingly enjoy the advantage of bronze equipment, and a greater variety of needs were satisfied.

In addition to swords and spears warriors could now carry circular targes of hammered bronze strengthened by embossed ribs and knobs. But smiths produced specialized tools for craftsmen and articles of domestic use. For the carpenter there were socketed gouges and chisels, with which he could carve wooden shields, cauldrons,[51] two-piece tubs [52] and canoes with a sternboard.[53] Knives for daily use were double-edged, with a flat tang or an oval socket [54] for the handle. Finally, the earliest sickles (Fig. 57) (apart from a very few imports) appear at the beginning of phase 4 [55] and develop locally till translated into iron in phase 6 (Period VII).[56] Fox points out that these sickles are not found in the great grain-growing districts of Sussex and Wessex and may not be agricultural

[49] *Arch. Camb.*, 16-22.   [50] *PSAS.*, lxxii, 159-162.   [51] *PRIA.*, xlii, C, 11-29.
[52] Body hollowed out of an (alder) trunk, bottom fitted into a groove: Clark, *Ant. J.*, xx, 53-56.
[53] *Arch. J.*, xc, 139.
[54] Perhaps developed, as in the spear-heads, from tanged blade plus ferrule: Evans, *Arch.*, lxxxiii, 190.
[55] An example with palstave and rapier from Downham Fen: *PPS.*, v, 227; Fig. 57, 1 here.
[56] *PPS.*, v, 238-239.

implements at all, but used rather for cutting reeds or in ritual. Partly ritual may be the double-edged razors that occur in hoards from phase 4.[57] Most have a terminal tang and a curious slit at the opposite end of the blade (they are hence called *bifid* (Fig. 58)). This feature is missing from the otherwise very similar razors found in graves (p. 154).

The greatest contribution of the new industry to raising the standard of life was, however, the provision of metal-ware usable for culinary purposes.

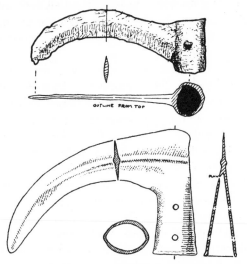

FIG. 57. SOCKETED SICKLES.
1. Downham Fen (Cambs.) ; 2. Llyn Fawr
hoard. ⅓. After Fox in *PPS*.

FIG. 58.   Bifid
razor, Heathery
Burn Cave. ½.

Hitherto our ancestors had been without any large vessel that could be suspended over a fire for boiling or seething. In heroic saga, both Greek and Celtic, and in the mediaeval Welsh laws the cauldron still figures as a standard and test of wealth. The Irish cauldrons (only 4 of class A and 5 of class B come from Great Britain as against 11 and 18 from Ireland) are all globular, built up out of three or more sheets of beaten bronze skilfully riveted together.[58] In class A (Pl. XIV, 1) the neck is straight but corrugated, while in class B (Pl. XIV, 2) the brim is very wide and its

[57] Found, e.g., with rapier and early spear-head at Glentrool, p. 171.

[58] Leeds, *Arch.*, lxxx, 1-36, none earlier than phase 5; in class A the staples are corrugated and cast on with T-shaped tongues of metal projecting downwards on both sides of the neck; in B the metal tongues are wrapped round the brim and supplemented by struts joining rim to belly.

edges are rolled over. The tubular staples into which the movable ring handles fit have been cast on in imitation of the brazed-on handles of the Greek *deinos*, which inspired the Irish cauldrons. Flat-bottomed sharp-shouldered buckets were fabricated in Ireland by the same method out of riveted sheets of bronze with semi-tubular staples cast on. Though in form these agree precisely with the *situlae* of the Hallstatt period in Central Europe and Upper Italy, the handle attachments are quite different; they are thus derived not through Central Europe but by the Atlantic route from the common Italic prototype.

3. THE STATUS OF THE METAL INDUSTRY IN THE LATE BRONZE AGE

'The completeness of the break which divides the Middle from the Late Bronze Age' has led Crawford,[59] Fox [60] and others to postulate an invasion—generally from Central Europe—to account for the innovations described in the last section. Admittedly the technical advances are not local inventions and could only be introduced by an actual influx of expert craftsmen or by the apprenticeship of insular artisans to practitioners of the new processes. But if metal-workers formed, as suggested on p. 163, a detribalized guild or caste, changes in their personnel need have no more ethnic or political implications than the settlements of Flemish weavers in England during the Middle Ages or the training of Japanese technicians in American factories. The novel processes were all East Mediterranean in ultimate origin, but the exotic types that accompany them do not all reach the British Isles from the same quarter. If swords, socketed axes and gouges and pegged spear-heads be Central European or Northern, trunnion celts (p. 173), targes,[61] cauldrons (p. 175) and bifid razors [62] come from the Mediterranean—either, like the double-looped palstave (p. 168), by the Atlantic route which had conveyed an Irish spear-head to Huelva, or across France. Our spear-heads with basal and protected loops, socketed knives and socketed sickles are purely native products betraying no foreign inspiration.

Peake [63] takes leaf-shaped swords as tokens of an invasion, and that with better logic, since the substitution of a slashing for a thrusting weapon denotes a change in methods of warfare. But, after all, the armament

---

[59] *Ant. J.*, ii, 27-35.   [60] *Arch. Camb.*, 52.

[61] If not based on native leather and wooden shields, the nearest analogies are those borne by the Sea Raiders in Egypt about 1200 and by Sardinian warriors in the Bronze Age.

[62] Childe, *Bronze Age*, 100.

[63] *The Bronze Age and the Celtic World* (1922).

industry is generally international. British warriors had been accustomed to smite with halberds and battle-axes as well as to stab with rapiers and spears. The migration might indeed be reversed if we accept Sprockhoff's view that the Bronze Age shields of North and Central Europe are derived from the Irish.[64]

Sunflower pins [65] (Fig. 59) could also be used as an argument for an intrusion of new people. Not only is the type derived from a Bohemian pin of Late Bronze Age I which gave rise to very similar pins in North Europe too, but the popularity of pins implies a break with the old Mediterranean fashion of buttoned garments in favour of the Anatolian–Central European style of pinned cloaks. The gold ornaments with trumpet-shaped ends termed fibulae by Irish antiquaries,[66] if really connected with the Northern two-piece safety-pins, might be interpreted in the same way. But these types are effectively confined to Ireland and Scotland and have no relation to the general industrial revolution. The ritual objects termed sun-discs in Ireland, discs of bronze ornamented with compass-drawn circles·and coated with gold foil,[67] might indeed be used, like the shields, to reverse the process. For while the idea can be traced in these islands to the Early Bronze Age (discs from Mere, p. 93), the Late Bronze Age Irish discs were reproduced in the same technique in the North during Montelius' Bronze Age II [68] when other Irish types were being imported (p. 171) there.

FIG. 59.
Sunflower Pin,
Ireland. ½.

There is no general correlation between the distribution of Late Bronze Age types and that of any culture defined by pottery or monuments. But one group—the carp's tongue sword complex (p. 172)—does occupy very much the same area as the invading culture defined in the funerary record by Deverel–Rimbury Urns and described in Chapter X. The industrial revolution as a whole can hardly be explained by the immigration thus attested. The latter is not demonstrably as early as the beginning of the Late Bronze Age; it cannot be detected in the Highland Zone or Ireland

---

[64] *Handelsgeschichte der germanischen Bronzezeit*, 4-32.

[65] Childe, *Bronze Age*, 110; Mahr, *PPS.*, iii, 394; *Germania*, xx (1935), 10.

[66] Childe, *Bronze Age*, 231; John Evans pointed out that these are very like the *manillas* used as currency in West Africa, so that the Irish ' fibulae ' may also have been ' ring-money.'

[67] Armstrong, *Catalogue*, 47; Childe, *P.S.*, 162-163 (Mull); Maryon, *PRIA.*, xliv, C, 196.

[68] *Ipek* (1931), 36-40; the best known, attached to a model horse and mounted on a wheeled stand, comes from Trundholm (Denmark).

at all; even in Cambridgeshire, where Late Bronze Age types and hoards are abundant, 'traces of exotic culture, as opposed to a change of fashion in metal types, are negligible.' [69] We shall see that an Irish smith arrived in Shetland to start manufacturing Late Bronze Age tools and ornaments without affecting the ceramic or architectural traditions of the local village.

The Late Bronze Age revolution, as such, changed not the ethnic conplexion of the British Isles but the economy of a detribalized industrial group already producing for an international market in the Middle Bronze Age. In phases 4 and 5 our bronze industry reached its zenith. Its markets extended to the southern coasts of Spain, the middle Elbe [70] and the shores of the Baltic. Imports from these islands are so numerous in northern Gaul that Breuil [71] speaks of a Britannico–Sequanian bronze province. And a hoard like that of Fresné-la-Mère, Calvados,[72] comprising metal-workers' tools, might belong to Britannico–Hibernian craftsmen travelling on the Continent.

Employment in the extractive, manufacturing and distributive branches of the metal industry can never have absorbed any large proportion of the superfluous rural population. But it must have offered economic and social freedom. This privileged status was, however, soon lost as a cheaper metal, iron, gradually ousted bronze from use for daily tools and weapons. The Continental market gradually contracted as the iron-using Hallstatt culture spread westward. The new industry, based on ores of relatively common occurrence but still technically unripe for large-scale production, could work with a simpler organization than the bronze industry requiring the combination of two rather uncommon metals. The days of the merchant-artificer himself selling on an international market what he had made of international materials were numbered. The bronzesmith had to meet the competition of the blacksmith and of fellow-craftsmen in like plight in the Atlantic west; quite a flood of square-mouthed socketed axes from Brittany were imported into southern England, apparently during Period VI.[73]

Blacksmiths soon reached Britain too. A hoard from a peat-moss at Llyn Fawr (Glam.) [74] (Fig. 60) comprised, together with socketed axes of South Welsh type, gouges and class B cauldrons, and a Hallstatt razor, a Hallstatt C sword, and a spear-head and a socketed sickle, all three of iron.

[69] Clark, *VCH. Camb.*, i, 282.

[70] Sprockhoff in *Nachrichten aus Niedersächsens Urgeschichte* (1932), 70.

[71] *L'Anthr.*, xiv, 517.

[72] Anvil, socketed hammer, socketed curved knife, funicular gold torque: Ashmolean Museum, Evans Collection.

[73] Fox, *Personality*, 20, Pl. IX.   [74] *Ant. J.*, xix, 370-386.

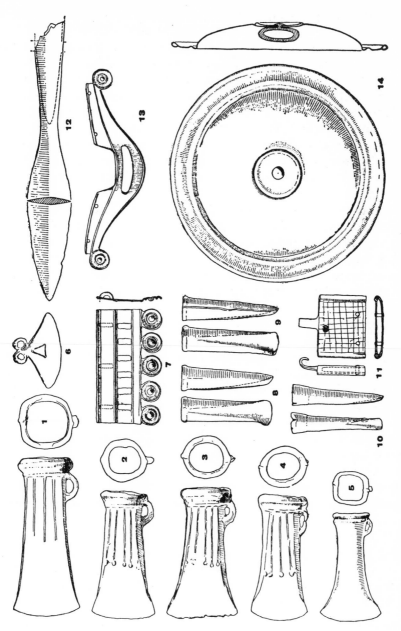

FIG. 60. PART OF LLYN FAWR HOARD. *Ant. J.* 6. Hallstatt razor; iron spear-head; 13. chape.

The sickle copies the native bronze type, so that a local iron industry must have been already established when the objects were collected.

The Late Bronze Age revolution had made bronze so cheap that in the Highland Zone and Ireland the old metal could hold its own even in Period VII. But the contraction of the market had destroyed the industry's prosperity and autonomy. The bronzesmith had to settle down to produce everyday tools and weapons for local consumption; politically emancipated from tribal society, he is forced back into it on an inferior status by economic pressure. The great founders' hoards vanish in the Hallstatt period. It was surely unemployment that drove an Irish smith to establish a workshop in the bleak Shetland Islands. Everywhere local types appear as the smith becomes attached to a territorial group. So Fox [75] has identified a Yorkshire type of socketed axe with sub-rectangular socket and three ribs cast on the face, John Evans and Wheeler [76] a South Welsh (Fig. 60) variety with a heavy cornice-like moulding round the mouth and three ribs, rather close set and sometimes converging. Such local variants cluster round their centre of origin though strays may percolate far; 35 out of 51 axes from South Wales belong to the local type, but strays reached North Wales, East Anglia and even Jersey.

It is precisely from this period of enforced localization that monumental evidence of the home-life of metal-workers is available. A group of smiths lived and worked in a limestone cavern excavated by a branch of the Heathery Burn near Stanhope in County Durham.[77] The cave was 500 ft. long, 2 to 30 ft. wide and never more than 10 ft. high, quite dark and traversed by the stream. Yet accumulations of charcoal and broken bones of Celtic short-horn, sheep, small horse and game prove its use as a habitation. Casting-jets, a mould, a tracer and tongs and long bone spatulae show that the occupants were metal-workers. Two swords, seven spear-heads and seventeen socketed axes (shown by high lead content to be made of Weardale ores [78]) may be accepted as their products. A bronze bucket and gold ornaments (including a lock-ring of triangular section) illustrate the wealth still to be derived from the industry. Antler cheek-pieces from bits (Fig. 61) may mean that the craftsmen travelled in a horse-drawn waggon and give the first definite indication both of the domestication of the horse and of the use of wheeled vehicles in the British Isles. An extended skeleton near a hearth might indicate the use of the cave for burial too. But broken human skulls near by remind us that in barbarous societies

[75] *Personality*, 69.
[77] *Arch.*, liv, 88-112 (Greenwell).
[76] *Wales*, 156, following Evans, *Bronze*, 119.
[78] *Arch. Ael.*, 4, ix (1933), 192.

metallurgical science is still bound up with mystic rites for which human blood may well have been required.[79] Typologically the bronzes could be as late as phase 6; the texture of the few surviving pot sherds is not incompatible with Period VII.

4. THE END OF THE BRONZE AGE IN SHETLAND

In Orkney and Shetland the culture sequence in post-megalithic times diverges substantially from that valid for the rest of the British Isles. An infiltration of Beaker folk, while the Skara Brae culture was still dominant in Orkney, is indeed attested by vases [80] from both archipelagoes and by brachycranial skulls from several graves. Moreover, battle-axes or maces

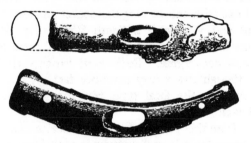

FIG. 61. Antler cheek-pieces from horses' bits, Heathery Burn Cave. ½.

were used in war. And everywhere collective burial gave place to individual interment of skeletons or cremated bones in cists of thin slabs. Several such cists both in Orkney and in Shetland were still two-storeyed,[81] just as collective tombs on Rousay and Eday had been. But typical Food Vessels and Collared or Cordoned Urns [82] are alike missing. In their stead we find plain urns, some shouldered and resembling the bronze situlae described on p. 176, or urns carved out of steatite, a soft stone native to Shetland but an import in Orkney. Some of these are barrel-shaped while others are sub-rectangular in plan, evidently in imitation of wooden vessels. They illustrate some sort of connexion with Norway, where steatite urns occur in the pre-Roman Iron Age, though the direction of influence is uncertain.

The position when Orkney and Shetland were reunited with the rest of the British Isles by incorporation in the Britannico–Hibernian province

[79] Even Assyrian chemical recipes mention a foetus among the ingredients.

[80] *PSAS.*, lxvii, 34-36; lxxiii, 26.   [81] Childe, *P.S.*, 140.

[82] An urn from Flemington (Shetland), however, is rather like the biconical degeneration of the Collared Urn: Childe, *P.S.*, Pl. X, d.

of the Late Bronze Age is best illustrated by a hamlet explored by Curle,[83] at Jarlshof, Sumburgh Head, the southernmost extremity of Shetland. The sandy isthmus that unites the rocky headland to the main island provided arable and pasture for a small community who built their stone houses in hollows between the dunes. The methods of excavation have not allowed the precise size of the settlement to be determined. Curle examined six dwellings, frequently reconstructed, so that not more than two or three were inhabited simultaneously, but jointly representing eight architectural phases.

From the first the settlement was surrounded by a light stone wall like a modern field dyke, pierced by a low gate or creep, exactly like the sheep-gates in such dykes today. The earlier houses (Nos. I, II, III, and V) are all variants on the so-called *courtyard house*—an oval court containing the hearth, with a pair of cubicles on each side and a larger transverse recess at the inner end (Fig. 62). The dune-dwellers depended, like the Skara Brae people, largely on stock-breeding; some sheep resemble the large-horned Soay breed, the Copper Age sheep of the Continent, while others belong to the older 'Turbary' stock whose descendants may survive in modern Shetland sheep. Similarly, the Jarlshof oxen are more like the Celtic short-horn than those from Skara Brae. Moreover, the large transverse cell at the back of the court (Fig. 62, V, ϵ) was used as a stall where the manure could be collected on a dished floor and one beast tethered to an ingenious 'ring' made from the vertebra of a whale built into the wall.[84] The arrangements illustrate a rural economy more advanced than that practised at Skara Brae. Indeed, the collection of stall-dung, presumably for manuring crops, is the earliest recorded instance of the use of fertilizers on the fields of Britain.

In any case, cereals were cultivated, actual grains of bere (barley) having been found. They were ground on *trough querns*, an insular derivative of the saddle quern in which the backward and forward motion of an oval grinder has worn a deep depression, open at one end. Seals, sea-birds and some fish, particularly cod, were caught and limpets collected in vast quantities as at Skara Brae.

Textile appliances (whorls)[85] are found only in the later houses. An immense number of scrapers made of quartz, a variety of heavy slate implements and some bone tools, including 'socketed chisels' like those described on p. 86, could be used for leather-dressing and might imply skin clothing.

[83] Reports in *PSAS.*, lxvi-lxx.   [84] *PSAS.*, lxix, 89.   [85] *PSAS.*, lxviii, 311.

At first the Jarlshof community seems to have been self-sufficing, making use of local materials—slate, quartz and bone. For clearing away the sand which was for ever threatening to bury the huts the villagers used heart-shaped tools of slate with a hole for the hand at the centre, as well as oxen's scapulae. Unpolished 'axes' were made of slate by processes similar to those used elsewhere by flint-workers making celts, but may have been used as clubs since they would never chop anything and there was no wood to chop! Other curious slate tools—T-shaped, L-shaped and serrated—are substitutes for wooden implements. Barrel-shaped and sub-rectangular bowls were carved out of steatite. A few rather coarse vessels of similar shapes were made in pottery of a vaguely Bronze Age fabric. But in the deepest levels pots, sometimes decorated with punctuations and possibly round-bottomed, are vaguely reminiscent of Windmill Hill.[86]

The culture described is a good adaptation to the exigences of life on a wind-swept treeless isle, so good that its origin is hard to decipher. The courtyard houses represent an Atlantic–Mediterranean plan, traceable already in Minoan Crete by 2000 B.C.[87] Some collective tombs on Orkney are houses of the dead, laid out on the same principle. The querns and the Celtic short-horn may have come in with the megalith-builders, or more probably with Beaker folk. The socketed chisels of bone and the slate implements are in a general way Baltic and might represent survivals of Maglemosean traditions or later contacts with Norway.

In the sixth phase the settlement's self-sufficiency and isolation were broken down. A bronzesmith, trained in Irish traditions of the Late Bronze Age, settled down at Jarlshof to produce socketed knives, leaf-shaped (V-type) swords, sunflower pins and other typically Britannico–Hibernian products. Hut I was converted into a smithy, and there Curle[88] found the casting-pit, the store of clay with kneading trough for making moulds, the broken moulds themselves and the jets from the castings. Copper was presumably obtained from local lodes, but unless driftwood sufficed, the charcoal[89] as well as the tin had to be imported.

Though the numerous broken moulds point to a considerable output of metal tools, such did not supersede the old equipment of quartz, slate and bone which continued to be made while the smith was at work. Nor can any change in pottery, nor yet in architecture, be connected with the establishment of a local bronze industry. It looks as if an Irish artisan had

[86] *PSAS.*, lxxii, 360. [87] Evans, *Palace of Minos*, i, 147.
[88] *PSAS.*, lxvii, 92.
[89] Scots fir, oak, hazel, birch and willow: *PSAS.*, lxviii, 233.

migrated to Shetland and was supplying the islanders' needs of metal without otherwise affecting the community's traditions in the very least.

But while the smith was still turning out bronze swords, architectural and ceramic conditions changed. A rough and very shallow underground gallery or souterrain (Fig. 62, *m*) was built under the court of dwelling III,

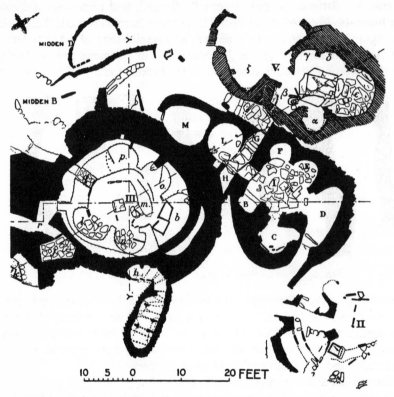

FIG. 62. PART OF SETTLEMENT AT JARLSHOF, SHETLAND. After *PSAS*. The earlier plans of house III are outlined, the final form alone shown solid.

which at the same time was remodelled and converted into a bronze-smithy.[90] A little later the whole house was reconstructed to form a roughly circular enclosure, 22 ft. by 26 ft. in diameter, with a round central hearth and cubicles around the walls, each with a private hearth of its own. A more commodious souterrain opened out of this round house (Fig. 62, *h*). The

[90] *PSAS.*, lxviii, 237-239.

structure is very much ruined, but the plan is suggestive of the Iron Age wheel-houses and may well be regarded as a new variant on the courtyard house.

About the same time as the first souterrain was built, a new sort of pottery came into vogue.[91] The clay is now tempered with steatite; the pot-rims are flattened or even internally flanged, and sometimes decorated with finger-tip impressions or dots; large vases have well-marked shoulders (Fig. 63). This pottery is in a general way reminiscent of what is termed Iron Age A in England (p. 203). Moreover, at the same general horizon iron slag is found in addition to moulds for bronze tools.[92] The new metal

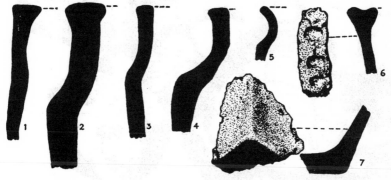

FIG. 63.   Pottery from Jarlshof. ¼. After Curle in *PSAS*.

industry had reached Shetland; the bronzesmith had to face the competition of a blacksmith or himself learn iron-working. Iron evidently did, not at once replace bronze for tools and weapons. On the other hand, the output of quartz scrapers, bone chisels and slate implements suffered a serious diminution, and the quality of these products declined.

The architectural changes—replacement of the courtyard house by the partitioned hut-circle and introduction of the souterrain—the adoption of new ceramic forms and techniques, and the gradual lapse into desuetude of the stone and bone tools on the manufacture of which so much care had previously been expended, taken together disclose a very definite break in the social tradition. The reports do not indeed establish the strict simultaneity of all these changes. But in effect they amount to the replace-

[91] *PSAS.*, lxviii, 283-298.
[92] *PSAS.*, lxviii, 303; but some iron slag is reported from the earliest occupation level in dwelling III associated with ' Bronze Age ' pottery, and Curle (*PSAS.*, lxx, 169) assigns a bloomery at Wiltrow to an earlier phase on the strength of many quartz and slate tools found there.

ment of one culture by another, in other words the immigration of a new society. Whence the new-comers reached Shetland is a question which must be discussed later in connexion with the general question of the Iron Age cultures in North Britain and Ireland. What is clear and relevant to this chapter is that the establishment of the Late Bronze Age industry in Shetland preceded the advent of any new culture and was itself accompanied by no general break in the traditions of a 'bronzeless Bronze Age' that went back to the Beaker period.

CHAPTER X

THE AGRICULTURAL REVOLUTION

1. Urnfield Invasions

It was not the abortive industrial revolution of the Late Bronze Age but an agricultural revolution during that period that actually provided sustenance for a vastly increased population. Well-balanced mixed farming with plough-tillage now, according to Curwen,[1] replaced pastoralism with scratch agriculture as the basis of life in Lowland England. The warrior-herdsman whose wife had tilled a little wheat and barley with the hoe was not converted into a settled ploughman by the mere example of neighbours overseas nor at the behest of a few conquering war-lords. It took an actual immigration of land-hungry peasants to effect the transformation. Such immigration is abundantly attested in the archaeological record from southern England by changes in settlement-form, architecture, pottery and the general mode of life. Indeed, while details are obscure, two main waves of invasion, each capable of subdivision, can be recognized and may be termed respectively the Urnfield (Deverel–Rimbury) and Hallstatt (Iron Age A) invasions.

Urnfield folk, peasant cultivators from East Central Europe expanding in the last quarter of the second millennium in search both of land and metals, encountered round the Alps and the Upper Rhine the more pastoral populations that had buried their dead under barrows—Tumulus Bronze folk—and other less well-defined groups, all more or less akin to our own Middle Bronze Age populations. The result was the formation of hybrid cultures combining Tumulus and Urnfield elements, and the westward spread of such composite societies.[2] Bodies of these, crystallized out between the Alpine slopes and the Lower Rhine, eventually crossed the Channel, to produce in Britain the Deverel–Rimbury culture. Invaders[3] occupied areas of easy settlement in East Anglia as far as Lincolnshire and the chalk downs of Sussex and Wessex, a major section entering by ports between

[1] *PPS.*, iv, 27-40; perhaps he underestimates the importance of agriculture in Neolithic-Middle Bronze Ages.

[2] Childe, *Danube*, 334-365; Hawkes, *Foundations*, 363, 367, 371.

[3] *Ant. J.*, xiii, 440–454 ; *PPS.*, iv, 181 ; viii, 34–44.

Weymouth and Christchurch, while a third party occupied Cornwall,[4] inspired no doubt by the need for tin and following a circuitous route, according to Hencken, via the Pyrenees. The colonization was explicitly southern; Yorkshire, like the part of the Highland Zone north of the Thames, was seemingly unaffected, so that there the old Urn folk presumably retained their more pastoral economy (Fig. 46).

The reality of the invasion of southern England, the origin of the invaders and their effect on population density, are best demonstrated from the cemeteries. Like the Urn folk with whom they mixed, the Deverel–Rimbury invaders practised cremation. In Wessex, indeed, they sometimes covered their burials with barrows, smaller and lower than those of native societies.[5] But the normal practice was burial in a cemetery, either a flat urnfield [6] or secondary burials clustered in one quadrant of an older barrow.

In several Wessex cemeteries biconical derivatives of the Overhanging Rim Urn[7] (Fig. 45, 4), sometimes modified in imitation of the exotic types, denote the absorption of native Urn folk in the new societies. The predominant foreign types of ossuary, which were used also as domestic pots, fall into several groups. *Globular Urns* with a rather smooth surface have a barely recognizable 'neck,' decorated with shallow flutings or tooling and distinguished by vestigial handles at the base (Fig. 64, 4). Their ancestor is in the last resort the 'amphora' of Lausitz and South-West German urnfields, more immediately the Weert type found in Lower Rhenish cemeteries.[8] Large *barrel*- and *bucket*-shaped urns are mostly made of coarser clay, often flat-rimmed and decorated with applied cordons embellished with finger-printing (Fig. 64, 1-2). Such cordon ornament had been in vogue in Gaul from the Copper Age, and somewhere between Champagne [9] and Holland had been incorporated in 'Bronze Age' pottery to form the Utrecht urns generally taken as the ancestors of our barrel urns. Thirdly, in Wessex and farther west the urns show features, like applied horseshoe ridges, resembling handles, that cannot be paralleled at all in the Rhenish cemeteries; such must be native traits, West European if not British, adopted by the Urnfield migrants from older stocks. Several of the foreign urns in Wessex, Devon and Cornwall exhibit on the inside of the base cruciform and wheel

---

[4] Hencken, *Arch. Corn.*, 94-97.   [5] *Ant. J.*, xiii, 429.

[6] Sometimes the urns are arranged in a ring as at Barnes (I. of Wight): *P.I.O.W.N.H.&A.S.* (1931), 108-109.

[7] *Ant. J.*, vii, 465-485; *PPS.*, iv, 175-180.

[8] Doppelfeld, *P.Z.*, xxi (1930), 361-375; Hawkes, *Ant. J.*, xiii, 437-439; Bursch, *Marburger Studien*, 20-25.

[9] Hawkes, *Ant. J.*, xiii, 439, n. 5.

patterns of applied ribs which would not be out of place in Hungarian urnfields but might locally be regarded as survivals of the reinforcements of Skara Brae bowls.[10]

A single Deverel–Rimbury urnfield may comprise 100 cremations, not all inurned. Such cemeteries cannot belong to isolated kinship groups or

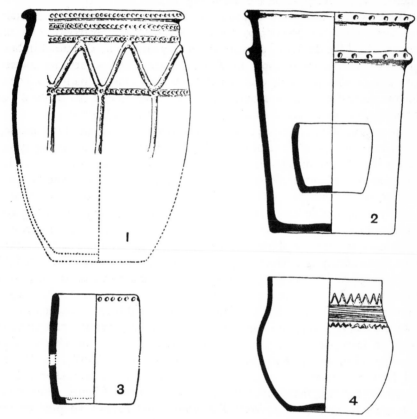

FIG. 64. Deverel–Rimbury urns from Latch Farm Urnfield (Hants). ⅛.
After Piggott in *PPS*.

nomadic herdsmen, but only to villages of a size and permanence hitherto unprecedented in Britain. The total number of Deverel–Rimbury interments in southern England exceeds that of burials recorded for any previous culture. In Dorset alone the figures are of the order of 600. Yet the cemeteries hardly cover more than three centuries. They thus really disclose an

[10] Clay, *WAM.*, xliii, 316-318; cf. Childe, *Danube*, 213.

enlarged population. Such could not have been supported on the old methods. It was made possible by improved methods of farming. Settlements prove this, for by a lucky chance their ancient fields are preserved.

If a hill slope be ploughed for any length of time, the disturbed soil from the top tends to be washed down to pile up against the unploughed bottom margin of the field. Thus arise *lynchets*—the shallow depression at the top being termed a negative, the bank at the bottom a positive, lynchet. Taken in conjunction with undisturbed strips running across the contours and interrupting the lynchets, they serve to define our ancestors' cornfields (Pl. V, 2). Lyncheted fields are connected with some Deverel–Rimbury settlements or interrupted by their cattle-kraals. All are of the type termed *Celtic*, irregular squares in contrast to the long narrow strips attributable to the Belgae or the Anglo-Saxons. The length of each is such that a pair of oxen could plough it comfortably without a breather; the

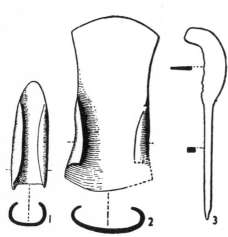

FIG. 65. Iron Ploughshares (¼) and Coulter (⅛), the Caburn and Bigbury. After Curwen in *PPS.*, iv.

pause then necessary could be profitably utilized for turning the plough. As length and breadth were approximately equal, Curwen infers that each field was ploughed twice—along and across the contours—as recommended by Pliny. The practice implies the use of a light plough, the Roman *aratrum* (ard), which really only scratches the ground without turning over the sod. The narrow ploughshares (Fig. 65, 1) which alone survive from England before 50 B.C. are in fact appropriate to this device.[11]

The earliest evidence for this ploughing comes from Sussex. On Plumpton Plain (near Lewes) Curwen and Holleyman [12] excavated steadings with which were associated Celtic fields (Fig. 66). Three were oval enclosures (125 ft. long by 100 ft. wide) and one sub-rectangular. All were surrounded by a bank, formed by scraping up the earth and presumably surmounted by a palisade; each enclosed a round hut, some 20 ft. in diameter. The pottery [13] from these farms, though partly cognate, is not classical Deverel-

[11] *PPS.*, iv, 42-46.   [12] *PPS.*, i (1935), 16-31.   [13] *PPS.*, i, 39-46.

Rimbury ware, but suggests that the farmers were recruited from the Middle Bronze Age population of North France with perhaps forerunners of the Urnfield folk. The settlements at site A were not occupied very long. Another group soon settled on an adjacent site, B. These too, judged by their pottery, should have come from North France and incorporated native

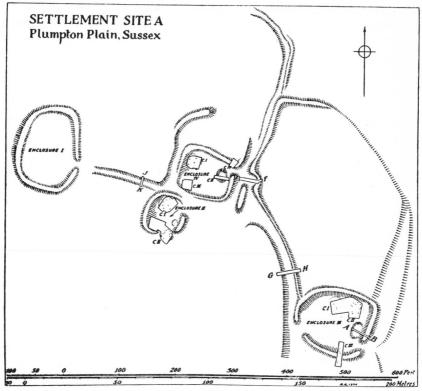

FIG. 66. Late Bronze Age steadings, fields and sunken ways. After Curwen and Holleyman in *PPS*.

British Urn elements together with Urnfield traditions derived both from the West Alpine province and from the Upper Rhine.[14] They used winged axes of Swiss type, such as define the carp's tongue sword complex of Late Bronze Age 2, and may even be identified with the sword-bearers. Another group, from Picardy, settled in Kent and introduced their own fashion in pins though these too used " Deverel urns " [14a].

[11] *PPS.*, i, 32, 46-59   [14a] *PPS.*, viii (1942), 26-47.

From these and the remaining settlements we see that grain was still ground on saddle querns and that no silos were dug for its storage. Cattle (Celtic short-horn), sheep and probably horses were bred.[15] The flocks and herds would be pastured on wastes, generally on the north slopes of downs, the southern slopes being preferred for cultivation. A series of travelling ditches in Dorset and Hampshire may mark the boundaries of cattle-runs. The ditch is typically 'a steep-sided, narrow-bottomed

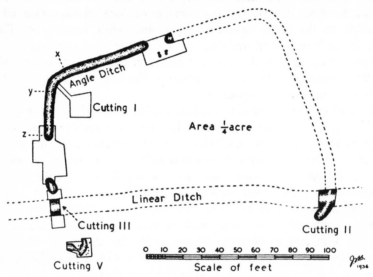

FIG. 67.   Rectilinear enclosure on Boscombe Down (Wilts.).   After Stone
in *WAM*.

cutting through the chalk, with a low bank on either or both flanks' which, Hawkes [16] thinks, served as cattle-ways as well as boundaries. The areas they demarcate are often bounded by streams on one side. The date of these travelling earthworks is by no means certain—they may well belong to Period VII. But one on Boscombe Down (Wilts.) was associated with one of the rectilinear cattle-kraals that are among the best-known monuments of the Deverel–Rimbury people (Fig. 67, 'linear ditch').[17]

These are rhomboid enclosures, one quarter to two acres in area, bounded by banks and ditches [18] (Fig. 67).   The rectilinear character of the earth-

---

[15] *WAM.*, xlvii, 484; *Ant. J.*, xvi, 33.   [16] *P. Hants F.C.*, xiv (1938), 142-146.
[17] *WAM.*, xlvii, 466-480.
[18] Classic are South Lodge Camp and Martin's Down, Dorset; Pitt-Rivers, *Excavations at Cranbourne Chase*, iv. (1898), 5, 185; cf. also *PPS.*, viii, 59-61.

works contrasts with the circular plan of pure Bronze Age sanctuaries and pounds, and with the irregular lines, following the contours, of neolithic camps and Iron Age forts. But it does recall the layout of larger enclosures termed *terremare* and built by immigrants from Central Europe in the Po valley, and the later quadrangular earthworks built by Celts in North France and southern Germany.[19] Both the rectilinear enclosures and the travelling ditches have at times been built on lands previously ploughed up into Celtic fields.[20] But normally they are connected with pastures on the north flanks of the downs; the more permanent habitations, connected with the arable on the sunny southern slopes, are hardly known. At Thorny Down, Stone [21] recovered the plan of a dwelling-house, standing in a yard protected on one side with bank and ditch; if the 33 post-sockets and 10 stake-holes recognized be all contemporary, the house thus supported may have been of the courtyard plan (p. 183).

In addition to transforming husbandry, the Deverel–Rimbury invaders brought improvements in secondary industries. For textiles spindle-whorls and *cylindrical loom-weights* are found in their settlements for the first time in Britain. Bronze was used in such quantities that broken pieces were left about in the ditches of kraals and on steading floors. These show that Deverel–Rimbury folk used winged axes attributed to phase 5 and thin double-edged razors, either oval or bifid (pp. 154, 175),[22] and wore ribbed bracelets of bronze.[23] Even iron-working may have been introduced while they were dominant in Wessex and Sussex.[24] But flint was still mined [25] and used for various tools, particularly scrapers with a high flaking angle and trimmed at the edge of the striking platform opposite the bulb.[26]

Even agriculture with a light plough could not provide for long adequate sustenance for expanding populations. Continued pressure on the land promoted further folk migrations in Central and North Europe, accelerated perhaps by a deterioration of climate from the genial Sub-Boreal to the cold Sub-Atlantic phase. Repercussions of these events set in motion communities settled over a wide area from the upper Marne to the Zuyder Zee. Fractions thus displaced invaded the English coasts along a broad

[19] ' Viereckschanze ': Bittel, *Die Kelten in Würtemberg*, 100-103.

[20] Crawford, *Air Survey and Archaeology*, 39.

[21] *WAM.*, xlvii, 640-660.

[22] e.g. Pitt-Rivers, *op. cit.*, Pl. 238; note that a leaf-shaped spear-head with loops on the socket was found *high up* in the silting of this ditch.

[23] Pitt-Rivers, *Cranbourne Chase*, iv, 20, Pl. 238, G.; *WAM.*, xlvii, Pl. V, 19.

[24] Iron-slag from ditch at Boscombe Down: *WAM.*, xlvii, 484; iron traces on whetstone from Plumpton Plain B: *PPS.*, i, 36.

[25] *WAM.*, xlvii, 482.   [26] *WAM.*, xlvii, 650; *Ant. J.*, xvi, 43.

front from Exeter on the south-west to Scarborough on the north-east. The colonists replaced or absorbed the Deverel–Rimbury populations of southern England and put an end to their culture.

2. THE COMING OF IRON

During the eighth century the knowledge of economical iron-working spread among the various mixed communities living round the Alps and in Central Europe. And iron for the first time put into the hands of every farmer cheap and durable tools for tree-felling and cheap but efficient weapons for warfare. All the earliest iron-using communities in the regions named share so many traits in common that it is legitimate to speak of a *Hallstatt civilization*, named after a rich cemetery in Upper Austria. The immigrants who now reached Britain were all more or less affected by the Hallstatt civilization, though to very different degrees. All may have been accompanied by blacksmiths, all had a rather more advanced rural economy and a more closely knit social organization than their Late Bronze Age precursors, and probably some traditions of fortification. Mixing with the not-unrelated Deverel–Rimbury folk they established in Britain a series of cultures—*All Cannings Cross* in Wiltshire (Fig. 83, 8), *West Harling* in Norfolk (*ib.*, 4) and *Scarborough* in Yorkshire may rank as type sites—that can easily be distinguished by pottery styles that relate them to distinct groups on the Continent, but are in other respects so closely allied that all can conveniently be embraced by the term *Iron Age A*, introduced by Hawkes.[27]

A century or so after the establishment of the Iron Age A farmers, England was harried by Marnian chieftains with a La Tène culture from Champagne. As will appear in Chapter XI, these actually conquered eastern Yorkshire, but were less successful in southern England where the Iron Age A peoples on the whole maintained their independence, or at least their cultural identity. But their culture was not unaffected, so that it is possible to distinguish within the continuous Iron Age A tradition an A 1 phase before and an A 2 phase after the invasion, as Wheeler[28] established. Since only a few aspects of the culture can as yet be accurately

[27] *Antiquity*, v, 67-74; *Arch. Eng. & Wales*, 153 ff. The division into A, B and C is not chronological but depends on the dominance of Hallstatt, Marnian–La Tène and Belgic features respectively.

[28] *Ant. J.*, xv, 274. *Maiden Castle*, 187 ff.

distributed between these two phases, both must be treated together here.

The Iron Age A culture was based on mixed farming more intensive than that practised by the Deverel–Rimbury communities, but supplemented, of course, by hunting. The quantities of red-deer's antlers used in the Wessex settlements are a timely reminder of the extent of surviving woodlands and of the utility of game as a variant on beef and mutton. Dart-heads, made from a sheep's metapodial, cut off obliquely at one end, hollowed throughout to take a shaft and perforated near the butt with peg-holes for attachment thereto, are common in most settlements and must rank as hunters' weapons.[29] But the main business of life was stock-breeding and cultivating Celtic fields with the appropriate two-ox plough. Wheat and barley were the favourite crops but oats (*Avena sativa*) was now also grown.[30a]

The fields were exploited from settlements of three distinct kinds: open villages generally on the slopes of the downs, lone steadings and hill-top forts. The classical site of All Cannings Cross[30] shows that nucleated villages go back to the beginning of phase A1, but none has been so fully explored as to afford a definite picture of the size of the social unit and its economy. Bersu's model excavation of the lone steading at Woodbury (near Salisbury)[31] throws light on the rural economy of the whole All Cannings Cross culture.

This steading was surrounded by a palisade enclosing an irregularly circular yard, 400 ft. in diameter. During the scare caused by the Marnian raids a defensive ditch had been started outside the fence but never finished— a phenomenon noted at other farms. In the yard stood a single circular house, supported by three rings of posts, walled probably with planks and perhaps enclosing an open central court. The posts of this house had been renewed three times, after which the whole structure was demolished and replaced by another house of similar plan.

The most prominent features in the yard were numerous pits, which showed up on an air-photograph even before excavation. They are familiar from many other steadings, from villages like All Cannings Cross and Scarborough, and from occupied hill forts.[32] They have been habitually described as 'pit-dwellings.' They may be bell-shaped, 8 to 10 ft. deep, 6 ft. wide at the mouth and as much as 10 ft. in diameter at the bottom.

---

[29] Cunnington, *A.C.*, 82; but these are also found on pure La Tène sites.

[30] Cunnington, *The Early Iron Age Inhabited Site at All Cannings Cross*, cited *A.C.*

[30a] Jessen and Helbaek, 48–50.   [31] *PPS.*, vi (1940), 30–111.

[32] At Maiden Castle Wheeler found 26 pits exceeding 5 ft. in depth in an area of ¼ acre: *Ant. J.*, xv, 269.

Even the largest would be singularly incommodious and uncomfortable dwellings. In reality they were silos for the storage of grain.[33] To be stored in this way the grain would have to be previously dried in a kiln. Even so, the same pit could only be used for storage for a few years. Then a new pit had to be dug, and the old hole turned into a refuse-dump or a working-place. Fires might be lit in the latter, and into the former would be thrown broken stones and baked clay from domestic hearths, together with ashes, bones and other rubbish. Such are the evidences of occupation which have been claimed as making the pits dwellings!

As silos they are more instructive, if less romantic. Woodbury was occupied for some three centuries. During that time no less than 360 silos, not to speak of other pits, must have been dug in the yard. In any one year they would have afforded storage room for 55 bushels. Now it is estimated that it would take 5 acres to produce such a yield. Hence, assuming a three-year rotation, some 15 acres of arable must have been attached to a lone steading like Woodbury.

Even during phase A 1 the Hallstatt colonists established strongholds or refuges on defensible hill-tops not only in Wessex and Sussex but also north of the Thames, even in Hertfordshire.[34] None were very large or strongly fortified; that on Quarley Hill was 1100 ft. long and 550 ft. wide, Thundersbarrow only 250 ft. across. The defences seem to have been confined to a stout palisade the trench for which survives. Such could have served as temporary refuges while the adjacent country was being pacified or during hostile campaigns. But during the third century some of these sites were converted into regular hill-top forts by enlarging and strengthening the defences. Some of the new fortresses were never finished [35]; others were abandoned almost as soon as they had been fortified, and the ditches allowed to silt up; half the total or less remained in occupation during phase A 2. The sudden outburst of fort-building must surely, as Hawkes [36] suggests, represent a common reaction to a common danger—the attacks by Marnian chiefs described below (pp. 213, 224).

[33] Silos (generally termed pit-dwellings) had been dug in the löss of Central Europe from neolithic times and throughout the Bronze Age (Childe, *Danube*, 26, 98, 234, 339). Less like the British are the straw-lined granaries of Merimde and the Fayum in neolithic Egypt (Childe, *NLMAE.*, 56, 58) and south-east Spain (Childe, *Dawn*, 251). Diodorus Siculus (v, 21, 5) expressly mentions as a peculiarity of British rural economy that the ears themselves (στάχυς αὐτούς) were cut off and stored in covered bins (καταστέγοι οἰκήσεις).

[34] Wilbury, near Letchworth (Herts., Fig. 83, 3) (*JBAA.*, xxxix, 352-357); the Trundle, Hollingbury, Cissbury, etc. (in Sussex); Quarley Hill and Meon Hill (Hants) (*P. Hants F.C.*, xiv, 187), etc.

[35] e.g. Ladle Hill (Hants): *Antiquity*, v, 474-485.   [36] *P. Hants F.C.*, xiv, 189.

This danger was repelled. But the panic may have had more permanent effects than to cumber the downs with grass-grown ruins. It may have promoted some degree of political unification expressed in permanent tribal refuges or capitals.

The hill forts of Iron Age A vary in area from 60 to 8 acres, but 14 to 24 acres is normal.[37] The defences, which always take advantage of the natural strength of the hill by following the contours, are constructed in accordance with a remarkably uniform plan. They consist of a deep V-shaped ditch, separated by a level platform or *berm*, 6 to 10 ft. wide, from

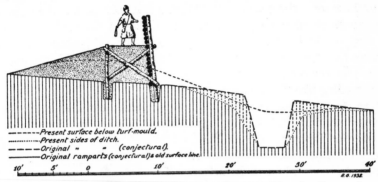

FIG. 68.   Rampart of Hollingbury, Sussex.   After *Ant. J.*

an earthen rampart. The latter, which appears today merely as a grassy bank, was in reality a formidable work, faced with an almost vertical timber revetment held in place by stout posts. The wood has of course decayed, but a skilled excavator can detect the sockets or trenches in which the uprights stood, and can even estimate the inward batter of the revetment. To support the thrust of the earth piled against it the batter of the revetment alone was insufficient; the frontal uprights had to be tied back by slanting beams grounded at the inner margin of the bank.[38] Often one can detect an inner line of post-holes or an inner trench, parallel to the revetment and 6 or 7 ft. behind it, to hold a second row of posts to which the revetment was cross-tied.[39] In either case the wooden revetment would be carried up to form a parapet above the top of the bank, which would thus form a rampart walk for the defenders (Fig. 68). At Maiden Castle (Fig. 83, 11)

[37] e.g. Cissbury, 60 acres; St Catherine's Hill (Winchester), 23 acres; Maiden Castle I, 16 acres; Figsbury, 15 acres; Wilbury, 14 acres; Quarley Hill, 8½ acres.

[38] e.g. Cissbury: Curwen, *Arch. Sus.*, Fig. 70, 1; Maiden Castle: *Ant. J.*, xvii, 265.

[39] e.g. Hollingbury as reconstructed by Bersu: Curwen, *Arch. Sus.*, Fig. 71; Wilbury: *Arch. J.*, xci, 323.

the wooden revetment near the east entrance was soon replaced by a built stone face, but even then the masonry was interrupted every 5 ft. by posts.[40]

The only stone-built fort of Iron Age A yet excavated, Chastleton (Oxon),[41] lacked the external ditch, and no timbering was observed, perhaps owing to the very short strip of outer face exposed.

The earthen ramparts being in any case some 12 ft. wide, the entrance took the form of a passage the sides of which, like the rampart face, must be reveted with timbers or, at Maiden Castle, with masonry. Additional strength was secured by prolonging the ends of the rampart inwards on both sides of the fairway, producing what is termed an *inturned entrance*. Often two pairs of stout post-sockets indicate a form of barbican gate over which the rampart walk could be carried by a wooden bridge.[42] At St Catherine's Hill and The Trundle the barbican plan replaces a simpler form with a single gate, but the gates in either case would be two-leaved.[43] A guardroom or cell was often constructed against the inturned rampart just inside the gate.

The uniformity of strategic architecture displayed in all well-excavated Iron Age A forts from Dorchester to Folkestone and northward to Letchworth is one of the best proofs of the homogeneity of the culture in southern England. It expresses traditions brought by the invaders from the Continent, since Bersu has described Hallstatt forts built on the same principles in south-western Germany.

The erection of such a number of imposing fortresses—at least 35 are known today—implies a substantial population. Curwen [44] estimates that the ramparts of Cissbury—admittedly the largest fort of the period—contained 35,000 cubic yards of chalk weighing about 60,000 tons, while the revetment would require 8,000 to 12,000 timbers at least 15 ft. long and 9 ins. thick! And the labour of digging the ditches and piling the upcast, felling and placing the timbers, could not be spread out over several seasons as could the building of a family vault or a sanctuary, but presupposes a very numerous labour force employed simultaneously on all the several hill-top forts and on many farms too.

3. THE FIRST CITIES?

Did the enlarged population deducible from the construction of the imposing works just described find support principally in the new improved

[40] *Ant. J.*, xvii, 266.   [41] *Ant. J.*, xi, 384-389.   [42] Bersu quoted in *Ant. J.*, xiii, 163.
[43] Hawkes, *Antiquity*, v, 74; Curwen, *Arch. Sus.*, 243-246.   [44] *Arch. Sus.*, 242.

farming, or had trade and manufacture progressed so far as to offer an urban livelihood to the overflow from the countryside? The granaries, providing for the storage of substantial supplies of grain, certainly prove that a surplus of food-stuffs could be produced and accumulated. And Curwen and Wheeler both speak of our hill forts as cities. They do not, of course, refer to unfinished or unoccupied works, which can incidentally only be distinguished by extensive excavation. In what sense is the term applicable to the rest?

On the South Downs four—Cissbury (Fig. 83, 6), the Trundle (Goodwood), Old Winchester Hill and St Catherine's Hill [45]—retained the status of permanent forts in phase A 2 (at Cissbury the A 2 culture was overlaid by that of victorious Marnians—p. 224). Each of them dominates a block of downland, delimited by river valleys, and presumably represents the capital of a tribe, grazing or cultivating the area thus defined—in the case of Cissbury, 35 sq. miles. Such forts might then denote the political unification of the communities occupying open villages and lone steadings in their areas—a consolidation perhaps accelerated by the Marnian scare.

To what extent did this political unification correspond to an economic unification? Were hill forts centres of trade and industry in which specialized merchants and artisans were supported by the surplus food-stuffs produced by the farmers? Curwen insists that lyncheted fields are not normally connected with the hill forts. He concludes that their occupants were not farmers but shopkeepers and artisans to whom the countrymen repaired for supplies of manufactured goods as they did to a Mediterranean or mediaeval city. Hill forts would be cities both in the political and in the economic sense.

Now hill forts are mostly very small, the enclosed area normally lying between 12 and 25 acres. Even the winter-quarters of a Roman garrison on the Scottish frontier like Inchtuthil (Perths.) exceed this, measuring 50 acres. Roman London covered 330 acres, Cirencester 240, and even Silchester 100, though Caerwent (Mon.) sinks to 44 acres.[46] In a hill fort only a small area at best was regularly occupied by dwellings. In the English climate of modern or Sub-Atlantic times a hill-top is a bleak spot if you have to live in a wooden house. The best place is immediately under the shelter of the ramparts, and that is where evidences of occupation are generally concentrated; the central area was probably an open space

[45] Curwen, *Arch. Sus.*, 236-240, and with map *SAC.*, lxxx, 214-215.
[46] Collingwood and Myres, *Roman Britain and the English Settlements*, 119, 197.

where flocks and herds could be gathered, at least in times of danger. The resident population cannot have been large.[47]

Secondly, the traces of occupation are relatively slight in most cases. Bersu indeed maintains that none of the large hill forts were really permanently inhabited. They would be rather just refuges to which villagers and farmers repaired during periods of danger, like the Hallstatt forts of Germany.[48]

In any case, there were silos in some forts, like Maiden Castle, just as much as in the rural villages and lone steadings. They presumably belonged to farmers resident within the enceinte. The crafts, industries, metallurgical and textile, demonstrably plied in hill forts, are equally attested in villages and farmsteads. In only two forts, founded by Iron Age A people, the Caburn and Hunsbury, do the relics suggest more intensive metallurgical activity, and both belong culturally to Iron Age B (*infra*, p. 244). The pure Iron Age A forts may then have been merely refuges like the German; at best they were tribal capitals in which periodical markets may have been held. They lack the economic, and probably also the spiritual, unity that gives coherence to an industrial town or cathedral city as it did to a Greek *polis* and a Sumerian city-state.

Industry remained on the whole in the stage of household crafts, though some improvements are manifest. Iron-working requires, as noted on p. 178, less extensive trade than bronze. But the sources of the iron used in Period VII are still undefined; the earliest settlements yet identified in the Weald, for example, date only from the last century B.C.[49] In the course of Iron Age A the blacksmith was able to provide the farmer with sickles, bill-hooks and even narrow ploughshares[50] (Fig. 65, 1). But some axes were still forged in imitation of the cast socketed axe of bronze, loop and all.[51]

In fact, at the beginning of Period VII bronze was still competing with iron for the manufacture of tools even in southern England. A socketed bronze axe was found in the village of All Cannings Cross, as was a bifid razor[52]; a Sussex hoard of the period comprised bronze spear-heads and palstaves.[53] And of course the old alloy was still current everywhere for ornaments. In the north, however, at Scarborough, bronze was cast into socketed axes and other implements in the native Late Bronze Age tradition,

---

[47] For the small fort of the Caburn, Curwen estimates 200-300 (*Arch. Sus.*, 248), but the pits used as the basis of his calculation may have been granaries, cf. p. 196.

[48] Ebert's *Real.*: *s.v.* Festung.　　　　　　　[49] Curwen, *Arch. Sus.*, 258.

[50] e.g. Frilford (Berks.): *Oxon.*, iv, 13; Hunsbury: *Arch. J.*, xciii, 66; the Caburn: *SAC.*, lxviii, Pl. IV.　　　　　　　[51] *Arch. J.*, lxxxv, 173.

[52] Cunnington, *A.C.*, 119, 121; another razor from Merlin's Cave: *PBUSS.*, iv (1931), 18-27, Pl. IV.　　　　　　　[53] Curwen, *Arch. Sus.*, 205, 227.

and only one piece of iron was recovered. The bronze was everywhere supplied by the organization described in Chapter IX, which must have still survived.

Moreover, flint was still in use everywhere. In Essex even axes were still produced by the old tranchet technique,[54] and at Scarborough a peculiar type of hollow scraper was manufactured.

The textile industry, at least in southern England, became increasingly important. Even in A 1 settlements, whether villages or lone steadings, some of the commonest finds are spindle-whorls and loom-weights, now always of a peculiar triangular type [55] (Fig. 69). By phase A 2 quite an elaborate set of bone tools had been invented—tools which are purely English and have no parallels abroad. The most striking are long-handled combs (Fig. 70) with coarse teeth supposedly used for separating the threads hanging

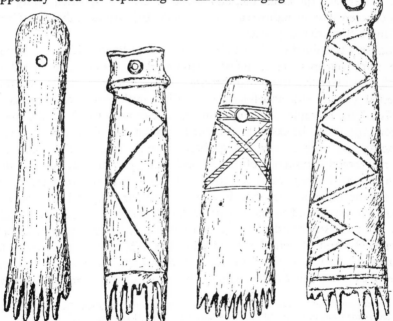

FIG. 70. Weaving Combs, All Cannings Cross. ⅔. After Cunnington.

[54] Kendrick and Hawkes, 167; *Essex Naturalist*, xxii, 131.
[55] e.g. Park Brow (Sussex): *Ant. J.*, iv, 350-355; Stutton (Norfolk): *Arch. J.*, xcvi, 21 and often.

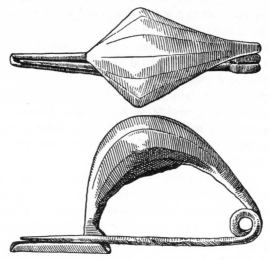

FIG. 71.   Hallstatt brooch, Boroughbridge.   ¾.   After *Ant. J.*

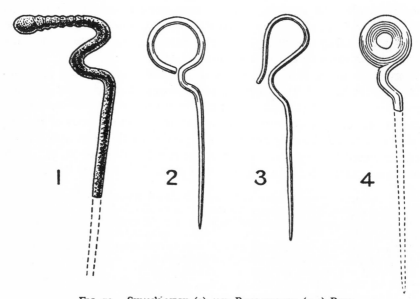

FIG. 72.   SWAN'S-NECK (1) AND RING-HEADED (2-4) PINS.
1. All Cannings Cross; 2. Hunsbury; 3. Laws of Monifieth; 4. Dunagoil.
⅔. After Dunning in *Arch. J.*

on the loom.[56] Whorls made from the heads of animals' femurs,[57] and tubular lengths of bone up to 2 inches long and perforated with a transverse slot,[58] may also have been used by Iron Age A spinners and weavers. This equipment is found in isolated farms just as much as in villages and hill forts, so that it must be used in household industry, though households may well have produced a surplus for sale.

The Hallstatt invaders had introduced the Central European fashion of pinned garments to supersede at length the Atlantic–Mediterranean buttoned costume. They may have brought with them or imported safety-pins or brooches of Hallstatt type (Fig. 71), stray examples of which have been found in the Iron Age A province from Yorkshire to Wessex,[59] but this fashion was not maintained. Though some Iron Age A people seem to have worn La Tène I brooches,[60] these, like a few penannular brooches,[61] were probably obtained from the Marnian invaders.[62] Pins, on the other hand, were locally made. The oldest type to be fashionable was the *swan's neck pin* [63] (Fig. 72, 1), popular among the Hallstatt peoples of Germany, Switzerland and eastern France. In England during phase A 2 this was improved to form the *ring-headed pin* (Fig. 72, 2) which was also worn by some B people. Jet armlets, too, had been popular among the Hallstatt peoples of the Continent and are first attested in southern England in Iron Age A, though they are found in the Highland Zone in a Late Bronze Age context, as for instance at Heathery Burn (p. 180).

Pottery, as in the Bronze Age, was still a hand-made product, generally of domestic industry. The almost universal coarse domestic ware is in fact quite in the Bronze Age tradition. It may be distinguished [64] by the careful flattening of the rim, decoration by finger-printing on the body of the pot as well as on applied mouldings, and by a preference for vases with a sharp shoulder placed high up and inspired by the metal situla (Fig. 73, 5). Such coarse ware persists for a long time, but in phase A 2 (Fig. 74) the flattened

[56] All Cannings Cross and often in Wessex, Chastleton (Oxon) and Radley (Berks.): *Ant. J.*, xi, 387; Park Brow (Sussex); Abingdon Piggotts (Cambs.): *VCH., Camb.*, i, 287. These pure A sites seem to demonstrate the antiquity of the appliance though it is better known from B sites.

[57] Cunnington, *A.C.*, Pl. 16, 7; cf. *Arch. J.*, xciii, 69 (Hunsbury).

[58] Cunnington, *A.C.*, Pl. 6, 38; *Arch. J.*, xciii, Pl. IX, 1.

[59] Kendrick and Hawkes, 168–169; *Arch. J.*, xcvi, 31, Pl. V.

[60] e.g. *All Cannings Cross* (Pl. 18, 13); cf. Fox, *Arch. Camb.* (1927), 70–90.

[61] *All Cannings Cross*, Pl. 18, 1.

[62] Hawkes, *Ant. J.*, xx, 120; *SAC.*, lxxx, 230–238.

[63] Dunning, *Arch. J.*, xci (1934), 270–287; and Wilbury, *ibid.*, xci, 323.

[64] Curwen, *Arch. Sus.*, 271.

rim and finger-printing tend to die out and the shoulders are rounded off and eventually lost. Finer wares serve to define local groups and disclose their Continental roots.

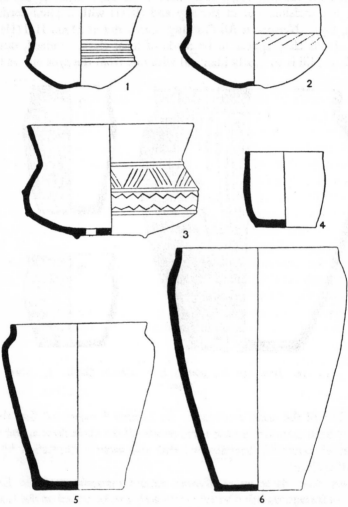

FIG. 73. Pottery from All Cannings Cross. ¼. After Cunnington.

Fine *haematite ware* is classically represented at All Cannings Cross, Meon Hill, and Hengistbury Head (Fig. 83, 7). The surface of the vases, often quite thin-walled, is coated with a ferruginous slip that turns red on firing. It was built up into jars, deep bowls and dishes, all with sharp angular profiles and often provided with an omphalos on the base pushed up from below. These may be decorated with corrugations (furrows) executed with smooth, blunt tools before the application of the red slip, or with fine incisions cut in the slip and (later) with applied cordons too (Fig. 73, 1-3). Neither at All Cannings Cross nor at Meon Hill (Hants) do vessels of this class appear to be made of local clays. Indeed, one vessel from Meon Hill is so nearly identical with one from the type site as to seem

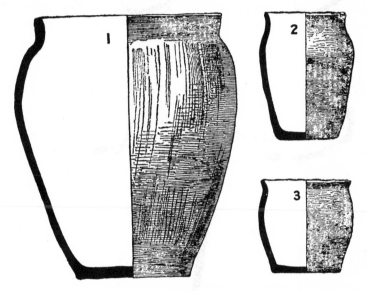

FIG. 74. Iron Age A2 pottery from Maiden Castle. ⅓. After Wheeler.

the product of the same workshop. So Liddell [65] suggested that the ware may have been manufactured at some centre off the chalk downs, and opened up vistas of industrial specialization that still await confirmation by petrographical analyses.

In any case, these vases, though almost certainly made in England, represent a foreign tradition which fortunately can be traced on the Continent with unusual accuracy. Just the same sort of vases were deposited in the graves of the Final Hallstatt cemetery of Les Jogasses near Epernay (Marne).[66] Now the people buried in this cemetery gave place to another

[65] P. Hants F.C., xiii, 23.   [66] Favret in Préhistoire, v (1936), 25-110, 105.

group possessed of a typically Marnian La Tène culture. The expelled Jogassians ultimately sought shelter in Wessex, but in the strain of an enforced evacuation lost much of their original Hallstatt culture and in the retreat mingled with remnants of older and less advanced communities.

The decorated Jogassian ware has a restricted distribution in Wessex, and the artistic tradition which inspired it soon died out in the insular environment. But it gave birth to a more persistent and widespread fabric that preserves its technical traditions, notably the haematite coating, and some Hallstatt shapes. This plain haematite-coated ware is found all over Wessex and even in Sussex, and spreads northward to the Upper Thames valley [67] and Hertfordshire.[68]

Farther east, another group of colonists settling near Eastbourne manufactured vases clearly inspired by the Hallstatt fashions of a south-west German homeland.[69] One was of reddish-brown ware adorned with lozenges painted in black in quite Central European style.

In East Anglia the surviving A pottery is coarser and less conspicuously exotic. But at West Harling (Norfolk) [70] we have a classical series of situliform urns with finger-printing on the rim and bowls with omphalos bases that can be traced as far inland as Hunsbury in Northamptonshire.[71] The home of this West Harling series must be sought on the Lower and Middle Rhine, very much in the area whence the Deverel–Rimbury invaders had started.

Finally, the pottery from Scarborough (Fig. 75), the only pure A site north of the Humber, is quite clearly derived from that of Holland.[72] It embodies one element of the Bronze Age tradition that underlay the Deverel–Rimbury ceramics, but to this have been superadded new Hallstatt shapes from the south and contributions from the Harpstadt group that had grown up east of the Rhine and is attributed to an infiltration of Teutonic tribes, precursors of those who fused with the Celts of eastern Gaul to become the Belgae.[73]

Of the carpenters and wheelwrights who must have made four-wheeled cars such as were used by the Jogassians and other Hallstatt peoples, the archaeological record has nothing as yet to tell. But we have some hints

---

[67] Frilford (Berks.), *Oxon.*, iv, 15.   [68] Wilbury, *JBAA.*, xxxviii, 249.

[69] *Ant. J.*, ii, 354-360; Curwen, *Arch. Sus.*, 226. Wasters (rejects from the kiln) demonstrate local manufacture.

[70] *PSEA.*, vii (1932), 111-122.   [71] *Arch. J.*, xciii, 83-85.

[72] Wheeler in Rowntree, *History of Scarborough*, 19 ff. Kendrick and Hawkes, 149-151, treat the site as Bronze Age.

[73] Stampfuss, *Mannus*, xvii (1924), 302 ff.

of one industry, highly developed among Continental Hallstatt folk, the manufacture of salt. For traces of salt-panning on the coasts of Essex and Lincolnshire [74] are associated with Iron Age A pottery.

With the settlement of the Iron Age A peasantry the funerary record breaks off, to reopen, only partially, in Period VIII. The Jogassians in Champagne had buried their dead, unburnt, with much pomp, sometimes in four-wheeled cars, but no comparable interments can be quoted from southern England. The Hallstatt societies on the Lower Rhine retained the Urnfield rite of cremation. There is one well-attested Iron Age A cremation from Park Brow (Sussex) [75] in a flat grave, and others under barrows have

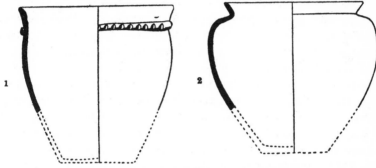

FIG. 75.   Pottery from Scarborough (Yorks.).   ¼.

been reported near Bristol and in East Anglia.[76] And some rough pots from Yorkshire, classed as Food Vessels or Incense Cups by Abercromby and Mortimer, are really Iron Age and may belong to the Scarborough group of invaders. But in general the farmers and warriors of Iron Age A did not waste their wealth and energy on funerary monuments that should survive to posterity.

The clearly recognizable Urnfield and Hallstatt immigrants, multiplying on the fertile unploughed soils of Lowland England, must have effected an almost total replacement of population. They established at least a rural economy that endured till the advent of the Belgae and in many parts throughout the Roman period till it was replaced by the Saxon system. When and how far did these events affect the Highland Zone?

[74] *Ant. J.*, xii, 239-256.
[75] *Ant. J.*, iv, 355.
[76] Kendrick and Hawkes, 172; *Arch. J.*, xcvi, 19; the 'house-urn' there illustrated by Rainbird Clark is really a portable oven and the 'grave' containing it a domestic rubbish pit (no human bones were found) according to Dr Bersu: *Arch. J.*, xcvi, 223-225.

4. Crannogs and Old Keig

Outside the areas mentioned on pp. 187-8, 194, no connected phenomena certainly disclose new societies apart from the old Urn folk during Periods VI and VII. Nevertheless, there are hints, like the Hallstatt sword and iron sickle from Llyn Fawr (p. 178), that Highland Britain had not been immune from infiltrations. And later we shall find that the Iron Age A technique of fortification was adopted in Wales and Scotland, and that the textile appliances here attributed to Iron Age A were in general use in Cornwall, Derbyshire and Yorkshire. In Ireland there is not a trace of the textile appliances, nor yet of the defensive architecture of the English Iron Age A.

On the other hand, a new type of settlement can now be traced back to Period VII and may denote an independent infiltration of new settlers. Some of the best-known Irish settlements of the Dark Ages are situated on artificial islands or *crannogs* in swamps and small lakes. Some are villages, substantially similar to that at Glastonbury described in the next chapter, but others are just lone steadings. Raftery [77] explored in 1936 a small crannog of the latter type at Knockanlappa on Rosroe Lough (Co. Clare), which yielded a leaf-shaped swòrd of degenerate V type, a socketed gouge and a sunflower pin of bronze, fragments from jet armlets and amber beads together with flat-rimmed vases of hard-baked black ware (not the least like Cinerary Urns), shaped on the model of the Hallstatt situlae (Fig. 76). Another crannog is reported to have yielded an iron socketed axe of Bronze Age form. The new type of settlement thus seems to go back to Period VII.

It is conceivable that the crannog developed in the British Isles out of lake-dwellings in the Western neolithic tradition such as may have existed on Ehenside Tarn (p. 43). But Mahr [78] pointed out that the genesis of the type can best be traced on the slopes of the Alps, the Late Bronze Age–Hallstatt village at Buchau on the Federsee in Würtemberg being in fact a classical crannog. He suggested that it may have been introduced into the British Isles by settlers of Alpine traditions.

Now, even in England there are indications of the settlement of peoples with traditions at least of lacustrine habitation. The only well-defined English crannogs, those of Somerset, indeed belong to Period VIII. But on the Thames near Southchurch (Essex) [79] and at Old England near

[77] *PPS.*, iii, 387-389.   [78] *CISPP.* (1932), 275-276.
[79] Kendrick and Hawkes, 145-146.

Brentford are remains of pile-dwellings, and at Old England there have been collected an iron copy of a socketed bronze axe, a winged Hallstatt sword-chape, horse-trappings, razors and chapes appropriate to the carp's tongue sword complex, some unusually 'Alpine' bronzes [80] and pot sherds, compared by Hawkes [81] to the Late Bronze Age pottery of Switzerland.

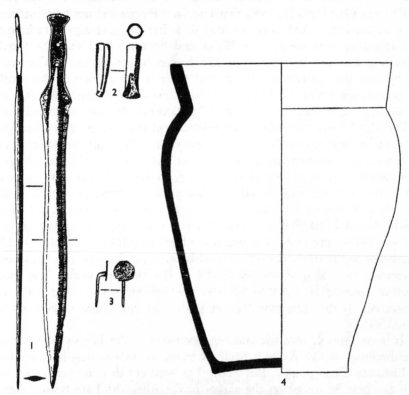

FIG. 76.   Sword, gouge and pin of bronze and pot from crannog of Knockanlappa.   ¼.   After Mahr in *PPS*.

The Old England settlement, like the carp's tongue sword group of bronzes and the pottery from Plumpton Plain B, may commemorate a distinct body of immigrants who were merged in the larger Deverel–Rimbury complex or swamped by the Hallstatt invaders.   As these latter types never appear

[80] e.g. the penannular razor, single-bladed knife and grooved sickle: *Antiquity*, iii, 20-32 (Pls. I, 6, 8, 9; II, 10); cf. Childe, *Danube*, Pls. V, 4a; VI, 13.

[81] *loc. cit.*

in Ireland, their bearers can hardly be the direct ancestors of the Knockan-lappa settlers.

Pile-dwellings in the Vale of Pickering (Yorks.) [82] are in the same case; for though the pottery is in the rough Iron Age A tradition, the dateable relics belong to the first century of our era. The numerous crannogs of

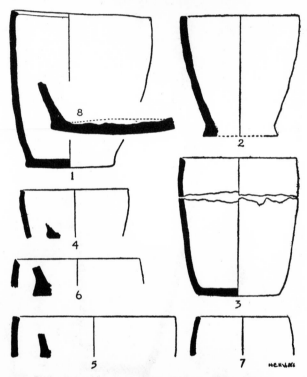

FIG. 77. Old Keig pottery from Loanhead of Daviot. ⅛.
After Kilbride-Jones in *PSAS*.

Galloway, Ayrshire and the Clyde valley, all lone steadings, are more like the Irish, but might just as well be derived from Ireland. The oldest dateable relic from any Scottish crannog is the ring of a class B cauldron.[83] If settlers of Alpine tradition did find lodgement in Ireland, they should, judging by the sunflower pins and amber, have belonged to the Northern stream of emigrants rather than the Western which reached the Thames.[84]

[82] *YAJ.*, xxx, 157-172.   [83] Childe, *P.S.*, 211-212.

[84] There are reports of pile-dwellings in Belgium, and the Dutch *terpen*, going back to the La Tène period, embody the same idea as a crannog: van Giffen, *Germania* (1936), 40 ff.

If they could not retain their identity over against the established Food Vessel and Urn folk, and even sank to a subordinate position, they may yet have influenced rural economy as well as architecture.

On the other hand in North Britain as in Ireland attention has recently been drawn to a class of flat-rimmed pottery which, though unconnected with crannog architecture, does resemble that from Knocknalappa, and, in its Continental affinities, is to some extent parallel to Iron Age A. In North-east Scotland " Old Keig ware " is harder fired than normal Cinerary Urns and is characterized by flattened rims, but the only common form is a barrel-shaped cooking pot (Fig. 77). In the Sculptor's Cave, Covesea (Elgins.),[85] this fabric was associated with Late Bronze Age types—Irish ring-money and massive penannular armlets of Central European type. In Aberdeenshire at Old Keig and Loanhead of Daviot[86] it accompanied cremated burials intruded into Recumbent Stone Circles and almost certainly later than those in Overhanging Rim and Enlarged Food Vessel Urns in an adjacent cemetery.[87] But it was found on a bloomery site too.[88] Seven precisely similar pots, filled with cremated bones, had been buried together, mouth upward, in an oval grave in an urnfield at Largs (Ayrshire)[89] and another, also containing a cremation, was exposed in 1944 in a sandpit near Creetown on Wigtown Bay. Some of the earlier domestic pottery from the great Iron Age fort on Traprain Law (East Lothian) (p. 254) and the few sherds from Heathery Burn Cave (Co. Durham) (p. 180) resemble Old Keig ware in a general way. At both these sites, as at Old Keig itself, lignite bracelets were also found. A number of Mortimer's " Food Vessels " from Yorkshire are really flat-rimmed barrel-shaped pots, but such occur also in graves of the Arras culture (p. 217).

In Ireland flat-rimmed situla-urns, more like Fig. 76, have turned up at two sites in Co. Antrim, once inverted over cremated bones[90], and even in Limerick one of the burial urns from Cush seems to belong to the flat-rimmed family. Finally, very similar is the domestic ware collected in a lake-side habitation under Crannog 2 at Ballinderry, Co. Offaly.[91] From the same layer came a socketed knife, rings and a flesh-hook of bronze, amber beads of Late Bronze Age type and shale armlets like the lignite bracelets from North British sites.

From these hints, together with the evidence from Jarlshof (p. 186), Dr. Hencken is inclined to deduce an invasion of Late Bronze Age folk, already influenced by Hallstatt culture, parallel to the Iron Age A movement but from a more northerly centre. Crossing northern Britain the invaders would eventually have reached Ulster from Galloway, like the Urn folk, and thence spread south. Nothing connects the hypothetical invaders with the building of crannogs nor yet of *souterrains*.[92] Yet the latter might well have been devised in the northern isles and thence diffused to the districts round the Moray Firth, perhaps with stone ladles[93] which have a somewhat similar distribution and are often made of steatite, a stone that occurs in Shetland.

(85) *PSAS.*, lxv, 180–90. (86) Childe, *PS.*, 175-6 ; *PSAS.*, lxix, 168–213.

(87) *PSAS.*, lxx, 290–310. (88) *PSAS*, lxxi, 401–5.

(89) *Arch.*, lxii, 245 ff. (90) Culmore, *UJA.*, viii, 40–2.

(91) Hencken, *PRIA.*, xlvii, C (1942), 6–27. (92) Childe, *PS.*, 213–7.

(93) *Ibid.*, 246. The distribution of the mainland is indicated by the following figures: north of the Moray Firth, 13 ; Moray Firth to the Mounth, 40 ; Mounth to Forth, 17 ; west of Scotland, 11. There are several strays in Ireland and one in Cornwall.

CHAPTER XI

THE LA TÈNE INVASIONS

THE *La Tène cultures* (called after a really rather late emporium on Lake Neuchâtel) arose through the impact of the urban civilizations of Magna Grecia and Etruria upon the Hallstatt populations of eastern France, Switzerland and southern Germany, with some contributions from the Scyths of South Russia. The contacts with Mediterranean States were at first commercial—across the Alpine passes with the Etruscans and along the Rhone with the Greek colony of Massilia (Marseilles). Trade in metals, amber, slaves, furs and forest products brought to the Celtic barbarians wealth, concentrated in the hands of war-chiefs. These could import jars of Mediterranean wine with complete table-services of Greek and Etruscan metal vessels and Attic or Italiote painted pottery. Foreign artisans came to share this wealth and taught native craftsmen to copy classical metal-work, to build light two-wheeled war-chariots on Etruscan models and to produce everyday necessities, like shears, chains, pot-hooks and tongs, hitherto unknown north of the Alps. The sudden access of wealth, superimposed upon a still primitive rural economy, promoted an expansion to find new lands for a growing population. In the fourth and third centuries the Celts spread far into the Danube basin, invaded Italy, South France and Spain.

In the third century they attacked Britain too. But the first invaders in the West lost much of the La Tène civilization on the way. They were warrior-bands, seeking new lands, perhaps the younger sons of Gaulish chiefs with their junior tenantry for whom no room was left on the ancestral farm. A few essential craftsmen—smiths and carpenters—must have accompanied them, but the highly skilled experts in luxury trades, and even perhaps the most competent potters, were more or less emancipated from tribal bonds in the new half-urban economy, and settled only where there was a market for their skill. Such would not embark upon overseas adventures until their success, yielding surplus wealth, offered inducements to migration. So in defining the new societies in Britain we are liable to be deprived of ceramic evidence, our best guide, and at first of art products too. Weapons and personal ornaments, like brooches, though very valuable for chronology, can so easily be traded or stolen that they do not in themselves accurately define peoples. Objects of parade—shields, scabbards, horse-trappings—decorated in the La Tène style, were the prerogatives of an upper class; they reveal the presence of La Tène chieftains, but say little about the cultural and ethnic affiliations of their subjects or their economic status. With these provisos we can distinguish four main groups in Britain enjoying some La Tène culture but differing in traditions and in the origins of their ruling classes.

1. THE ABERNETHY CULTURE

The La Tène invaders are most easily recognizable in Scotland, where they seem, in fact, to have introduced the first iron-using economy. Bands of warrior-farmers landed round the Firth of Tay and northward to the Moray Firth, and eventually spread across Scotland to the west coasts of Inverness and Argyll,[1] and thence perhaps to Galloway and North Wales.[2] On arrival in their new untamed home they promptly entrenched themselves in powerful fortresses. These they girt with stupendous stone ramparts, 10 to 20 ft. thick, and constructed in a technique similar to that described by Julius Caesar as *murus gallicus*. The facing walls, built of roughly squared stone blocks, were tied together at intervals by stout timbers, laid horizontally at right angles to the faces. The interspace was filled with timbers, laid parallel to the faces, and with rubble.

Walls built on this plan are very stable, but they are liable to be set alight by fires kindled against them. Many were in fact ignited, whether by accident or by hostile design. Experiment[3] has shown that, once ablaze, such a Gallic wall becomes a kiln, the combustion of the wood between the faces generating a temperature of the order of 1000° to 1300° C. The faces, of course, for the most part collapse when the tie-beams are consumed, but the rubble core may be partly melted by the intense heat, forming huge *vitrified* masses in which the component stones are literally fused together. The vitrified walls, which have puzzled antiquaries since 1760, are just Gallic walls that have been destroyed by fire.

The ramparts thus constructed do not as a rule follow the contours of the hill as do the defences of Iron Age A forts in England. Many Gallic

---

[1] The most important excavated sites are: Castle Law, Abernethy (Fig. 83, 22); Castle Law, Forgandenny (Perths.); Laws of Monifieth and Finavon (Angus); Rahoy (L. Teacuis) and Duntroon (L. Crinan) (Argyll); Dunagoil (Bute); and Burghead near Elgin.

[2] Childe, *P.S.*, 193-197; near Corwen in North Wales is at least one classical vitrified fort agreeing in plan and siting with the Scottish.

[3] Childe and Thorneycroft, *PSAS.*, lxxii, 44-49.

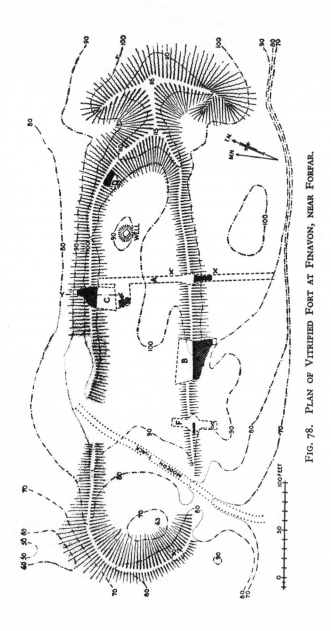

FIG. 78. PLAN OF VITRIFIED FORT AT FINAVON, NEAR FORFAR.

forts in Scotland, and at least one in Wales, are trapeze-shaped, the long parallel sides running dead straight across gullies and ridges (Fig. 78).

Most were occupied as regular hill-top towns—or rather villages, for their dimensions are modest. At Finavon[4] the area enclosed by the walls was barely an acre. Yet at least one row of small houses was ranged under the shelter of the north rampart to the number of at least 20. And, as in other Gallic forts, a well had been sunk through the living rock to provide a permanent water-supply within the enceinte. Some of the villagers may, however, have dwelt in peace-time beside their fields outside the walls. Many hut-circles may be seen on the slopes of Tap o' Noth (Aberdeens.), which is crowned by a vitrified wall. In any case, the quarrying of 250,000 cubic feet of stone, the felling of the timbers and the construction of the ramparts of Finavon seem beyond the powers of twenty households.

In the West Highlands a different social structure, appropriate to the local geography and foreshadowed even in megalithic times, is indicated. The circular fort at Rahoy (Fig. 83, 23) on Loch Teacuis (Argyll)[5] measured only 40 ft. in internal diameter and could thus accommodate only a single household. It was, in fact, the castle of a clan chief whose tenants presumably cultivated fields in the isolated glen dominated by the fortress.

The forts' occupants were farmers, breeding Celtic short-horn cattle, sheep and a few pigs, and cultivating cereals which they ground on saddle querns. Ovens found behind a hearth in a house at Finavon and under the floor at Rahoy[6] may have been used for drying grain, but granaries have not been identified. Industries on a small scale were carried on within the forts—metal-working, attested by thick clay crucibles and sandstone moulds for bronze bars; textiles, denoted by flat stone spindle-whorls; and, at Dunagoil, the manufacture of jet ornaments and steatite ladles from local materials. But the invaders had brought with them no expert potters to make fine vases. Instead they used wooden vessels,[7] supplemented where clay was available by coarse cooking-pots, unskilfully built up by hand out of very badly levigated clay and imperfectly fired. Technically and artistically the Abernethy pots are inferior to even the most degraded products of the Bronze Age and are just what might be expected from amateurs who had been accustomed to purchase earthenware from expert craftsmen.

Nor were arms and ornaments decorated by expert artists. Cloaks were fastened by simple bronze or iron La Tène I brooches of the pattern

[4] *PSAS.*, lxix, 49-80.　　　　　　　　　[5] *PSAS.*, lxxii, 23-43.
[6] *PSAS.*, lxix, 63; lxxii, 32-34.
[7] Part of a wooden vessel was actually recovered from Castle Law, Abernethy.

fashionable on the Continent before 250 B.C.,[8] but also with ring-head pins of English Iron Age A type.[9] Thick rings of jet, obtainable in the occupied areas, were worn as pendants as among continental La Tène peoples; armlets, sometimes fluted, were made of the same material, and spiral finger-rings of bronze.

The settlements were indeed nearly self-sufficing. Flint scrapers, including the hollow type found at Scarborough, bone pins and needles, and perhaps even stone axe-heads, were still used. No certainly imported manufactures appear in the record. Most tools were of iron; a forged socketed iron axe of Late Bronze Age type from Rahoy [10] shows that the new metal was still competing locally with bronze. And the old commercial system doubtless provided the new lords with the bronze used for their ornaments and bulbous spear-butts.

Assuming that fashions in safety-pins in North Britain marched with those of the Continent, the Abernethy invaders must have arrived and spread even to the west coast by 200 B.C. How long they retained their identity is doubtful. Part of a rotary quern was found at Finavon, others at Dunagoil, but no Roman objects. Very likely it was the Roman army under Agricola that burned the Gallic forts in Perthshire and Angus. The invaders must have been prominent agents in introducing iron-working and intensive agriculture and in initiating forest clearance in Scotland. But with these improvements they seem to have introduced the wasteful Celtic system of perpetual internecine war. Perhaps they started fighting from chariots, though the antler cheek-pieces [11] that alone survive belong to the old-fashioned Hallstatt bits, not the new La Tène type. They do not seem to have succeeded in popularizing at all widely the fashion of wearing brooches.

2. THE ARRAS CULTURE

During the third century part of a tribe of Marnian Celts occupied the Wolds and Limestone Hills of eastern Yorkshire. The origin of this band of invaders is demonstrable historically as well as by the agreement of their burial rites, armament, horse-trappings and artistic tastes with those of the Marnian cemeteries in Champagne. In the second century A.D. the geographer Ptolemy mentioned a Celtic (not Belgic) tribe named Parisii as living in eastern Yorkshire. They must be a branch of the Parisii who

---

[8] Abernethy and Rahoy (bronze); Dunagoil (iron; too corroded for dating).
[9] Abernethy, Dunagoil, Laws of Monifieth (Fig. 72, 3-4).
[10] *PSAS.*, lxxii, 39.   [11] From Dunagoil.

since Caesar's time had been living on the Seine and have given their name to Paris. As there is no evidence for any migration into Yorkshire later than that to be described here, the tribal name must have been introduced by the invaders [12] to whose archaeological remains we now turn.

Meeting no effective resistance, the invaders did not have to build hill forts; the relatively sparse Iron Age A population and survivors of the Urn folk could be easily subdued; the occupied territory is protected naturally by the marshy Vale of York, by the Humber and by the North Sea. In Ptolemy's day the Parisii had a town, Petuaria, and a village site of the Roman period is now being excavated at Elmswell.[13] But no pre-Roman settlement attributable to them has been identified. They have left a sepulchral record instead. The cemeteries near Arras (Fig. 83, 1) and near Driffield (Danes' Graves) are said once to have comprised as many as 500 barrows. These may of course have been used from 200 B.C. to 100 A.D., though no Roman relics have been actually reported from them. But in any case these large cemeteries must belong at least to villages more compact and permanent than anything heretofore encountered in northern England. If the usual Celtic economy of mixed farming supplemented by hunting has to be deduced *a priori*, the rich furniture of some graves gives positive hints as to the social structure of the communities concerned.

The little barrows, 33 ft. or less in diameter, and surrounded with trenches, usually cover a simple pit grave containing a skeleton, extended or more often contracted. The grave-goods are normally limited to a rough barrel-shaped pot, quite in Iron Age A tradition, containing joints of pork, with perhaps a brooch or pin. Contrasted to these commoners' burials are the rich graves of the local ruling families. The nobles were buried richly caparisoned with their chariots, just as in the Marnian graves of Champagne. At least three nobles were interred in the Arras cemetery, and Elgee [14] enumerates a total of a dozen known chariot-burials in eastern Yorkshire. Their rarity emphasizes the oligarchic character of La Tène society; their rich furniture illustrates the wealth concentrated in the hands of the ruling class and the demands it was used to satisfy. If warfare were their main concern, the rulers provided employment for skilled wheelwrights, armourers and other artisans, and for traders who supplied raw material and Continental manufactures, and were patrons of art. Artist-craftsmen did settle at the Yorkshire courts and founded a local school of La Tène art.

[12] Elgee, *N.E.Y.*, 200.

[13] *Hull Museum Publications*, Nos. 193, 198; *Ant.J.*, xx, 338; the pile-dwellings in the Vale of Pickering may also belong to Parisii, p. 210.   [14] *N.E.Y.*, 186.

The chariots had wooden wheels with perhaps 16 spokes,[15] cased in iron tyres $1\frac{1}{2}$ ins. wide and measuring $2\frac{1}{2}$ to nearly 3 ft. in diameter. Lynch-pins with decorated bronze terminals (very similar to those from a chariot-burial at Nanterre, Marne [16]) fastened the wheels to the axles. Two

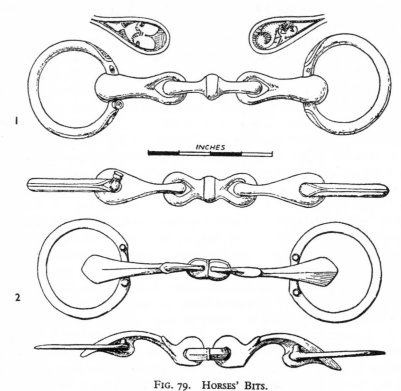

INCHES

FIG. 79. HORSES' BITS.
1. Tripartite bit, Walthamstow; 2. Irish derivative.
After Ward Perkins in *PPS.*, v.

horses drew each chariot and were buried with their owners. They were controlled by jointed snaffle-bits, terminating in large rein-rings like modern bits, not in cheek-pieces as in the Bronze Age–Hallstatt pattern. In the Yorkshire variety, as in five specimens from Champagne,[16] the mouth-pieces consist of three pieces—a central figure-of-8 link and two branches of the same figure but each twisted (Fig. 79, 1). Each rein-ring normally carries

[15] Greenwell, *Arch.*, lx, 281.
[16] Ward Perkins, *PPS.*, v, 177-187; *Ant.J.*, xx, 358-365.

a pair of studs to restrict the play of the ring in the terminal link and so limit the area of wear. Bits were normally made in iron, but the fine ones were either cased, wholly or in part, in bronze or cast in bronze throughout and always decorated. The links of the mouth-piece have gracefully swelling profiles and the rings may be incised. The harness mounts, termed *terrets* and probably used for crossing the reins, are sub-oval rings of bronze or iron, plain or embellished on the upper part with lip-like protuberances.[17]

The Arras charioteers were not buried, as on the Marne, in the full panoply of war. Enjoying uncontested sway over the Wolds and Limestone Hills, the Parisii need no longer regard military eminence as the sole qualification for chieftainship. But some graves do illustrate the prestige a successful warrior could acquire and the armament employed. As on the Continent, the warrior relied on iron daggers and broadswords carried in bronze-sheathed scabbards terminating in ornate chapes, and was protected by a wooden shield adorned with bronze plates and boss. But for hunting a spear or dart tipped with a socketed bone head like those described on p. 195 might be used.

The Parisii introduced the La Tène costume with appropriate brooches. Only one extant brooch from their territory conforms to the old La Tène I type (Fig. 80, 1-2). Those from the Danes' Graves, Driffield, illustrate a purely British variant that grew up late in the second century, parallel to the continental La Tène II—the *involuted brooch*[18] (Fig. 80, 3). Originating in a late form of La Tène I brooch in which the bow has been flattened till it is parallel to the pin, the new fashion bends both pin and bow into a graceful curve. At the same time the 'foot' is cast in one piece with the bow, as in La Tène III, the spring is suppressed and the pin made to work on a neat hinge. Penannular brooches with very long pins were also worn while the Danes' Graves were still used as a cemetery, and a variant on the ring-headed pin with cast head was adapted for use as a hairpin.[19] In one form the ring-head has become a cast four-spoked wheel and been embellished with bosses of coral.

Bracelets of jet or bronze, the latter ornamented with swellings, and even anklets, were worn. To assist in arranging her finery, a lady buried with her chariot at Arras was provided with a bronze mirror—a refinement that played a prominent part in the later La Tène civilization of Britain.

Comparatively few imported articles are included in the Yorkshire

---

[17] Leeds, *Celtic Ornament*, 18.

[18] Fox, *Arch. Camb.*, lxxxii (1927), 93; cf. *PPS.*, v, 185.

[19] *Arch.*, lx, 270.

graves. Amber and coral sparingly used must have been brought from the Continent; blue glass beads, sometimes embellished with white inlays, may have been imported; but before the Roman conquest glass-workers had established factories in Britain. Objects of parade, decorated in the

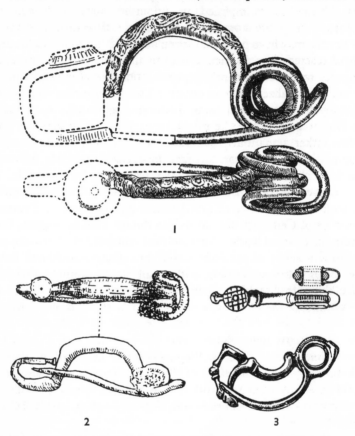

FIG. 80. 1-2. La Tène I brooches: 1. Hunsbury; 2. All Cannings Cross. 3. Involuted (La Tène II) brooch, Danes' Graves. ¼.

Yorkshire style, are found as far away as Wales, Galloway and even Ulster. Such need not result from an export trade; there is no evidence for the existence on Parisian territory of factories turning out metal-work on a large scale. Some may be loot, others the treasures of nobles who had migrated from the east coast; others local products executed by craftsmen trained in the Arras school.

For a British school of Celtic art had grown up under the patronage of the Charioteers. The foundations of the La Tène decorative style had of course been laid over a century before the colonization in the Alpine cradle of Celtic culture. Its original inspiration had been the art of fifth-century Greece as exemplified in imported metal-work and pottery. Subsequently the peculiar variations on the Oriental animal style, introduced by the Scyths, may have presented stimulating models to the Celtic artificers. But these reacted in a distinctive way to the models. The decoration of the imports was predominantly representational—naturalistic animals and rather conventionalized plant motives. The Celtic artist was not content just to copy these, and soon made them unrecognizable. As he had never seen a lion or a palm-tree, he might be excused for making his lions and palmettes rather unnatural. Ignorance will not excuse the conventional treatment of a dog or a horse. In fact, no excuse is needed; for decorating scabbards and bowls the portrait of a lion was felt to be unsuitable.

The native craftsman lacked the courage to reject out of hand themes vested with all the prestige of rich Hellenic and Etruscan civilization. But the tendency of Celtic art was 'to reduce the naturalistic motives, borrowed by it from the classical world, to geometrical schemes.' [20] It let 'the palmette design grow a series of repoussé scrolls branching into formal leaves and terminating in engraved tendrils with small closely wound spiral coils and a tender half-closed leaf.' [21] Some of the scrolls end in a round or oval motive producing the effect of a bird's head at the end of a long winding stalk.[22]

The purely curvilinear figures were rendered not only in two, but also in three, dimensions. The swelling curvatures imparted to the links of a bridle-bit are plastic renderings of the linear figures, which are themselves often enhanced by repoussé work. The patterns might be enlivened by coloured inlays—first studs of red coral, then of red glass, later still champlevé enamel.[23]

The Celtic school had already progressed far along the path of stylization before any of its exponents settled in England. But some objects from eastern England, like the Whitham shield and the scabbard-mount shown

[20] Arthur Evans, *Arch.*, lv, 404.
[21] Leeds, *Celtic Ornament*, 8.
[22] The effect is very Scythian, cf. Borovka, *Scythian Art*, Pl. 3 B.
[23] Coral became so costly after the opening of a market for it in the East that Celtic chiefs had to be satisfied with 'synthetic coral' (glass). Some Yorkshire products are decorated with coral studs (Leeds, *Celtic Ornament*, 43). White and blue enamels were added only after the Roman conquest.

in Pl. XV, are so like those found in Gaul that they may rank as imports.[24] In the sequel, cut off from Mediterranean products decorated in naturalistic style, craftsmen settled in Britain developed pure geometric forms faster than their Continental colleagues. Notable British peculiarities were: breaking the back of curves [25] and basketry hatching.[26] The first-named device may have been suggested by the Yorkshire trick of breaking the back of a La Tène brooch (p. 219). Even on the Continent incised figures were often distinguished by hatching. In Britain the lines of the hatching alternate in direction giving precisely the effect of the fibres of a basket, hence Leeds's term, *basketry style* (Fig. 79, 1). Leeds regards the style as early and South-Western. Its most famous embodiments in south-western England are, however, assigned by most authorities to the first century A.D. On the other hand, it is applied to some distinctively North-Eastern (Yorkshire) [27] products, like bits, which may probably be substantially earlier.

3. MARNIAN CHIEFTAINS IN SOUTHERN ENGLAND

Only in eastern Yorkshire did the Marnians succeed in planting a compact colony. But elsewhere in eastern England objects of parade in the La Tène I tradition demonstrate influence from this colony or more probably from the parent societies of Gaul. Such objects might of course be due to trade and nothing else. But a few grave-groups and settlement finds suggest the rule of La Tène chieftains over a Hallstatt peasantry. Stray finds of princely war-gear and horse-trappings from Lincolnshire,[28] a couple of chieftains' graves in Cambridgeshire [29] and Suffolk [30] might point to landings all round the Wash. It is suggested that the East Anglian burials and stray objects in the same tradition belong to the intruders who founded the ruling houses of the Iceni. The latter were a non-Belgic tribe who preserved till the Roman conquest a predominantly Iron Age A culture. But the rulers, who made submission to Rome and then led the great revolt of A.D. 61, can, Rainbird Clark [31] argues, hardly have sprung from the poor Iron Age A peasantry, but were more probably descended from B chieftains.

[24] Leeds, *op. cit.*, 8.   [25] Leeds, 49.   [26] Leeds, 21.

[27] Ward Perkins, *PPS.*, v, 188-190.

[28] e.g. shield, dagger and trumpet from R. Witham, three-piece bit from Ulceby, etc.: Phillips, *Arch. J.*, xci (1934), 103-107.

[29] Contracted burial of long-headed man with ornate La Tène II brooch, two penannular brooches, hinged armlet, etc.: *VCH. Camb.*, i, 293.

[30] Extended skeleton found at Mildenhall in 1812 lying between two horses' skeletons and armed with iron sword and wearing a gold torque: *Arch. J.*, xcvi, 43.

[31] *Arch. J.*, xcvi, 42.

The little round fort of Hunsbury near Northampton, only 4 acres in area, occupies a site first settled by Iron Age A invaders from East Anglia [32] attracted perhaps by the iron-stone which doomed the fort to destruction in the Victorian éra. But it has yielded an unusual wealth of objects of

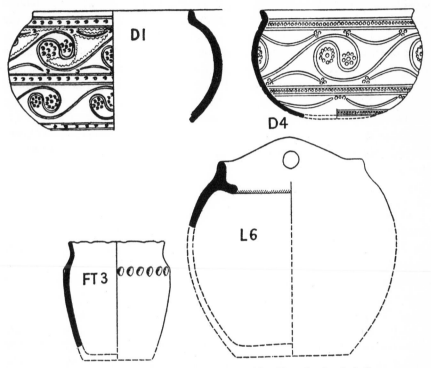

FIG. 81. Pottery from Hunsbury. ¼. After Dunning in *Arch. J.*

Marnian or Yorkshire character—remains of a chariot with lynch-pins, three-piece bits,[33] Yorkshire terrets, iron swords in bronze-plated scabbards with heart-shaped chapes, two La Tène I brooches (Fig. 80, 1) and an unprecedented quantity of iron tools and weapons. Much of the pottery is richly decorated with spiral and other motives (Fig. 81, D1, D4). Hawkes regards this as the work of native Iron Age A potters, copying true La Tène patterns in wood or metal.[34] But the similarity to South-Western Glaston-

[32] Attested by pottery of A 2 style, 9 weaving combs, 9 femur-head whorls, triangular loom-weights, a ring-headed pin, etc. The site is marked 2 in Fig. 83.

[33] But also 14 antler " check-pieces." Rye was cultivated at some time.

[34] *SAC.*, lxxx, 250-251; cf. *Arch. J.*, xciii, 74-79.

bury ware is admittedly significant.[35] At least commercial relations with the Glastonbury traders are attested by a lead lump and a currency bar, and the potter's metal models might have come from that quarter, as might the labour-saving device of the rotary quern which here assumed a new form, improved upon the Glastonbury model (Fig. 88, 2). But it still seems likely that a party of Marnian invaders conquered the Hallstatt community and the iron ore it controlled and established themselves as a local dynasty or oligarchy. They may later have been supplanted by South-Western lords or merely attracted to their courts South-Western traders and artisans. The chariots, swords and horse-trappings would in any case belong to La Tène chiefs whether North-Eastern or South-Western.

The attacks on southern England deduced on p. 196 must be part of the same general movement of Marnians. They were not everywhere beaten off. In places conquerors established themselves long enough to import or manufacture locally pottery in true Marnian style. From Worth in Kent, a good port of entry, Hawkes[36] has identified comb-roughened keeled pots, lids, goblets, and pedestalled bases every one of which can be matched in the Marne cemeteries (Fig. 82). Similar pottery was found in Sussex at Findon Park and Park Brow near Cissbury,[37] accompanied as at Worth by La Tène I brooches, at Hengistbury Head and even in Wiltshire.

Cissbury itself, the largest Iron Age A hill fort on the downs, was, according to Curwen[38] and Hawkes,[39] occupied by Marnian invaders, perhaps already mixed with A people. As a military class ruling the original A inhabitants, the conquerors created a mixed, AB, society and culture— the Cissbury culture—which cut off the pure A population of eastern Sussex from their kinsmen in Wessex. This composite tribe was the first to move against the forested Weald to secure control of its iron ores.

In Wessex some A societies maintained their independence, and after the storm of invasion had passed were able to allow their fortifications to decay. Maiden Castle was enlarged to its present size of 46 acres, but protected no longer by a timber-faced rampart rising from a berm, but by a simple glacis sloping up from the inner lip of the ditch.[40] On the other hand, some south Wiltshire farms, like Fifield Bavant and Swallowcliffe Down[41] may, judging by sherds of Marnian pottery, have become manors

[35] Cf. pp. 239, 244 below.
[37] *Ant. J.*, iv, 352; viii, 453-458.
[39] *SAC.*, lxxx, 239-242.
[41] *WAM.*, xlii, 476-477; xliii, 60-93.

[36] *Ant. J.*, xx, 115-121.
[38] *SAC.*, lxxx, 214-216.
[40] Wheeler, *Maiden Castle*, 36.

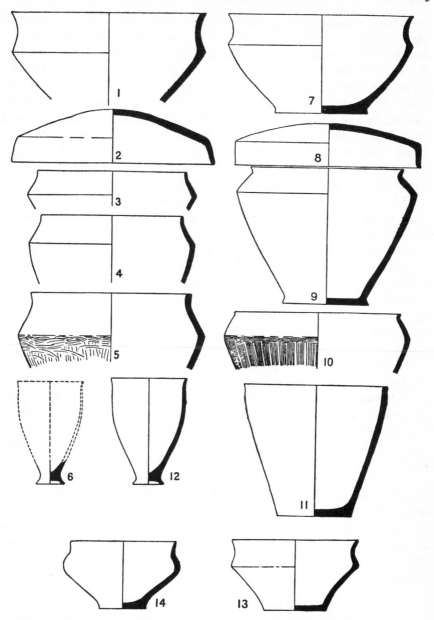

FIG. 82. POTTERY FROM WORTH, KENT (1-6), AND FROM CHAMPAGNE (7-12). After *Ant. J.*, xx.

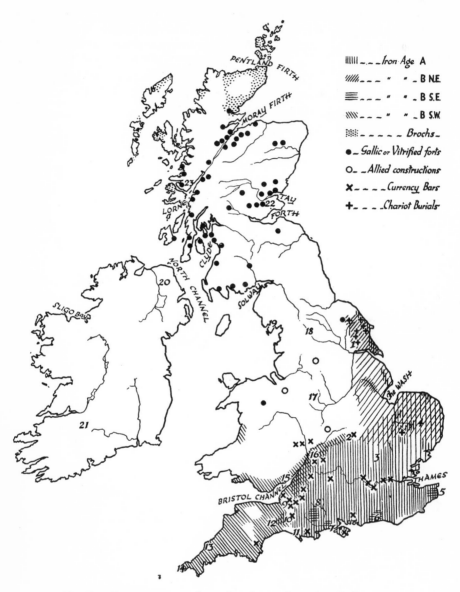

FIG. 83.   DISTRIBUTION OF IRON AGE A AND IRON AGE B CULTURES.

of Marnian chiefs. Whether as landlords concentrating and redistributing the surplus produce of the Hallstatt peasantry, or merely by their example to free neighbours, the La Tène invaders did contribute to raising the standard of life, to promoting new industries and fostering trade. The partial adoption of the safety-pin and the elaboration of flat British variants on the continental La Tène I model are just archaeological clues to this process. The enlargement of Maiden Castle may be taken as an indication that population expanded as a result.

CHAPTER XII

CELTIC TRADERS IN SOUTH-WESTERN BRITAIN

1. The Iron Age in Cornwall

A COMPLICATED series of invasions, following devious routes, brought La Tène civilization to south-western England and spread it by a process only completed during Period IX. Celts from eastern Gaul spread by various ways to the Atlantic coasts, to the metalliferous regions of north-western Spain, to Brittany and so at last to Britain. The bearers of Iron Age culture here, following, like the megalith-builders, a long sea route, arrive as societies disrupted by overseas migration and with their culture impaired by the voyage.

The first object of the immigration was control of Cornish tin, just as the tin of Galicia had attracted post-Hallstatt Celts to Spain. Literary evidence suggests that tin from Cornwall was being brought to Marseilles and Narbonne by the Pyrenaean isthmus route [1] in the third century. The earliest really dateable object definitely associated with tin-streaming is a La Tène I brooch found in a working at Redmore near St Austell.[2] The Celtic prospectors found Cornwall already in possession of the Deverel–Rimbury peoples, themselves probably Celtic, who had presumably improved farming there as much as in Wessex.

The invaders can be recognized by inhumation cemeteries, contrasting with the cremations of the Bronze Age populations; by stone fortresses unlike anything put up by Iron Age A peoples and commanding settlements of a novel type; and by a regrettably small number of distinctive relics with Breton and Iberian affinities.

To dominate the tin-producing districts the invaders established round stone forts, built without the aid of timbers in fine masonry. In the only excavated example, Chun Castle[3] (Figs. 83, 14; 84), a wall 14 to 15 ft. thick with a marked external batter encloses an area some 170 ft. in diameter. Outside the wall was a shallow ditch the upcast from which had been banked against

---

[1] Hencken, *Arch. Corn.*, 166-170; Diodorus Siculus, v, 22, 4, and v, 38, 5, says the tin was carried by sea from Ictis to Gaul, and thence, some thirty days' journey on foot, was brought on horseback to the mouth of the Rhone to Massilia and Narbo.

[2] Hencken, *Arch. Corn.*, 109.   [3] *Arch.*, lxxvi, 205-239.

a stone revetment to form an outer rampart with a second ditch beyond it. Radial walls served to partition off some 11 elliptical hutments against the interior face of the wall. One of these served as a workshop where tin and iron ores were smelted in an elaborate furnace with a well beside it. Other

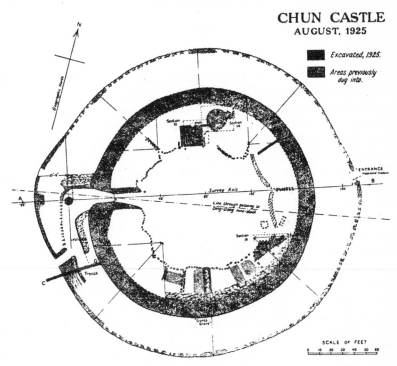

CHUN CASTLE
AUGUST, 1925

■ Excavated, 1925.

▨ Areas previously dug into.

FIG. 84.   PLAN OF CHUN CASTLE.   After Leeds in *Arch.*

ring forts are twice or even thrice the size of Chun, and even more elaborately defended.[4]

Chun Castle dominates three unwalled clusters of courtyard houses, and in two other cases such open villages are similarly related to hill-top castles.[5] In the Land's End district Colonel F. C. Hirst[6] has identified no less than 23 such open villages. All belong to small farming communities of not more than 8 households. Little irregular garden plots are attached to the houses, while around the villages are the lynchets of ploughed Celtic

[4] Hencken, *Arch. Corn.*, 127-128.   [5] *Arch.*, lxxxiii, 278.

[6] *JBAA.* (1937), 71; he gives an ideal synthetic description of such villages illustrated by equally 'ideal' and inaccurate plans.

fields. Only the village at Chysauster[7] has as yet been scientifically excavated. It is dependent on the hill-top ring fort of Castle-an-Dinas, half a mile away. The houses were occupied over a long period during which they had often been remodelled; house 7 yielded a few duck-stamped or incised sherds which should go back to the second century B.C., and plenty of Roman pottery coming down as late as the third century A.D.!

Owing perhaps to the many reconstructions the plans (Fig. 85) seem less uniform than in the corresponding houses at Jarlshof, but the general idea of a central court with cellular chambers in the walls is the same. On one side of the court a broad shallow alcove—45 ft. long in one instance— may have been the stable, while the remaining cells would be for human habitations.[8]

About 200 yards south of the Chysauster village was a souterrain (locally called a *fogou*), and Hirst[9] reports a similar association of fogous and courtyard houses in at least five other cases. In that at Carn Euny[10] a beehive chamber, roofed by corbelling, opens off the main gallery-like chamber, a plan reproduced exactly in the Scottish souterrains at West Grange of Conan (Angus)[11] and at Castle Law, Glencorse (Midlothian).[12] There is of course no guarantee that souterrains, circular forts and courtyard houses are really integrally associated in a single complex. Indeed, souterrains occur also in irregular contour forts with earthen banks.[13] None of the three architectural forms can be traced with confidence to a single source.

We have already met the courtyard house in Shetland and traced it to megalithic traditions. In Cornwall it might represent an otherwise unattested survival of the megalithic tradition, an importation from the north or a contribution from the Deverel–Rimbury people (cf. p. 193). We have met the earth-house too in Ireland in a Late Bronze Age that is no earlier than Period IX, and in Shetland in an Early Iron Age that need be no earlier. In eastern Scotland a southward spread might be followed in Period X till south of the Forth the dateable examples were built after A.D. 180.[14] But abroad souterrains are very common in western Gaul. Blanchet[15] records over 50 each in the Departments of Vendée, Tarn, Vienne, Haute–Vienne, Creuse and Dordogne, and quite a cluster in Morbihan, Finistère and Côtes du Nord. So, though the Gaulish souterrains do not

[7] *Arch.*, lxxxiii, 237-284.

[8] Hencken, *Arch.*, lxxxiii, 278.

[9] *JBAA.* (1937), 82.

[10] Hencken, *Arch. Corn.*, 139.

[11] Anderson, *Scotland*, i, Fig. 259.

[12] *PSAS.*, lxvii, 378.

[13] Hencken, *Arch. Corn.*, 143-146.

[14] Childe, *P.S.*, 215.

[15] *Les Souterrains Refuges de la France* (1923).

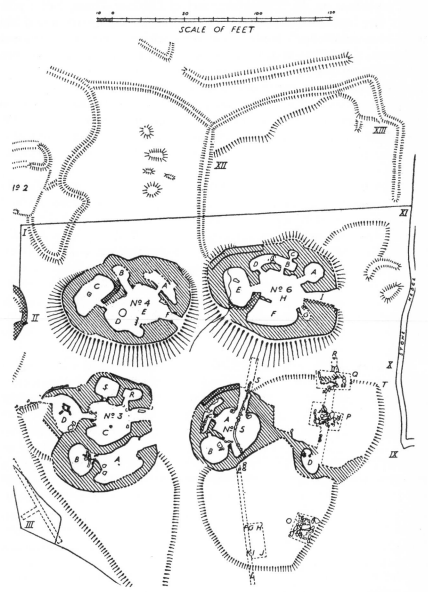

FIG. 85.   PART OF VILLAGE OF CHYSAUSTER.   After Hencken in *Arch.*

agree very closely with fogous, the idea might have come from the same quarter as the other innovations mentioned below.

Finally, Leeds [16] has compared the masonry of Chun with that of the much larger *castros* of Galicia and northern Portugal. But the circular plan had been consecrated in Britain and Ireland from the Bronze Age, and even the masonry should not be beyond the capacity of the masons who built the Dartmoor pounds, once equipped with iron tools.

On the whole it looks as if disparate traditions had been welded in western Cornwall in a single stratified society. The hill forts would be the citadels

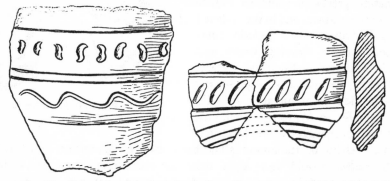

FIG. 86.   Stamped and incised sherds from Chun Castle.   After Leeds in
Arch., lxxvi.

of chiefs whose tenant farmers lived in the open villages. In their economy the extraction and export of tin supplemented agricultural pursuits, as tin-stone from Chun Castle and Carn Euny shows. But the sole archaeo-logical trait which defines this society is its decorated pottery.[17] A few sherds from Chun and Chysauster bear stamped impressions, recognized by Leeds as conventionalized versions of the Villanovan–Hallstatt *duck pattern* (Fig. 86). Others show incised ribbons (generally forming chevrons), filled with dots or hatchings, which recur at Carn Euny too. These may betray both the extension of the culture and the source of the foreign element that differentiated Iron Age society in Cornwall.

The actual settlement of foreigners in Cornwall at the dawn of the Iron Age is proved by the inhumation burials. The cemeteries wherein the west Cornish villagers were buried have indeed not yet been found, but one, which must have belonged to a sandhill settlement such as are so familiar

[16] *Arch.*, lxxvi, 228.
[17] *Arch.*, lxxvi, 231, Figs. 11 and 12; lxxxiii, 264, Fig. 7, 1-2; *Arch.J.*, xcv, 89-96.

in Orkney and Shetland, has been explored at Harlyn Bay (Fig. 83, 13).[18] No less than 140 cist graves containing contracted skeletons were explored without reaching the limits of the cemetery. Their occupants were rather short, the men standing only 5 ft. 4½ ins. high. Of eleven skulls, five were long, only one round, and it not of Beaker type. The cemetery was admittedly in use for a long time, as relics of the first century A.D. were found in some graves, but no Roman objects. The oldest and most significant grave-goods were two brooches (Fig. 87) of a type, derived from the Jogassian, such as are common in the 'post-Hallstatt' cremation graves of southern France and northern Spain, and in the Galician *castros*. Other relics include ring-headed pins, a weaving comb and sherds of incised and hatched pottery.

FIG. 87. Brooch from Harlyn Bay.
⅓. After Leeds.

So the Cornish Iron Age society was founded by inhumationists with strongly South-Western traditions, attracted primarily by the local tin. Leeds,[19] relying on the brooches and the duck-stamped pottery which recur in the *castros*, would bring them from the stanniferous region of Galicia by the same maritime route as the double-looped palstaves. Hencken [20] points out that a derivation via the tin trade route, ultimately from South France, immediately from Brittany, is more probable. In either case the invaders would be Celts. They would doubtless have blended with, or been superimposed as a ruling military and commercial class upon, the established Bronze Age peasantry. The analogy with the megalith-builders is significant, and the recognition of indubitably South-Western imports and equipment in the Iron Age substantially confirms the account of Stone Age culture given in Chapter IV.

The traders spread eastward to establish an Iron Age commercial system dealing in iron and lead as well as copper and tin. Duck-stamped ware can be traced up the Bristol Channel and right to Bredon Hill fort (Glos.) (Fig. 83, 16).[21] The new element it symbolizes constitutes the differentia of the Glastonbury culture, the classical B culture of south-western England.

[18] *Ant. J.*, i, 283-299; Hencken, *Arch. Corn.*, 115-118.

[19] *Arch.*, lxxvi, 230-237. So too Pokorny, *ZfkP.*, xxi, 158.

[20] *Arch. Corn.*, 156; in Iberia the Hallstatt-Urnfield rite of cremation was retained. Direct trade with the Peninsula is demonstrated by Iberian votive bronze statuettes from Aust-on-Severn as from Sligo and Dorset: *BM. Iron*, 148; Jacobsthal, *JRSAI.*, xlviii, 51-54.

[21] *Arch. J.*, xcv, 4-13, 94; cf. *T.B. & G.A.S.*, lviii, 160-164.

But in it an Iron Age A substratum must be admitted too. At Bredon Hill pottery in Iron Age A tradition, mixed with duck-stamped ware, reveals the blending of two societies. And Iron Age A peasants must have spread still further west. Pure Iron Age A pottery [22] from the great hill fort on Ham Hill (Somerset) (Fig. 83, 10), over 200 acres in area, implies that it began as a Hallstatt stronghold. The original post-neolithic ramparts at Hembury fort near Honiton (Fig. 83, 12) seem to have been reveted with timbers set in a trench in the Iron Age A fashion.[23] Weaving combs, symbolic of the Iron Age A textile equipment, occur as far west as Kent's Cavern near Torquay and Harlyn Bay (Cornwall), and indeed form an integral constituent of the Glastonbury culture itself. The South-Western traders must have joined forces with or dominated communities of expanding Hallstatt peasants. They may later have been reinforced by a further immigration from north-western Gaul.

2. THE GLASTONBURY CULTURE

The developed South-Western culture of Iron Age B is classically illustrated by the marsh villages of Glastonbury (Fig. 83, 9) and Meare. These two sites are exceptional both from the unique wealth of material preserved in the peat and also for their situation and the economy it implies. Both lie among 'impenetrable swamps' in the valley of the Brue close to Glastonbury.[24] Though the marshes were impassable on foot, the Brue provided a waterway from the Bristol Channel only 12 miles away, and the Glastonbury village stood close to its tributary, the Old Rhyne, which was apparently still navigable in the Middle Ages. At Glastonbury begins a ridge of solid ground connecting with a spur of the Mendips. Along this ran an old trackway that can be barred by an earthwork, Ponter's Ball, where Gray [25] reports the discovery of 'Late Celtic' (? Glastonbury) pottery. Only 9 miles away on this route lies Charterhouse-in-Mendip where the Romans mined lead and where Gray again found Glastonbury pottery.[26] Eventually the ridgeway leads by the Jurassic zone to iron-mines round Hunsbury and to the downs of Wessex and Sussex.

The site thus offered a well-guarded haven where water-borne imports could be safely unloaded for distribution by land-transport along the ridgeway and where merchandise brought by land could be stored in security

[22] Kendrick and Hawkes, 179.   [23] *PDAES.*, ii, 163.
[24] The Glastonbury site has been fully described by Bulleid and Gray, *The Glastonbury Lake Village* (1914); Meare remains unpublished.
[25] *Glastonbury*, i, 37.   [26] *Glastonbury*, ii, 497.

for shipment. The founders of the Glastonbury village took advantage of this situation and planted a colony consisting at one time of some 60 households, devoted to trade and industry as well as primary production. But to obtain a footing on the yielding peat an artificial island or crannog had to be constructed with immense labour. An irregular area of over 2 acres beside the Rhyne was surrounded by a multiple palisade of pointed posts, 5 to 14 ft. long and up to 9 ins. thick. From this a long causeway on piles and a stone mole projected obliquely and led to a landing-stage on the stream. The whole, or at least the major part, of the enclosed area was occupied by a platform of logs and brushwood supplemented by rushes, bracken, clay and stones, laid upon the peat.

Here were erected some 90 buildings, marked before excavation only by low clayey mounds. At least 61 such mounds were the sites of round houses, 18 to 28 ft. in diameter, bordered with stakes driven into the substructure at intervals of 6 to 15 ins. The house floors were of clay, laid on a timber platform, and each supported a central hearth of clay or stones. The walls and roofs were probably of wattle and supported by a central post, planted beside the hearth. Not all these buildings can have stood simultaneously, since the floors of adjacent mounds overlap and some post-rings intersect. Moreover, a single mound often comprises several superimposed floors; in one there were no less than 10 floors, in thirteen there were 4. Hearths were renewed as many as fourteen times! So the settlement must have been occupied for a long time; 150 years would seem a modest estimate.

The villagers doubtless supplied themselves with food by hunting, by fishing, by breeding cattle (*Bos longifrons*), sheep, goats and pigs, and by cultivating wheat, barley and beans. In addition to the remains of plants and animals' bones, the handle of a plough and iron sickles or bill-hooks have been recovered. Posts grouped to form a square [27] have been taken as marking the foundations for granaries.

For grinding their grain the Glastonbury housewives were no longer content to push the old saddle quern; of the 56 querns recovered, 38 belong to a new *rotary* type (Fig. 88, 1), which embodies one early mechanical application of the wheel idea to the reduction of human labour. Curwen [28] believes that the device is an adaptation of the Greek donkey or slave mill, but can cite no earlier or geographically intermediate examples. In any case, the adoption during the life of the settlement of this labour-saving contriv-

[27] e.g. *Glastonbury*, Pl. XIV, between mounds XIV, XXIX and XXXIII.
[28] *Antiquity*, xi (1937), 137-142.

ance is a good indication of the higher standard of life prevailing in the South-Western province as contrasted with Hallstatt Wessex or even La Tène Yorkshire.

A similar deduction can be drawn from the textile industry. In addition to using numerous whorls of stone, clay and femur-heads, triangular loom-

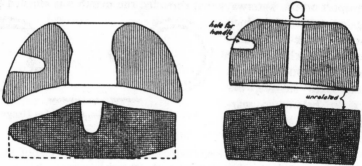

FIG. 88. ROTARY QUERNS.

1. Maiden Castle ; 2. Ham Hill. $\frac{1}{10}$. After Curwen in *Antiquity*.

FIG. 89. Bobbins, Glastonbury. $\frac{1}{2}$. After Bulleid and Gray.

weights and 89 weaving combs, the Glastonbury women wound the thread for the shuttle on spools made from marrow-bones of sheep, generally perforated lengthwise and transversely (Fig. 89). Bobbins of this kind, placed within wooden shuttles, were still used by Hebridean weavers in the nineteenth century A.D.

Metal was worked at four points near the edges of the settlement. At each site the evidences of metallurgy were restricted to a single floor in a composite mound. So not all four smithies were functioning at the same period. The smiths now used bellows provided with clay-protected nozzles, iron tongs and thin triangular crucibles of fire-resisting clay in addition to the old globular type made in softer clay.

Transport on the waterways that threaded the marsh was effected partly by dug-out canoes, of which two survive. For land trans-port wheeled vehicles were available. The wooden naves and axle-boxes survive, but such might belong to war-chariots as well as to four-wheeled carts. Some at least

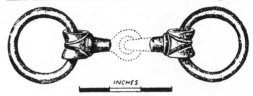

FIG. 90.   Bipartite Bit, Carneddau Hengwm.
After Ward Perkins in *PPS*.

were drawn by horses. The steeds were controlled by iron *bits* of the *two-piece type* (Fig. 90) distinctive of the South-Western cultures; in such the jointed mouth-piece consists of only two links with large round rein-rings in the outer loops. But the older form of bit of rope or leather ending in antler cheek-pieces was still current. Lipped terrets carried the reins.

The peat has preserved exceptional testimony to the skill of the carpenters and wainwrights who built the vehicles, houses, platforms, loom-frames and

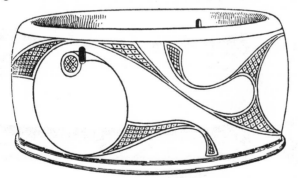

FIG. 91.   Wooden tub, Glastonbury.   ¼.
After Bulleid and Gray.

other articles which the archaeologist has generally to infer. Even tubs built up of staves have survived as well as smaller vessels made from a single piece of timber turned on the lathe. The woodwork may be decorated with flowing scrolls in the La Tène style, first engraved and then deepened by burning in (Fig. 91).

FIG. 92. DECORATED POTTERY, GLASTONBURY. ⅓. After Bulleid and Gray.

Potters produced a fine grey ware, but, despite the use of the wheel idea for querns and lathes, it was built up by hand. As in Cornwall, a taste for stamped and hatched patterns is in evidence. But the duck is no longer recognizable, giving place to impressed circles suggested by contemporary metal-work.[29] Hatching is used to fill in splendid scrolls and other La Tène patterns, equally inspired by the bronzesmith's and the woodcarver's art (Fig. 92). Many pots copy wood and metal vessels. Imitation of the reinforced rims of metal vases leads to the *bead rim* produced by an incised groove parallel to and immediately below the brim. The conspicuous similarity of Glastonbury ware to the decorated pottery of Hunsbury might be due to the imitation of widely traded metal vases by two schools of potters each trained in the Iron Age A tradition. The occurrence at All Cannings Cross as well as at Glastonbury and Hunsbury of *loop-rimmed vases* (Fig. 81, L6)[30] might support this view. The differences would then be due to the Cornish element at Glastonbury. An alternative would be to treat Hunsbury as an outpost of the Glastonbury culture. Or finally the decorated pots at each site may be due to fresh immigrants not yet considered. In any case, Glastonbury pottery was not mass-produced for export, but manufactured almost as a household industry at several centres; local styles of Glastonbury ware can be recognized by close study.[31]

In addition to these practical refinements provision was made for the diversions of the villagers. A dice-box, complete with dice (Fig. 93), was found at Glastonbury.[32] The game goes back to 3000 B.C. in the Orient and was as popular among the continental Celts as among the Vedic Indians and the Greeks. But the Glastonbury dice are parallelopipeds—the first examples of an exclusively British variant on the common cube form. And a variety of ornaments were of course worn. Of the safety-pin brooches 2 were of La Tène II pattern, 10 La Tène III, and 8 might pass for La Tène IV.[33] Penannular brooches, generally with spiral terminals, were also worn, as were glass beads and shale armlets.

The wealth and prosperity of the marsh village is clearly due not merely to farming and the modest domestic industries plied at the site, but also to trade. The reality of such trade is attested in the first place by the variety

[29] The horn stamps used have been recovered: *Glastonbury*, ii, 465.
[30] i.e. vessels with a perforated projection rising from the rim: Cunnington, *A.C.*, 176; *Arch. J.*, xciii, 80; *Glastonbury*, Fig. 169.
[31] e.g. *PPS.*, iv, 155, n. 5; *Arch. Camb.*, lxxxviii (1933), 291.
[32] *Glastonbury*, ii, 408.
[33] *Glastonbury*, i, 189-205; a La Tène I brooch has been found at the adjacent village of Meare: Kendrick and Hawkes, 180.

of imported materials left in the village—tin from Cornwall, lead from the Mendips, rings and bracelets of Kimmeridge shale from Dorset [34] and glass beads from Gaul, but more explicitly by *currency bars*. The merchants of the Glastonbury culture had agreed upon a standard of value expressed in a metallic currency. But the medium of exchange socially sanctioned

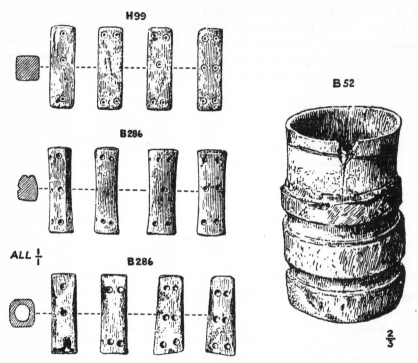

FIG. 93. Bone dice and dice box, Glastonbury. After Bulleid and Gray.

took the form not of minted coins but of flat iron bars (Fig. 94) the edges of which have been hammered out to form a flanged 'handle' at one end.[35] The standard unit weighed about 309·7 grammes or 4770 grains, and bars were issued weighing ¼, ½, 1, 1½, 2 and 4 such units. These are the *taleae ferreae* still used among the Britons in Caesar's day. Their distribution defines an economic system, not a political unit; they extend far beyond the range of the Glastonbury culture into the AB province of Sussex and

[34] Imported ready-made: *Glastonbury*, i, 242; for the local workshops see *Arch. J.*, xciii, 200-219.

[35] Smith, *BM. Iron*, 165; Kendrick and Hawkes, 176; cf. *Antiquity*, vii, 61-68.

the AC province of the Lower Thames.   On Fox's [36] map and on our Fig. 83 they fan out from the Glastonbury district along the Mendip-Cotswold ridge and so north-east along the Jurassic zone to Hunsbury, eastward down the Thames, along the downland ridgeways towards Sussex, the Isle of Wight and Weymouth, southward to the Cornish border and up the Severn with outliers in Anglesey and near Settle (Yorks.).

The marsh village was not a political capital, but no more was it a refugee settlement.   It was an emporium, designed as such by its location and proved to function as such by the recovered relics.   At the same time it is the type station of a culture, defining a society distinguished

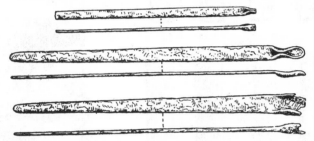

FIG. 94.   Iron currency bars of 1, 2 and 4 units. $\frac{1}{10}$.   By permission of the Trustees of the British Museum.

by its own fashions in pottery, decorative art, bits, weaving apparatus and ornaments.   The political aspect of that society is better illustrated from other sites.

As defined by its pottery the Glastonbury culture is represented both in inhabited caves in Cornwall, Devon, Somerset and Gloucestershire and across the Bristol Channel in South Wales.   The caves in the Mendips [37] and near Torquay may have been inhabited by herdsmen and refugees sheltering from the Belgic attacks of Period X.   The hill forts may, on the contrary, be tribal capitals or chieftains' seats, as in Cornwall, or refuges in the Hallstatt tradition.   Some, like Leckhampton (Glos.),[38] Hembury (Devon) and Ham Hill (Somerset), had already been occupied in Iron Age A.   None preserve the regular form of the West Cornish castles.   But many, on stony ground, are girt with stone ramparts faced with fine masonry; at Worlebury there are three external and two internal faces to the ramparts.[39] Most are now protected by two or more ramparts as a defence against the

[36] *Anglesey*, 32 ; the centre of production may have been the Forest of Dean, *Antiquity*, xiv, 427 ff.
[37] Balch, *Wookey Hole*: Dobson, *Arch. Som.*, 114-118.   [38] *T.B. & G.A.S.*, xlvii, 81.
[39] For these forts see in general Hawkes, *Antiquity*, v (1931), 80-86.

sling-stone strategy described below, but only excavation can decide whether this multiplicity of defences was original. Ham Hill in Somerset is large enough to hold a town, measuring 230 acres. But most B forts are much smaller. Quite a number occupy less than 10 acres.[40] Kingsdown Camp (Somerset) [41] indeed was originally only ⅜ acre—in fact, a castle or defended farm.

In a few of these forts, like Hembury, Worlebury and the anomalous Salmonsbury,[42] silos ('pit-dwellings') may be accepted as evidences of regular occupation. Others, like Cranbrook Castle, have yielded so little domestic rubbish that they may have been merely refuges. The discovery of currency bars in six forts of the South-Western B province [43] enhances the probability that markets were held periodically at such sites.

Finally, a number of stray finds of fine Celtic metal-work may be regarded as the ornaments of Glastonbury chieftains. But the majority, notably the beautiful mirrors,[44] are so late that they may belong to Belgic lords. Some of these ornate objects are in any case explicitly South-Western, like the two-piece bits and terrets from Polden Hill (Somerset). But the craftsmen who made them may have been trained in the Yorkshire school. Basketry ornament, for instance, reached its crowning beauty on the mirrors, but seems to have originated earlier in the North-Eastern province (p. 222). On the other hand, it was in the South-Western province that enamel decoration developed most spectacularly. So, in the Glastonbury society as in Cornwall and Yorkshire, we have to reckon with war-chiefs and traders in addition to a mixed peasantry.

The Glastonbury culture in the West seems to have been wrecked by Belgae who sacked its citadels, massacring the garrisons,[45] disrupted the economic system but substituted coined money for currency bars. This catastrophe hardly preceded the Claudian conquest of A.D. 43. If the end of the Glastonbury culture thus coincide with the end of Period IX, when did it begin? It was long customary to put the foundation of the culture well back into the second century B.C., but the general tendency since 1938 has been to bring it down to the second half of the first century. The predominance of La Tène III brooches at the type site admittedly establishes the culture's survival to that sort of date. But a century is too short for the

---

[40] Hembury 8, Cadbury 6¼, Llanmelin 5¼.   [41] *Arch.*, lxxx, 63-77.

[42] Dunning, *CISPP.* (1932), 273-274. The pottery is not typical ' Glastonbury.'

[43] Listed by Fox, *Antiquity*, xiv (1940), 432, and Wheeler, *Maiden Castle*, 384 ff.

[44] Dunning, *Arch. J.*, lxxxv, 69-79. Leeds, *Celtic*, 28-32, dates them much earlier despite the late objects in all closed finds.

[45] e.g. *Arch. J.*, xcv, 17-20.

life of the village (p. 235). The La Tène II brooches point to the second century, while even a La Tène I brooch was found at Meare.[46]

The most cogent argument against admitting the emergence of the Glastonbury culture during Period VIII is derived from observations in Wessex. The Glastonbury culture never effectively penetrated to the fertile downs where the Iron Age A population, stiffened in places by an infusion of Marnian chiefs (p. 224), survived during Period VIII. But some Wessex hill forts were strengthened by the addition of one or more extra lines of defence, assuming the multivallate form so common in forts classed as Iron Age B. Thus after Maiden Castle had already attained its maximum extent, its whole defences were remodelled with the addition of two outer lines of defence.[47] Now Wheeler has pointed out that the multiplication

FIG. 95. Iron Age AB pottery with bead rims and (right) countersunk handles ; from Maiden Castle. ⅙. After Wheeler in *Ant. J.*

of ramparts was conditioned by the methods of attack against which they had to give protection. The causative factor was identified as 'the developed use of the sling with an effective range of something like 100 yards on the level.' In fact, hoards of sling-stones, one comprising as many as 22,000 pebbles, and sling-platforms arranged along the main rampart were exposed at Maiden Castle. Wheeler[48] has traced the origin of the sling-complex among the Veneti of southern Brittany whose prowess as slingers is emphasized by Caesar and where multivallate forts do exist.

But the changes in military architecture in Wessex were accompanied by no radical break in cultural tradition as exemplified in the ceramic record. The old Iron Age A tradition in pottery persists; the chief innovations distinguishing B from A here are bead rims and the so-called *countersunk handles* (Fig. 95)—a type appearing also in south Breton forts and at

[46] Kendrick and Hawkes, 180. *N.B.*—While in a closed find (including a single occupation-floor) the *latest* object is decisive for dating, the foundation date of a complex monument in long use is given by the *earliest* dateable relic.

[47] *Ant. J.*, xvii, 274-275. [48] *Antiquity*, xiii, 70-74.

Glastonbury, but here only on late floors accompanied by Belgic imports.[49] Wheeler [50] accordingly concludes that the reconstruction of Maiden Castle was indeed due to an actual influx of new people, Veneti from southern Brittany. But these 'arrived in small numbers with no considerable train of craftsmen (or craftswomen), but obtained complete dominion over the large but unenterprising population of the Wessex downs. . . . The bulk of the population of *oppida* such as Maiden Castle remained of the old stock; but their potters, with the usual imitativeness of the craft, adopted the forms of the metal vessels and, to some extent, of the pottery vessels which accompanied the invader. . . . Only in the actual mechanism of warfare had the change been instant and drastic—the reflection of the act of military domination with which the new régime had come into being.'

He further suggests tentatively that these immigrants were refugees who had escaped destruction at Caesar's hands after the Venetic war of 56 B.C. This account and the chronology it implies may be accepted as valid for Wessex. It need not apply to the Glastonbury culture as a whole, nor to all the multivallate forts associated therewith. Wheeler himself draws attention to Strabo's [51] statement that the Veneti 'had an emporium' in Britain before the Roman aggression, and writes: 'The multiple earthworks of Cornwall represent Venetic trade before the time of Julius Caesar.' Indeed, the marsh villages have a good claim to be regarded as entrepots of Venetic trade, and the maritime culture, at once commercial and warlike, reflected in the Cornish castles, exhibits a significant parallelism to that of the Veneti as described in the Classical authors. Nevertheless in the light of Wheeler's observations a fresh influx of peoples from north-western Gaul, strong enough to introduce an Armorican tradition of ceramic decoration and the rotary quern, as well as new defensive and offensive tactics, not only into the Glastonbury area and to Hunsbury but even into Sussex, has become a possibility.[52]

3. THE BROCH CULTURE OF NORTH SCOTLAND

Beyond the Bristol Channel the coasts of South Wales,[53] and presumably the iron-mines in the hinterland, became a transmarine province of the South-Western culture. A coastwise expansion from Cornwall still farther

---

[49] Gray, *Glastonbury*, ii, 518.

[50] *Antiquity*, xiii (1939), 73–76; cf. *Maiden Castle*, 56, 217.

[51] Strabo, iv, 4, 1, says χρώμενοι τῷ ἐμπορίῳ.

[52] cf. Hawkes in *SAC.*, lxxx, 252 ff.

[53] e.g. *Arch. Camb.*, xciv, 210-219: the multivallate 'Knave's Fort,' Gower, yielded slingstones and Glastonbury ware.

north might be deduced from a sherd of duck-stamped ware found in the reconstructed hill fort of Pen Dinas (Aberystwyth) whose earliest defence had been a rampart, reveted with timbers in Iron Age A style.[54] But it is only when we reach the north and north-west of Scotland, beyond the area dominated by Gallic forts, that we can discern in the archaeological record a distinct society, reproducing the warlike maritime economy of Cornwall and Brittany and using much of the distinctive Glastonbury equipment. There conquerors of South-Western B traditions, coming by the western sea route, founded the *broch culture*.

Halting-places on their way may indeed possibly be represented on the one hand by textile appliances from a cave at Borness in Galloway and a Glastonbury die from Bute,[55] on the other by a number of tiny forts or *dùns*[56] built without timber in fine masonry in Arran, Bute, Argyll and the Western Isles. Some dùns are irregular hill-top or promontory forts whose single walls follow the contours; others are circular, like Rahoy, and not always situated on naturally defended hills. The age of these dùns is very uncertain. All seem later than the vitrified Gallic forts of the same area.[57] Some in Argyll have yielded second-century Roman pottery. Many of the circular castles may have been built in the Dark Ages by Dalriadic Scots. But the dùns of Coll and Tiree sometimes yield pottery similar to that of the brochs, and the vases from the ring fort at Clettraval have been compared by Scott[58] to Iron Age A pottery.

In any case, each dùn is a castle designed to hold the household of a petty chief. As in Period II beside each strip of arable land and in each narrow glen had stood the communal tomb of a leading family, so now each of these tiny natural units was dominated by the dùn of a clan chief. Indeed, at Clettraval (North Uist) the circular fort had been built from the stones of the long cairn.[59] All illustrate an economy based on farming, but supplemented by fishing, piracy and reiving, and a social system of small communities constantly at war and ruled by war-chiefs—an organization, in fact, naturally adapted to the topography of the Western Highlands and Islands. On the more fertile northern isles and the wind-bared moors of Caithness and Sutherland a similar organization assumed a peculiar form, and castle architecture attained an unprecedented grandeur in the brochs.

[54] *Ant. J.*, xviii, 77-81.
[55] Childe, *P.S.*, 239-241. Roman pottery was found in Borness Cave.
[56] Childe, *P.S.*, 197-201.
[57] Vitrified stones from a burned Gallic fort on the same hill were incorporated in the walls of the circular castle of Dun Skeig (Kintyre).
[58] *PSAS.*, lxix, 532-534.   [59] *PSAS.*, lxix, 481-484.

A *broch* (Fig. 96) is essentially a circular castle with an internal diameter of 25 to 35 ft. But in the massive walls of the ground floor, 12 to 15 ft. thick, are contrived circular chambers, often four in number, disposed round the circular court rather like the cells in a courtyard house. One serves as a guardroom into which opens the socket-hole for the bar that fastened the door; another, on the left of the entry, is the vestibule to a staircase. Superimposed upon this foundation is a cylindrical tower that may rise 40 ft. above the ground (Pl. XVI, 1). The walls are nearly vertical inside, but steeply battered externally. And they are hollow, the two faces being tied together at intervals by horizontal transverse slabs. In the interspace a stair winds up clockwise from the left-hand cell on the ground floor. The tower was probably open at the top. But the central area, which is in any case almost dark even on a sunny day, was sheltered by a verandah roof, running all round 6 to 8 ft. above the ground. There is generally a hearth and a well or cistern in this court.

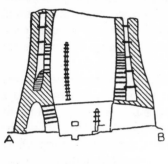

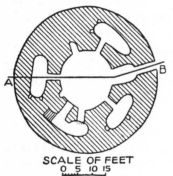

SCALE OF FEET
0 5 10 15

FIG. 96. Section and plan of the broch of Mousa, schematized after Hencken in *Arch*.

The tower in most cases stands in an enclosure, protected by stout ramparts often built in the same massive style as the tower's foundations. Within this enceinte cluster the flimsy round or oval huts of the lord's tenants (Pl. XVI, 2).

Quarrying the stone and building therewith a lofty tower was a task requiring a much stronger labour force than the erection of a long cairn. Yet no less than 425 brochs are still traceable in Shetland, Orkney, Caithness, Sutherland, the Outer Hebrides and Skye.[60] Along the coast of Caithness near Keiss there are three brochs in a distance of two miles and so too on the north-west of Rousay. Moreover, clusters of wheel-houses with attached souterrains,[61] belonging no doubt to an older, perhaps Bronze Age population, have yielded relics of broch type and must have been

[60] There are 145 in Caithness, 78 in Orkney ; cf. *Ant. J.*, xxiii, 19–26.
[61] Especially on North Ronaldshay, North Uist and Lewis: Childe, *P.S.*, 217–221.

inhabited contemporaneously with the castles. These facts betoken a dense population.

It was supported primarily by intensive farming. Brochs normally stand on good agricultural land. Saddle and flat rotary querns are among the commonest broch relics. Considerable quantities of barley (bere) have been exposed, as well as bones of Celtic short-horn cattle,[62] sheep, goats and pigs. But the location of many brochs and wheel-houses along the coast emphasizes maritime enterprise as a supplementary source of livelihood. Coastal brochs are situated by preference beside narrow clefts which would offer secluded havens to light boats. At Midhowe, Rousay, rock-cut steps lead down from the enceinte to such a haven [63] (Pl. XVI, 2). There were artificially protected boat-harbours attached to clusters of wheel-houses on North Uist.[64] These arrangements recall Caesar's account of the seamanship of the Veneti. It cannot be doubted that the light craft, very probably coracles, lurking in these clefts were used not only for fishing, but also for Viking raids, which have in fact left a mark on the Lowlands (p. 248).

No one denies that the broch as such was developed in the north of Scotland. But its very masonry suggests comparison with Cornish castles. Such comparison seems justified by the relics. The broch-builders used the whole specialized textile equipment of the Glastonbury culture [65]— femur-head whorls, bobbins, weaving combs and slotted lengths of bone. They presumably brought the tradition of using these with them, and so must have arrived accompanied by their wives. They played with the same peculiar parallelopiped dice; for hunting they employed the same hollow bone dart-heads; for metal-work the new triangular crucibles of fire-resistant clay.

On the other hand, apart from a loop-rimmed vase from a dùn at Tota Dunaig (North Uist),[66] the broch pottery is not of Glastonbury type. Most of it is plain and crude. A few decorated pieces do recall south English vases, but from All Cannings Cross, not Glastonbury. Feathered oblique lines can be paralleled at that site [67]; chevrons filled with a single row of dots also in Cornwall.[68] The commonest decoration is, however, by means of applied cordons, notched, finger-printed or most often crinkled.

---

[62] One skull from Midhowe (Orkney) belongs to *Bos frontosus*, a Scandinavian type of domestic ox: Ritchie in *PSAS.*, lxviii, 515-516.

[63] *PSAS.*, lxviii, 469.　　[64] *PSAS.*, lxv, 320-356; lxvi, 39.　　[65] Childe, *P.S.*, 239.

[66] National Museum, Edinburgh. The site was never fully excavated: Beveridge, *North Uist*, 232.

[67] Cunnington, *A.C.*, Pl. 48, 1; Childe, *P.S.*, Pl. XVIa.

[68] *Arch.*, lxxxiii, 264, Fig. 7, 1; Cunnington, *A.C.*, Pl. 48a, 3.

The South-Western chiefs may have been accompanied to the north by a substantial contingent of Iron Age A subordinates.

And all the refinements of the South-Western La Tène culture seem to have been jettisoned on the voyage. No fine metal-work has survived. No safety-pins were worn. But cloaks were sometimes fastened by pen-annular brooches with knobbed terminals, more often by bone pins with carved heads or by bronze pins derived from the ring-headed pin, but with the ring-head bent forward out of the plane of the shaft like a modern tie-pin. This latter is a distinctively Scottish form, developed from the English type under the influence of the Bronze Age sunflower pin either in the broch or in the Abernethy culture.[69] Jet armlets were indeed popular, but horses were controlled (if at all) by old-fashioned bits with antler cheek-pieces.

The remote northern broch folk could obtain few foreign materials by trade or robbery. Bronze and iron were indeed worked in brochs and wheel-houses, as furnaces, crucibles and moulds have been found. But metal was so scarce that all sorts of tools and ornaments were laboriously copied in stone or bone. Yet a few vessels of first and second century Roman pottery and stray Roman coins found their way to Caithness and the Islands. The stone ladle was adopted, perhaps from earlier settlers (p. 211), as a substitute for wooden ladles, and for striking fire a quartz pebble replaced flint. The resultant *tracked stones*—quartz pebbles with a shallow V-shaped groove on one face, very common in the brochs—were carried south when the Lowlands were raided and were later adopted in Scandinavia.[70]

The broch culture endured for a long time, probably indeed till the advent of the Norsemen. But it seems to have degenerated. But long before that degeneration set in, the population, multiplying in prosperity, found an outlet by colonization beyond their bleak northern homeland. There are a few brochs on Mull, Lismore and Islay, perhaps three on the coast of Galloway, two near Stirling, two near Galashiels and one on the Lammermuirs in Berwickshire. These colonial establishments give the most reliable date for the broch culture's origin. A large amount of first century Roman pottery was found on the broch site at Torwoodlee near Galashiels. Assuming that this comes from the broch, not from an older 'fort,' and that the Romans would not tolerate the establishment of a robber stronghold beside a main road through newly conquered territory, Dr Curle [71]

[69] Childe, *P.S.*, 263.
[70] *PPS.*, ii, 233-236. To the list of finds add the Gallic fort of Dunagoil (Bute).
[71] *PSAS.*, lxvi, 341.

infers that the broch must have been standing by A.D. 80.   The broch culture in the north must, then, go back to at least the beginning of our era.

So an actual immigration from south-western England reproduced in the remote northern isles a barbaric version of that maritime warlike and commercial culture, known from Roman history in Brittany and deduced by archaeology round the Bristol Channel.   The main body of migrants might have been refugees from the Belgic invasion, but the process of colonization must not be over-simplified.   What culminated in the broch culture may have been preceded by smaller emigrations along this same route.   It might be to such that we should attribute the first Iron Age settlements at Jarlshof, which are apparently pre-broch, the earth-house complex and the isolated finds of allegedly Hallstatt pottery from the Western Isles.   But that is just guesswork.   The South-Western origin of the broch culture remains an archaeological fact which helps to confirm our account of the spread of the megalithic religion to the north.

CHAPTER XIII

GERMANS, CELTS AND PICTS

1. The Belgic Invasions of England

In the latter half of the second century Teutonic tribes from beyond the Rhine had conquered northern Gaul, replacing the Marnian chiefs, and to some extent their subjects too, and creating mixed States with a preponderantly Germanic population, as Caesar states in his 'Commentaries on the Gallic War.' Archaeology confirms the historian's statements. In the valleys of the Somme, the Seine and the Marne a hybrid culture replaces that of the Marnian chieftains. Most of the refinements of the older La Tène culture indeed survived. Even in pottery former traditions persisted; the pedestal urn, distinctive of the new Belgic culture, was simply taken over from the Celtic population of La Tène I-II. On the other hand, the rite of cremation that had been retained by the Teutons since their Late Bronze Age replaces the Celtic practice of inhumation. And a new rural economy, adapted to the wooded soil of the North European plain and employing the heavy wheeled plough—Latin *caruca*—was superimposed upon the Celtic system, based on the light *aratrum*.

An invasion of south-eastern England about a generation before the British campaigns of Julius Caesar is a historical fact, duly vouched for by Caesar himself. It too is reflected in the archaeological record.[1] The earliest and most explicit testimony is provided by the spread of cremation cemeteries and settlements, characterized by wheel-made pedestal urns of Continental pattern. Archaeologists agree with historians in dating this invasion somewhere about 75 B.C. It was evidently a genuine folk-movement, involving mass settlement of Belgic farmers and craftsmen, not merely a conquest by a handful of foreign warriors. Nevertheless, in settlement sites[2] so much of the ceramic traditions linger on from Iron Age A as to show that some of the old peasantry too remained to live alongside and under the new lords of the soil.

The Belgae occupied first Kent, where the *Aylesford* cemetery[3] in

---

[1] Hawkes and Dunning, ' The Belgae of Gaul and Britain,' *Arch. J.*, lxxxvii, 150-270.

[2] e.g. at Bigbury (Kent): *Arch. Cantiana*, xlviii (1936), 166,

[3] *Arch.*, lii, 317-388,

particular is so rich that the site might give its name to the culture, and subsequently crossed the Thames into Hertfordshire, extending northward to the Nene and the Fen borders and westward to the Cherwell, but leaving Essex unconquered till some time after the Julian invasion. Before the Roman attack the Belgae had created a genuine State-organization, a kingdom instead of a loose tribal group. At its head was Cassivellaunus, who established a capital, a great oppidum about 100 acres in area, above Wheathampstead.[4] After his submission to Rome, in 54 B.C., the capital was transferred to the more convenient and larger, if less defensible, site in Prae Wood above the Roman Verulamium (St Albans),[5] and finally, under Cunobellinus (Cymbeline, A.D. 5-43), to Colchester when the old Iron Age A tribe of the Trinobantes had been absorbed.

Ere this another Belgic State had been established in eastern Wessex, governed by Commius, a prince of the Atrebates of Gaul, who is believed to have taken refuge in Britain about 50 B.C. The State's existence is fully attested numismatically, but it is not now clear how far 'the second Belgic invasion'[6] which created it was a mass migration. Some of the hand-made bead-rimmed pottery that should have distinguished the invaders is now ascribed to Wheeler's Venetic refugees (p. 244), to whom Hawkes[7] himself now attributes the multivallate Wessex hill forts that had formerly been taken as marking Belgic frontier posts. But the potter's wheel was probably introduced in this area by followers of Commius. If the second Belgic invasion did not involve such a general displacement of population as the first, and did not so thoroughly transform rural economy, it did result in the establishment of new States and the foundation of cities on valley sites to replace hill forts. Chichester replaces the Trundle; St Catherine's Hill was deserted, but Belgae lived at Winchester.[8] Minted coinage[9] takes the place of currency bars; the ceramic industry was industrialized, specialist potters turning out en masse bead-rimmed vases of Continental pattern. It was probably from this western Belgic centre that Glastonbury and the west were eventually attacked somewhere between A.D. 20 and 40.

In the conquered territory the Belgae established relatively large and stable kingdoms instead of the small and unstable tribal groups that can

---

[4] Wheeler, *Antiquity*, vii, 27-33.

[5] Wheeler, 'Verulamium,' *Report No. 11 of the Research Committee of the Society of Antiquaries of London.*

[6] *Arch. J.*, lxxxvii, 280-309; *Ant. J.*, xii, 411-430.

[7] *P. Hants F.C.*, xiii, 162.   [8] *P. Hants F.C.*, xiii, 211.

[9] The 'British Remics,' and later those inscribed with the names of Commius and his descendants: *Antiquity*, vii, 279-281.

alone be suspected in Periods VII and VIII even in southern England. The new capitals, Verulamium, Camelodunum (Colchester), Calleva (Silchester), come nearer the modern idea of a city than do hill forts or marsh villages. Physically indeed they still seem a disorderly aggregation of squalid huts. But economically they were truly urban—centres of specialized industries and far-flung trade. Even the ceramic industry had been removed from the sphere of a household craft to that of mass production by the immigration of specialist potters, skilled in the use of the wheel, who accompanied even the first Belgic invaders to Kent. Trade is now attested not only by the coinage but by masses of Gaulish and Roman manufactures, including vases. The exports of corn, fat stock, gold, silver, iron, leather, slaves and hunting-dogs mentioned by Strabo [10] brought in a more enduring return than the rare trinkets that have in earlier pages been hailed as witnesses to foreign purchases from Britain!

But above all, the Belgic farmers effected a revolution in rural economy where they settled in force. Traditions of forested plains and valleys were still alive among these new colonists. And so as riverside villagers 'they exploited the rivers in a scheme of valley and cross-country highways.' [11] They were prepared, too, to tackle the drainage and clearance of the fertile wooded soils—the loams and even the Lowland clays. For they possessed a heavy wheeled plough that could turn over the sod instead of just scratching the soil. Broad-bladed ploughshares and coulters (Fig. 65, 2-3) have been found at Bigbury and other Belgic sites.[12] The Belgae thus initiated the agricultural revolution, consummated by the Saxons, and laid the foundations of English farming as it remained till the Improvers.

2. NON-BELGIC BRITAIN IN PERIOD IX

Thus in south-eastern England prehistory gives place to history before the Roman conquest, though we have to rely on Latin authors even for the names of the several tribes and cities. From these, too, we learn of other peoples, all apparently Celtic. Some are already familiar from the archaeological record. We can recognize in the Iceni (Norfolk), the Regni (Sussex), the Dumnonii (Devon and Cornwall) and the Parisii (eastern Yorkshire) descendants of peoples whose A and B cultures have already been described. But other tribes and States mentioned might, from all that has been said hitherto, be unmixed descendants of Urn folk still preserving a Bronze

---

[10] IV, 5, 2. [11] Wheeler, *Antiquity*, vii, 33.
[12] Karslake, *Ant. J.*, xiii, 455-462; Curwen, *PPS.*, iv, 45.

Age economy. And indeed Strabo [13] alleges that some British tribes did not know how to make cheese, while others were ignorant of gardening and the remaining agricultural pursuits. On the other hand, by the Conquest the greater part of northern England was comprised in a single potent State, that of the Brigantes, who even coined money. And after the Conquest they, like the Silures, Dobuni and Cornovii of Wales and the Marches, were practising Celtic agriculture just like the non-Belgic peoples of southern England. Was the growth of a State-organization among such peoples and the development of plough cultivation just the result of imitation by Urn folk, or were these changes inspired or accelerated by immigration or conquest on the part of groups already identified as Iron Age?

Of course in the Highland Zone agriculture has never played such a predominant role in rural economy as in Lowland England. The hill country is admirably suited for grazing, but offers limited scope for tillage. Nevertheless, even outside the areas marked in Fig. 83 as immediately affected by the Hallstatt and La Tène invasions, mixed farming was the rule in Roman times. If the accent were on stock-breeding, cereals were generally cultivated. The direct proof of Iron Age agriculture afforded by the lynchets of southern England is indeed seldom available; for the Celtic system of small square fields was not often abruptly replaced by the 'Anglo-Saxon' strip system as on the downs. Celtic fields were still cultivated in the Middle Ages or later.

But in the Brigantian area of western Yorkshire remains of prehistoric Celtic fields can still be discerned as preceding the long strip cultivations of the Teutonic Middle Ages.[14] They are associated with unfortified hamlets—clusters of stone huts. Similar hamlets are common, too, on the moors of Cumberland and Westmorland and in parts of Northumberland. Such, writes Wheeler,[15] 'find their counterparts in hut villages which swarm upon the Downs of southern England and there represent the peasantry of the Early Iron Age and Roman periods.' Hill forts, on the contrary, are rare in Brigantian territories, but the area of their capital, Stanwick, a mile and a half square, suggests a barbaric city.

In the Scottish Lowlands, on the other hand, every large continuous area of plain or vale is dominated by a hill fort of substantial size, representing, as in southern England, a tribal capital or refuge. Some of these were demonstrably occupied before the Roman conquest under Agricola (A.D. 80). Burnswark in Annandale was probably besieged by the legions;

---

[13] IV, 5, 2.   [14] Raistrick, *Antiquity*, iii, 165-181; *YAJ.*, xxxiv, 117-130.
[15] RC. *Westmorland*, p. xxxiv.

Bonchester Hill (Roxburgh) and Traprain Law (Haddington) have both yielded ring-headed pins and other relics of pre-Roman Iron Age types.[16] Some, like Traprain, assumed a semi-urban character in Period X.

But everywhere the country round these oppida is dotted with 'small forts.' These are in reality just fortified farms, or at best castles in the enceinte round which might be grouped a hamlet of tenants' huts. Some can be shown to have been inhabited in the second century A.D.; others may be Dark Age. Many are clearly the direct precursors of mediaeval and modern farms, located farther down the same hill-spur in more commodious if less defensible situations. But economically they were as self-sufficient in the Roman period as the Iron Age A steadings of Wessex. For instance, iron was smelted at Castle Law, Glencorse, in the second century; its inhabitants did not have to repair to the hill-top town of Traprain, clearly visible above the forests 10 miles away, to purchase essential tools and weapons.[17] The hill forts themselves were no more urban than English oppida of Iron Age B. Glass bangles were indeed manufactured on Traprain and exported thence,[18] but similar glass trinkets were also manufactured in a 'small fort' (Castlehill, Dalry) in Ayrshire.[19] A very similar system prevailed in Wales, though there open villages are commoner than in Scotland.[20]

The fantastic numbers of hill-top towns and fortified steadings in Scotland and Wales present a striking contrast to their relative sparsity in the Brigantian territory. It is not entirely explicable by the difference between an area enjoying barbaric freedom or a frontier territory and the Province benefiting by the Pax Romana.[21] The political unification, already effected by the Brigantes before the subjugation, undoubtedly contributed to the differentiation. But the crucial question here is how far this rash of villages and forts reflects just the growth of the Urn population when they had learned from intrusive neighbours an improved rural economy and acquired iron tools to clear the land therefor. Admittedly Bronze Age survivals can be detected in Iron Age forts. On Traprain Law people had been buried in Cinerary Urns of the Overhanging Rim family, and leaf-shaped swords had been cast in clay moulds.[22] A Bronze Age bracelet and a socketed bronze axe were found in a hut under the ramparts of Breiddin Hill fort (Montgomery).[23] Admittedly, too, no connected group

---

[16] Childe, *P.S.*, 206-208. [17] Childe, *P.S.*, 226.
[18] *PSAS.*, lxxii, 394. [19] Childe, *P.S.*, 228.
[20] Kendrick and Hawkes, 222, 267-269.
[21] Collingwood and Myres, *Roman Britain and the English Settlements*, 144.
[22] Childe, *P.S.*, 229. [23] *Arch. Camb.*, xcii (1937), 92.

of cultural changes demonstrates beyond cavil the advent of new peoples in these areas during the Iron Age.

Nevertheless, isolated phenomena do suggest that the immigrants described in Chapters X to XII eventually spread beyond the boundaries there assigned. In the Brigantian area outside the Parisian territory the sparse relics recovered from graves and villages are inconclusive. But people took refuge, too, in the caves of Derbyshire [24] and Staffordshire,[25] round Settle in the West Riding [26] and in Lancashire north of the sands.[27] The refugees who squatted in these caverns all plied a textile industry with the familiar Iron Age A or AB equipment of weaving combs and femur-head whorls. And some of the pottery is in the Iron Age A tradition. All sites have yielded also Roman pottery; many, however, also earlier objects going back to the Bronze Age. Even if the caves be hiding-places to which Brigantian families fled after the tribe's subjugation under Petillius Cerialis (A.D. 71-72), the textile equipment [28] may be taken as proving that the Brigantian peasantry had assimilated Iron Age culture to such an extent that a bodily expansion, or rather retreat, of Iron Age A farmers might be postulated to explain it. The Brigantes would, in other words, comprise a real core of Iron Age A farmers injected among the more pastoral survivors of the Urn folk.

In Wales and the Marches a spread—or again more probably a retreat—from south-western England has been deduced from the distribution of hill forts with inturned entrances.[29] But neither relics nor structural details have yet confirmed this impression. 'Culture has been left behind; warriors are on the march accompanied by such camp-followers as could tolerate an uncivilized existence.' The impetus may well have been the pressure exercised by the invading Belgae and Venetic refugees upon the population of the South-Western hill forts. At the same time, raids by Abernethy people from Scotland may have resulted in some permanent settlements in North Wales and even the Midlands, comparable to those effected by the broch-builders in the Scottish Lowlands. Apart from the vitrified fort

[24] Harborough Cave (Fig. 83, 17): *DAJ.*, xxxi (1909), 91-106. Yielded also a bridle-bit of the Arras series, a leaf-shaped arrow-head, a Late Bronze Age knife, etc.

[25] Thor's Cave.

[26] Victoria, Attermire and Dowkerbottom (Fig. 83, 18): *YAJ.*, xxxiv, 130.

[27] Dog's Hole, Warton Crags: *T.C. & W.A. & A.S.*, xiii, 155. Yielded also Beaker ware.

[28] Note that weaving combs, doubtless brought by camp-followers, were found in the Roman stations of Camelon and Newstead.

[29] Chitty, *Arch. Camb.*, xcii (1937), 132-135; Radford too notes the similarity of Border forts to those of south-west England: RC. *Hereford*, iii (1934), p. xiv.

near Corwen, mentioned on p. 213, Corley Camp near Coventry [30] is built in true Gallic masonry. Varley has detected modified versions of the Gallic wall technique at Almondbury near Huddersfield [31] and at Maiden Castle, Bickerton (Cheshire).[32] The quite inconclusive evidence for dating the excavated sites points to a date after 50 B.C. As several of these forts are multivallate, they may turn out, after all, to belong to the South-Western complex, since Gallic masonry was in use also in Brittany and Normandy by the first century B.C.

Finally, the younger sons of Arras chiefs, or splinters from the original North-Eastern invasion, may have followed the old Bronze Age trade routes from Yorkshire across the Spine of Britain to the golden West. Stray objects of parade decorated in La Tène style might be interpreted in that sense. Such might of course have been lost on a fruitless raid, looted by Bronze Age reivers or simply traded. But by the first century A.D. at least we do find craftsmen, trained in the Yorkshire school, producing in northern England and southern Scotland distinctive variants on the Arras style on equipment in the North-Eastern tradition. Their patrons might well be scions of the Arras houses who had carved out for themselves little domains in the barbarous North.

If so, their expeditions must have begun relatively early. From Torrs (Kirkcudbrightshire) comes a chamfrein, the helmet for a warhorse,[33] weirdly embellished with a pair of horns terminating in birds' beaks. It is adorned with embossed palmettes, elaborated in the style of the Whitham shield and enhanced with fine incised designs. Stylistically this bizarre piece of armour should belong to Period VIII.

Other horse-trappings of a later date disclose a further dissemination of the charioteers. By the first century A.D. the Arras three-piece bit was simplified by the fusion of the two outermost links with the rein-rings, the central link being lengthened in compensation. The now functionless extremities of the outer links, projecting into the rings, became vehicles for decoration. One end of each bit was more ornate than the other; for, the horses being yoked in pairs, only the outermost end of each bit would be conspicuous. This new form of bit is represented at Rise, Holderness, in the Parisian territory, and at Stanwick, the Brigantes' capital, but also in the West—in Westmorland, Annandale and Galloway.[34] One may have belonged to the chief who commanded the defence of Burnswark (p. 253).

---

[30] *Antiquity*, v, 82-85.
[31] *PPS.*, v, 255.
[32] *LAAA.*, xxii, 97-110; xxiii, 101-112.
[33] Childe, *P.S.*, 252 and Pl. I.
[34] Leeds, *Celtic Ornament*, 115-118; Childe, *P.S.*, 230, Fig. 66.

But terms taken from linguistics would at least indicate the sort of language a culture's authors spoke.

Celtic is such a term.   It implies nothing whatsoever about physical appearance, head-form or complexion.   It does mean that those to whom it is applied spoke one of the great Indo-European family of languages (miscalled Aryan) spread by the beginning of our era from India to Ireland. As no one supposes that Indo-European languages originated in the British Isles, it is legitimate to ask when the Celts reached Britain.   The question is generally posed in a more complicated form.

Existing Celtic languages fall into two quite distinct groups: Goidelic (Irish, Manx and Scots Gaelic) and Brythonic (Welsh, Breton and Cornish). A convenient shibboleth for distinguishing the two is found in the treatment of Indo-European QU.   Goidelic preserves the guttural (velar) sound; Brythonic labializes it, changing qu to p.   The antiquity of the cleavage is very uncertain, since hardly anything survives of Celtic speech before 300 B.C.   It is quite conceivable that the divergence took place within an already extensive continuum of 'proto-Celtic' somewhat in the same way as Low and High German were differentiated in the Dark Ages.   Phonetic changes spread 'in an almost mysterious way through languages.   Their spread may be arrested by a geographical barrier so considerable as the Irish Sea, but is not likely to have been brought to a stand by the waters of the Seine and Marne.' [40]

Most prehistorians, however, assume, perhaps erroneously,[41] that Goidelic and Brythonic were brought to the British Isles as already differentiated languages by distinct peoples or waves of invaders who can be labelled respectively Goidels and Brythons.[42]

Now by Roman times the population of Great Britain was admittedly Celtic.   This follows not only from the statements of the Classical authors themselves but also from the place-names they have recorded and which indeed in many instances have survived the subsequent Anglo-Saxon, Danish, Norse and Norman immigrations.   The place-names of Roman Britain, and (with a few exceptions in the north-east) of Caledonia too, are almost exclusively Brythonic.[43]   So we may call the Britons not only Celts,

[40] MacNeill, *Phases of Irish History*, 46.

[41] See Peate's criticism in *Antiquity*, vi, 156-160.

[42] So Edward Lhuyd, *At Y Kymry*, 16, and most English authorities since Sir John Rhys; Déchelette, Hubert and Loth in France; Meyer, Pokorny and Zimmer in Germany.

[43] Ekwall, *Introduction to the Survey of English Place-Names*, 32; Watson, *Celtic Place-Names of Scotland*, 15-19; Pokorny, *ZfkP.*, xxi, 124-129, claims many river names as Illyrian, and Kent as Goidelic.

but also Brythons. Hence the linguistic term 'Celts' may be applied not only to the Belgae but also to the La Tène invaders and their outposts, as we have already done in Chapter XI for a different reason; wherever La Tène remains are found in Central Europe, Upper Italy or Spain, as in Gaul, there the ancient authors and toponymy attest the presence of Celts. On the English evidence the qualification Brythonic may be added. A large proportion of our Brythonic place-names may thus commemorate the advent of the La Tène Celts as described in the last two chapters.

But these were hardly the first Celts to arrive. It is generally agreed that the western Hallstatt cultures were in some sense Celtic, and the Hallstatt invaders of southern England might even be called Brythons if such a term have any meaning before 300 B.C. Considering the tenacity with which the Iron Age A tradition in culture persisted in Wessex, Kent and East Anglia, something of their language should surely have persisted too. It is likely that some non-Brythonic place-names should have survived there had the firmly rooted population that so stubbornly preserved its cultural traditions spoken a different language from its ultimate Brythonic conquerors.

The replacement of population attested archaeologically and anthropologically over the greater part of Britain during the first millennium B.C. was so complete that we can hardly anticipate the survival of a single place-name from earlier times—our Periods I-V. Hence we cannot infer from the absence of Goidelic place-names in England that no sort of Goidelic speech had been current there in the second millennium B.C., though this absence makes the immigration of Goidels into or across England during the first millennium eminently unlikely. Ireland, then, provides a good negative instance. There we have no Brythonic Celts and no wholesale replacement of Bronze Age culture by La Tène or Hallstatt cultures as in Britain. The sprinkling of La Tène warriors and artisans was manifestly numerically too weak to affect language any more than culture.

But the presence of Celts in Ireland before the La Tène incursion and in the north of Scotland before the advent of the broch-builders can be deduced from place-names preserved by Festus Avienus; the relevant portions of his poem *Ora Maritima* are supposed to be based on the reports of a Massiliote Greek, Pytheas, who sailed the Atlantic in the fourth century.[44] Now it mentions *insula Albionum* (Britain), *Hierni* (Ireland) and the *Orcades* (Orkney). The first coincides with the Irish name for Britain (*Albù*) and cannot be Brythonic; it may be Illyrian and not really Celtic at all. *Orcas,*

---

[44] Schütte (*Our Forefathers*, i, 3) and others think that Avienus used the Carthaginian Himilco who lived about 500 B.C.

on the contrary, is unambiguously Celtic and most probably Goidelic,[45] and *Hierni* (Lat. *Iuverna* or *Hibernia*) can also be explained as Celtic. With what stratum in the archaeological record, older than Period VIII, can these Celts in Ireland and the north of Scotland be connected?

Common to both areas are souterrains which reached even Shetland in pre-broch times (p. 184) and were adopted also just on the coast of Jutland in late pre-Roman times,[46] just as the idea spread down the east of Scotland to appear south of the Forth first in the second century A.D. (p. 230). In England they were confined to a corner of Cornwall, but they were common in the Armorican peninsula, in Poitou and farther south. If an invasion on the requisite scale could be deduced from the distribution of a single architectural type unassociated with other cultural changes, the souterrain, spreading from western Gaul, might be symbolic of the Goidels. The 'post-Hallstatt' Celts in northern Spain who came from the same sort of region included obviously Goidelic tribes like Querquerni. And in north-eastern Scotland where the broch was never superimposed upon the souterrain, river-names like Devana and Loxa recorded by Ptolemy seem to have remained Goidelic till they became Don and Lossie.[47]

Souterrain-diggers are frankly rather tenuous figures to bear the trappings of the Goidel There are other claimants, even more ghostly—crannog-builders, sword-bearers—whom we have tried to clothe with flesh in previous chapters. And benind them another candidate remains, more substantial and supported by weighty backers [48]—the Beaker folk, with their descendants the Urn folk. At least the A and B 2 groups of round-headed invaders started from an area between the Rhine and the Elbe, which, although Teutonic at the dawn of history, had once been Celtic on the testimony of river-names. Indeed, British rivers like the Weaver and the Wear still bear the Celtic names of north-west German rivers the Wippur and the Weser.[49] Hawkes [50] has recently restated the claims of the Beaker folk to be regarded as in some sense Celtic in the light of the latest archaeological data. He claims, too, that the Food Vessel society had absorbed so much from the conquerors that 'the spread of the Food Vessel in Ireland implies an immigration of Bronze Age people taking over to Ireland their share in the great European entity that was the real making

---

[45] Pokorny, *MacNeill-Festschrift*, 237-243 ; *ZfkP.*, xxi, 124.

[46] Hatt, *Antiquity*, xi, 172, insists that this very restricted group of souterrains in Denmark must denote foreign influence there—very likely from Scotland and Ireland.

[47] Diack, *Revue celtique*, xxxviii, 119; Fraser, *Scottish Gaelic Studies*, ii, 187-189.

[48] e.g. Abercromby (*B.A.P.*, ii, 99) and Hubert (*The Celts*, 207).

[49] Loth, *Revue celtique*, xxxviii, 282.   [50] *Foundations*, 372.

of the original Celts.'[51] In any case, we now know that some Beaker folk reached both Orkney and Ireland where Celts are so early attested historically.

The Urn folk too, who after all were dominant in Ireland at the beginning of our era (p. 162), owe so much to their Beaker constituent culturally, that their language too should belong to the same family. In 1940 it really looks as if the first Celticization of Britain were effected by the Beaker folk. They themselves, or later peoples dominated by their cultural traditions, made Ireland too Celtic. In Britain the Beaker folks' descendants were so completely replaced by the invasions of the first millennium that nothing remains to show what sort of language they spoke. But their Irish kinsmen appear speaking what we call Goidelic. So if anyone feels he will gain in knowledge by attaching the label Celt, or even Goidel, to the Beaker folk he is at liberty to do so. No linguistic label can at present be attached to the earlier neolithic or mesolithic populations. To call megalith-builders or Windmill Hill folk Iberian would be legitimate only if the adjective reassert their cultural connexions with the Peninsula already emphasized in Chapters III and IV. It would be confusing if it were taken to imply connexion with the historical Iberians of eastern Spain, conquered by the Romans.

Even less informative would be the label Picts. And it really has no place in prehistory. For Picti are first mentioned in A.D. 297. No doubt by 600 a Pictish realm embraced north-eastern Scotland and the northern isles—an area that in prehistoric times had twice been linked by exclusive cultural communities into a single archaeological province; carved stone balls have been taken as proving the dominion of the Orcadian Skara Brae culture over Aberdeenshire too (p. 88), and souterrains together with stone ladles may again denote a cultural unity interrupted by the arrival of broch-builders in the north. It may be a legitimate subject for speculation whether these cultural agreements reflect an ethnic identity that later gave stability to a Pictish kingdom.

But the word Pict has been freely, but with questionable propriety, used in a much wider sense as denoting a general element in the prehistoric populations. By a series of precarious and even contradictory equations the *Picti* (meaning in Latin 'the tattooed' or 'painted') have been equated with the *Cruithni* of Ireland, Welsh *Prydyn*—words which mean the same in Celtic as Picti in Latin; and so with the hypothetical *Qretani* who gave to the British Isles their oldest recorded name—in a Brythonic version— *Pret(t)anikai nesoi*, but also (or alternatively) with the *Pictones* who in

---

[51] *Ibid.*, 376. Pokorny, *ZfkP.*, xxi, 157, still identifies Goidels and Hallstatt invaders.

Caesar's time occupied what is now Poitou.[52]   On this unstable foundation even more speculative hypotheses have been reared.   One school [53] regards the Picts in the above sense as an aboriginal population with Arctic, Esquimoid or Finnish affinities.   In this case they should be represented in the archaeological record by the mesolithic Forest or Maglemose culture which provides the requisite Baltic connexions.   To Mahr [54] its continuation into a period when 'Picts' might really be contrasted with other societies is provided by the Riverford culture (p. 90).

A larger body of authorities regard their 'Picts' as Celtic.   In this case, if there were a people responsible for diffusing the tradition of building souterrains, such would have a good claim to be called 'Picts.'   For souterrains are common in the territories of the Pictones, of the Cruithni and of the historical Picts.   It could even be argued that the inhabitants of the Cornish tin-land, the most interesting part of Britain to early Greek or Carthaginian voyagers, should have given to the whole island the name by which it was first known in the Ancient World.   So there would be an almost exclusive coincidence between the distribution of 'Picts' and that of souterrains.   It would apparently follow that the 'Picts' were more Goidelic than Brythonic.[55]   The claim of the Beaker folk to be accepted as Celts would not thereby be impaired.   But earlier populations would remain altogether nameless.

[52] e.g. Hubert, *The Celts*, i, 203-208, 246; cf. MacNeill, *JRSAI.*, lxiii, 1-28. Watson, *Celtic Place-Names*, 11, rejects the equation of Picti and Cruithni, but maintains the connexion with Pictones. Pokorny, *ZfkP.*, xxi, 115-117, regards both Picti and Prydyn as Illyrian words introduced by the Urnfield invaders whom he considers Illyrians.

[53] Pokorny, *History of Ireland*, 16; Macalister, *Ireland in Pre-Celtic Times*, 255; *MacNeill-Festschrift*, 184-223.

[54] *PPS.*, iii, 327-331.

[55] Cf. pp. 162, 261. In Adamnan's *Vita S. Columbae* some Pictish chiefs bear Gaelic names, but not their king, Brude; cf. Fraser, *Scottish Gaelic Studies*, ii, 190.

BIBLIOGRAPHY

(Only books and periodicals frequently cited
by abbreviated titles are listed here)

ABERCROMBY, JOHN, *The Bronze Age Pottery of Great Britain and Ireland*, Oxford, 1912.

ANDERSON, JOSEPH, *Scotland in Pagan Times:* I, *The Iron Age;* II, *The Bronze and Stone Ages*, Edinburgh, 1883, 1886.

ARMSTRONG, E. C. R., *Catalogue of Irish Gold Ornaments in the Collection of the Royal Irish Academy*, Dublin, 1920.

BATEMAN, T., *Ten Years' Diggings in Celtic and Saxon Grave Hills in the Counties of Derby, Stafford and York*, 1861.

BULLEID and GRAY, *The Glastonbury Lake Village*, London, 1911-17.

CHILDE, V. G., *The Bronze Age*, Cambridge, 1930; *The Danube in Prehistory*, Oxford, 1929; *The Dawn of European Civilization*, London, 1939; *New Light on the Most Ancient East*, London, 1934; *Prehistory of Scotland*, London, 1935; *Skara Brae*, London, 1931; *Scotland Before the Scots*, London, 1946.

CLARK, J. D. G., *The Mesolithic Age in Britain*, Cambridge, 1932; *The Mesolithic Settlement of Northern Europe*, Cambridge, 1936; *Archaeology and Society*, London, 1939.

COFFEY, *New Grange*, Dublin, 1912; *The Bronze Age in Ireland*, Dublin, 1913.

COON, C. S., *The Races of Europe*, New York, 1939.

CUNNINGTON, M. E., *The Early Iron Age inhabited Site at All Cannings Cross*, Devizes, 1923; *Woodhenge*, Devizes, 1929.

CURWEN, E. C., *The Archaeology of Sussex*, London, 1938.

DOBSON, D. P., *The Archaeology of Somerset*, London, 1931.

EBERT, *Reallexikon der Vorgeschichte*, Berlin, 1924-29.

ELGEE, F., *Early Man in North-East Yorkshire*, Gloucester, 1930; *The Archaeology of Yorkshire*, London, 1933.

EVANS, JOHN, *The Ancient Bronze Implements of Great Britain*, London, 1881.

FORSSANDER, E. J., *Der ostskandinavische Norden während der ältesten Metalzeit Europas*, Lund, 1936.

FOX, CYRIL, *Archaeology of the Cambridge Region*, Cambridge, 1923; *The Personality of Britain*, Cardiff, 1938; *A Find of the Early Iron Age from Anglesey*, Cardiff, 1945.

GARROD, D., *The Upper Palaeolithic Age in Britain*, Oxford, 1926.

GREENWELL, W., *British Barrows*, London, 1877.

GRIMES, W. F., *Guide to the Collection illustrating the Prehistory of Wales, National Museum of Wales*, Cardiff, 1939.

HAWKES, C. F. C., *The Prehistoric Foundations of Europe*, London, 1940; see also under KENDRICK.

HENCKEN, H. O., *The Archaeology of Cornwall*, London, 1932.

JESSEN AND HELBAEK, *Cereals in Great Britain and Ireland in Prehistoric Times*, K. Danske Videnskab. Selskab. *Biologiske Skrifter*, III, 2, 1944.

KENDRICK and HAWKES, *Archaeology in England and Wales, 1914-1932*, London, 1932.

LEEDS, E. T., *Celtic Ornament*, Oxford, 1933.

MACALISTER, R. A. S., *Ireland in Pre-Celtic Times*, Dublin, 1921.

MacNeill-Festschrift=Féil Stríbinn Eóin MicNeill, Dublin, 1939.

MORTIMER, J. R., *Forty Years' Researches in British and Saxon Burial Mounds of East Yorkshire*, London, 1905.

PITT-RIVERS, Lieut.-Gen., *Excavations in Cranbourne Chase*, IV, Oxford, 1898.

WHEELER, R. E. M., *Prehistoric and Roman Wales*, Oxford, 1925 ; *Maiden Castle, Dorset* (Report XII of Research Committee of Society of Antiquaries of London), 1943.

BM.=British Museum, *Guide to the Antiquities of the Bronze Age; Guide to the Antiquities of the Stone Age; Guide to the Antiquities of the Early Iron Age.*

CISPP.=*Report, International Congress of Prehistoric and Protohistoric Sciences*, London, 1932.

RC. = Royal Commission on Ancient and Historical Monuments :

    England: *Herefordshire.*   *Westmorland.*
    Scotland: *Berwickshire.*   *Fife and Clackmannan.*
               Caithness.   *Sutherland.*
               The Outer Hebrides, Skye and the small Isles.
    Wales: *Anglesey.*

Survey = *A preliminary Survey of the Ancient Monuments of Northern Ireland*, Ancient Monuments Council, Belfast, 1940.

VCH. = *Victoria County Histories:*
    Cambridgeshire. *Cumberland.* *Devonshire.* *Derbyshire.*

PERIODICALS

AJA. . . .	*American Journal of Archaeology.*
Amer. Anthrop. .	*American Anthropologist.*
Antiquity . .	*Antiquity*, Gloucester.
Ant. J. . .	*Antiquaries' Journal* (Society of Antiquaries), London.
Arch. . . .	*Archaeologia* (Society of Antiquaries), London.
Arch. Ael. . .	*Archaeologia Aeliana*, Newcastle-on-Tyne.
Arch. Camb. . .	*Archaeologia Cambrensis*, Cardiff.
Arch. J. . .	*Archaeological Journal* (R. Arch. Institute), London.
BBCS. . . .	*Bulletin of the Board of Celtic Studies.*
BMQ. . . .	*British Museum Quarterly*, London.
BPI. . . .	*Bullettino di Paletnologia Italiana*, Parma.
Co. Louth AJ. . .	*County Louth Archaeological Journal.*
DAJ. . . .	*Derbyshire Archaeological Journal*, Derby.
GFF. . . .	*Geologiska Föreningens Forhandlingar*, Stockholm.
INJ. . . .	*Irish Naturalists' Journal*, Belfast.
IPEK. . . .	*Jahrbuch für prähistorische und ethnographische Kunst*, Köln.
JBAA. . . .	*Journal of the British Archaeological Association*, London.
J. Ches. A. & H.S. .	*Journal of the Chester Archaeological and Historical Society.*
J. Cork H. & A.S. .	*Journal of the Cork Historical and Archaeological Society.*
J. Galway H. & A.S.	*Journal of the Galway Historical and Archaeological Society.*
JRAI. . . .	*Journal of the Royal Anthropological Institute*, London.
JRIC. . . .	*Journal of the Royal Institute of Cornwall*, Truro.
JRS. . . .	*Journal of Roman Studies*, London.
JRSAI. . . .	*Journal of the Royal Society of Antiquaries of Ireland* (formerly *R. Historical and Archaeological Assoc.*), Dublin.
LAAA. . . .	*Annals of Archaeology and Anthropology*, Liverpool.
L'Anthr. . .	*L'Anthropologie*, Paris.
MZ. . . .	*Mainzer Zeitschrift*, Mainz.
Oxon. . . .	*Oxoniensia*, Oxford.
P.B.N.H. & P.S. .	*Proceedings of the Belfast Natural History and Philosophical Society.*

PBUSS. . . *Proceedings of the Bristol University Spelaeological Society.*

PCAS. . . . *Proceedings of the Cambridge Antiquarian Society.*

PDAES. . . *Proceedings of the Devonshire Archaeological Exploration Society*, Exeter.

P. Hants F.C. . . *Proceedings of the Hampshire Field Club*, Southampton.

P.I.O.W.N.H. & A.S. *Proceedings of the Isle of Wight Natural History and Archaeological Society*, Newport.

POAS. . . . *Proceedings of the Orkney Antiquarian Society*, Kirkwall.

PPS. . . . *Proceedings of the Prehistoric Society*, Cambridge.

PRIA. . . . *Proceedings of the Royal Irish Academy*, Dublin.

PRS. . . . *Proceedings of the Royal Society*, London.

PSAS. . . . *Proceedings of the Society of Antiquaries of Scotland*, Edinburgh.

PSEA. . . . *Proceedings of the Prehistoric Society of East Anglia* (continued as *PPS.*).

PZ. . . . *Prähistorische Zeitschrift*, Berlin.

Reliquary . . *The Reliquary and Illustrated Archaeologist*, new series, London.

SAC. . . . *Sussex Archaeological Collections*, Lewes.

T.B. & G.A.S. . *Transactions of Bristol and Gloucester Archaeological Society.*

TBNHS. . . *Transactions of the Buteshire Natural History Society*, Rothesay.

T.C. & W.A. & A.S. *Transactions of Cumberland and Westmorland Archaeological and Antiquarian Society*, Kendal.

TDA. . . . *Transactions of Devonshire Association.*

T.Som.A.S. . . *Transactions of Somersetshire Archaeological Society*, Taunton.

UJA. . . . *Ulster Journal of Archaeology*, new series, 1937 ff., Belfast.

WAM. . . . *Wiltshire Archaeological Magazine*, Devizes.

YAJ. . . . *Yorkshire Archaeological Journal*, Leeds.

ZfkP. . . . *Zeitschrift für Keltische Philologie*, Halle.

INDEX

PLATE I.

1. FALSE PORTAL, BELAS KNAP.

Photo : W. J. Hemp, F.S.A.

2. MASONRY OF RETAINING WALL, BLACKHAMMER CAIRN, ROUSAY.

Photo : V. G. Childe.

PLATE II.

1. BEACHARRA VASE, CLACHAIG, ARRAN.

National Museum of Antiquities, Edinburgh.

2. UNSTAN BOWL, TAIVERSO TUICK, ROUSAY. ½

National Museum of Antiquities, Edinburgh.

PLATE III.

1. ENTRANCE TO TOMB OF NEW GRANGE.

Photo : Mason.

2. SITE OF VILLAGE (A) AND CAIRNS (B), CARROWKEEL.

Photo : V. G. Childe.

PLATE IV.

1. PETERBOROUGH BOWL, MORTLAKE. ¼.

British Museum.

2. CARVED STONE BALL, SKARA BRAE. ¾.

National Museum of Antiquities, Edinburgh.

PLATE V.

1. HUT 1, SKARA BRAE.

Photo : V. G. Childe.

2. FORT AND CELTIC FIELDS, BATHAMPTON DOWN.

Air photo : O. G. S. Crawford, F.S.A., and Alexander Keiller, F.S.A.

PLATE VI.

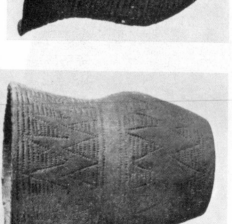

3. A BEAKER, ERISWELL, SUFFOLK. ⅓.

University Museum of Archaeology, Cambridge.

A BEAKER (1) AND B BEAKER (2) FROM WICK BARROW. ⅓.

Taunton Museum.

PLATE VII.

2. C BEAKER, RUDH'AN DUNAIN, SKYE.

National Museum of Antiquities, Edinburgh.

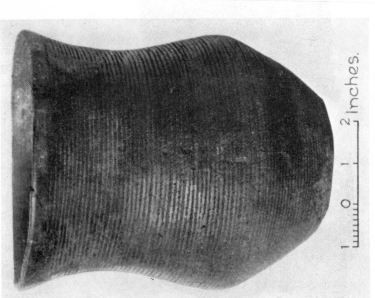

1. B BEAKER, BATHGATE, MIDLOTHIAN.

PLATE VIII.

1. HANDLED BEAKER, BOTTISHAM FEN. ⅓.

University Museum of Archaeology, Cambridge.

2. TYPE 1 FOOD VESSEL, KILBOWIE,
DUMBARTON. ⅓.

PLATE IX.

1. TYPE A FOOD VESSEL, MOUNT STEWART, CO. DOWN. $\frac{3}{8}$.

Municipal Museum, Belfast.

2. TYPE F FOOD VESSEL, BALLON, CO. CARLOW.

National Museum of Ireland.

PLATE X.

1. TYPE C FOOD VESSEL, MT. STEWART, CO. DOWN. $\frac{7}{12}$.

Municipal Museum, Belfast.

2. ALDBOURNE CUP, CAMERTON, SOMERSET. $\frac{1}{1}$.

British Museum.

PLATE XI.

1. AMBER CUP, HOVE. $\frac{7}{10}$.

Photo : Dr. C. E. Curwen, F.S.A.

2. GOLD CUP, RILLATON, CORNWALL.

British Museum.

PLATE XII.

ENCRUSTED URN AND FOOD VESSEL,
BURGAGE MOR, CO. WICKLOW.

National Museum of Ireland.

PLATE XIII.

SKARA BRAE SHERDS, RINYO, ROUSAY. ⅜.

Museum of Antiquities, Edinburgh.

ENCRUSTED URN, AGOWER, CO. WICKLOW. ⅓.

National Museum of Ireland.

PLATE XIV.

CAULDRON OF TYPE A FROM R. CHER.

Ashmolean Museum.

CAULDRON OF TYPE B, LLYN FAWR, GLAM.

National Museum of Wales.

PLATE XV.

LA TÈNE SWORD (¼) WITH DECORATED SCABBARD-
MOUNT (½) FROM R. WHITHAM.

British Museum photograph.

PLATE XVI.

1. BROCH OF MOUSA, SHETLAND.

Photo : V. G. Childe.

2. BROCH OF MIDHOWE, ROUSAY.

Photo : V. G. Childe.

45096